Palgrave Studies in Compromise after Conflict

Series Editor
John D. Brewer
Queen's University Belfast
Belfast, UK

Stellenbosch University
South Africa

This series aims to bring together in one series scholars from around the world who are researching the dynamics of post-conflict transformation in societies emerging from communal conflict and collective violence. The series welcomes studies of particular transitional societies emerging from conflict, comparative work that is cross-national, and theoretical and conceptual contributions that focus on some of the key processes in post-conflict transformation. The series is purposely interdisciplinary and addresses the range of issues involved in compromise, reconciliation and societal healing. It focuses on interpersonal and institutional questions, and the connections between them.

More information about this series at
http://www.palgrave.com/gp/series/14641

Linus Nnabuike Malu

The International Criminal Court and Peace Processes

Côte d'Ivoire, Kenya and Uganda

palgrave
macmillan

Linus Nnabuike Malu
International Law Consultant
Armidale, NSW, Australia

Palgrave Studies in Compromise after Conflict
ISBN 978-3-030-19904-3 ISBN 978-3-030-19905-0 (eBook)
https://doi.org/10.1007/978-3-030-19905-0

Cover credit: Alamy C6JFY6

This Palgrave Macmillan imprint is published by the registered company Springer Nature Switzerland AG
The registered company address is: Gewerbestrasse 11, 6330 Cham, Switzerland

Preface

This book examines how the International Criminal Court (ICC) influences the peace processes in Côte d'Ivoire, Kenya and Uganda. It explores how the prosecution of those who bear the greatest responsibility for the gravest crimes committed, negatively or positively, influences the process of making peace after the violent conflicts in these counties. The deployment of international justice mechanisms, such as the ICC, may be justified on several grounds, including the argument that such involvement in conflict and post-conflict situations could assist in ending wars, and in promoting peace. But, this belief has not been properly studied to understand whether international justice actually contributes positively or negatively to the peace process. It is not yet clearly determined whether it is the retributive or restorative or the truth-telling functions of the Court that has most impact on the peace process. Drawing upon interviews with national experts in these three countries, this book provides evidence-based responses to these questions and reviews the controversies surrounding the involvement of international justice mechanisms in conflict and post-conflict situations. Relying on an analytical framework that is based on four variables: deterrence, victims' rights, reconciliation and accountability to the law, it argues that the ICC's intervention has had multiple impacts on the situations across these countries, and that, despite some acknowledged arguments to the contrary, the ICC does promote peace processes through deterrence and the promotion of accountability to the law. However, there is minimal evidence that the ICC effectively contributes to peace processes in these countries through the promotion of reconciliation and victims' rights.

Armidale, Australia Linus Nnabuike Malu

Acknowledgements

This book is based on my Ph.D. thesis which was completed at the University of New England, Australia, in 2017. During my studies, and thereafter, I worked with several persons to complete the book. I am immensely grateful to all the experts and other individuals who agreed to be interviewed for this study. I highly appreciate their time, expertise and insights. Without these interviews, this study would not have been successfully carried out. Also, my special thanks go to my principal supervisor, at the University of New England, Australia, Professor Helen Ware for constructive and objective criticisms/suggestions and motivation. I am also very grateful to my second supervisor, Dr. Marty Branagan, for critical comments, encouragement, support and assistance in developing my thesis. My particular gratitude goes to the Staff of the School of Humanities for providing invaluable assistance, and being always willing to help, and making my study less stressful. I am thankful to Dr. Ray Nickson, who was at that time a Lecturer at the Department of Criminology, University of New England (UNE) for reviewing three chapters of my thesis and providing criminology perspective, and to Dr. John Adeleke of the School of Arts, UNE, for editing some chapters. It is important to acknowledge with profound gratitude the research funding provided by the Australian government (International Post-Graduate Research Scholarship) and the University of New England (UNE Research Scholarship and the Keith and Dorothy Traveling Scholarship). Without those funds, it may have been almost impossible to have this book. Last, but not the least, I appreciate the inputs of experts at two research seminars at the University of New England in 2013 and 2014, at the UNE Peace Conference in Sydney in 2015, and at the African Studies Association of Australasia and the Pacific Conference in 2015 in Melbourne.

Contents

Acronyms

ARLPI	Acholi Religious Leaders' Peace Initiative
AU	African Union
BBC	British Broadcasting Corporation
CAR	Central African Republic
CDVR	Commission Dialogue Vérité et Réconciliation
CIPEV	Commission of Inquiry on Post-election Violence
CNE	Commission Nationale d'Enquête
CONARIV	Commission Nationale pour la Reconciliation et l'Indemnisation des Victims
DPP	Director of Public Prosecutions
DRC	Democratic Republic of Congo
ECOWAS	Economic Community of West African States
FN	Forces Nouvelles
FPA	Final Peace Agreement
FRCI	Forces Républicaines de Côte d'Ivoire
GDP	Gross Domestic Product
GoC	Government of Côte d'Ivoire
GoK	Government of Kenya
GoU	Government of Uganda
HSM	Holy Spirit Movement
ICC	International Criminal Court

ICTR	International Criminal Tribunal for Rwanda
ICTY	International Criminal Tribunal for the former Yugoslavia
IDP	Internally Displaced Persons
JPT	Juba Peace Talks
KNDR	Kenya National Dialogue and Reconciliation.
LRA	Lord's Resistance Army
NGO	Non-Governmental Organisation
NRA/M	National Resistance Army/Movement
OTP	Office of the Prosecutor
PEV	Post-Election Violence
PNCS	Program National de Cohesion Sociale
TFV	Trust Fund for Victims
TJRC	Truth, Justice and Reconciliation Commission of Kenya
UN	United Nations
UNDP	United Nations Development Programme
UNGA	United Nations General Assembly
UNOCI	United Nations Operation in Côte d'Ivoire
UNSC	United Nations Security Council
UPDA	Uganda People's Democratic Army

Table of Cases

1.	The Prosecutor v. Ahmad Al Faqi Al Mahdi	ICC-01/12-01/15
2.	The Prosecutor v. Akayesu	ICTR-96-4
3.	The Prosecutor v. Bagaragaza	ICTR-05-86
4.	The Prosecutor v. Biljana Plavšić	Case No. 1T-00-39&40/1-S
5.	The Prosecutor v. Charles Blé Goudé	ICC-02/11-02/11
6.	The Prosecutor v. Dominic Ongwen	ICC-01/04-01/07
7.	The Prosecutor v. Dusko Tadic (Appeal Judgement)	IT-94-1-A
8.	The Prosecutor v. Francis Kirim Muthaura, Uhuru Muigai Kenyatta and Mohammed Hussein Ali	ICC-01/09-02/11-383 ICC-01/04-01/07
9.	The Prosecutor v. Germain Katanga	
10.	The Prosecutor v. Jean-Pierre Bemba Gombo	ICC-01/05-01/08
11.	The Prosecutor v. Kambanda	ICTR-97-23
12.	The Prosecutor v. Laurent Gbagbo and Charles Blé Goudé	ICC-02/11-01/15
13.	The Prosecutor v. Paul Gicheru and Philip Kipkoech Bett	ICC-01/09-01/15
14.	The Prosecutor v. Ruggiu	ICTR-05-86
15.	The Prosecutor v. Saif Al-Islam Gaddafi and Abdullah Al-Senussi (Decision on the admissibility of the case against Abdullah Al-Senussi)	ICC-01/11-01/11-466 ICC-02/11-01/12
16.	The Prosecutor v. Simone Gbagbo	

17. The Prosecutor v. Thomas Lubanga Dyilo	ICC-01/04-01/06
18. The Prosecutor v. Uhuru Muigai Kenyatta	ICC-01/09-02/11
19. The Prosecutor v. Walter Osapiri Barasa	ICC-01/09-01/13
20. The Prosecutor v. William Samoei Ruto and Joshua Arap Sang	ICC-01/09-01/11
21. Uganda v. Thomas Kwoyelo, Constitutional Appeal	No. 01 of 2012

List of Statutes Referred To

1. Decree No. 2013–93 of December 30, 2013
2. Degree 24 of March, 2015
3. Rome Statute of the International Criminal Court, 1998
4. Rules of Evidence and Procedure of the International Criminal Court, 2013
5. The Constitution of Kenya, 2010
6. The International Criminal Act, Kenya, 2008
7. The International Criminal Court Act, Uganda, 2010
8. The Judicial Services Act, No. 1 of 2011, Kenya
9. The Ordinance No. 2011–167 of 13 July 2011, (as extended by Order No. 2014–32 of 3 February 2014)
10. The Vetting of Judges and Magistrate Act, No. 2 of 2012, Kenya
11. The Witness Protection Act, 2006 (as amended in 2012), Kenya
12. The Supreme Court of Kenya Act, No. 7 of 2011, Kenya
13. The 2000 Constitution of Côte d'Ivoire
14. Order No. 020/MEMJ/DSJRH/MEF of June 24, 2011 (Special Investigation Unit of Côte d'Ivoire)

List of Tables

Series Editor's Preface

General Editor's Introduction

Compromise is a much used but little understood term. There is a sense in which it describes a set of feelings (the so-called spirit of compromise) that involve reciprocity, representing the agreement to make mutual concessions towards each other from now on: no matter what we did to each other in the past, we will act towards each other in the future differently as set out in the agreement between us. The compromise settlement can be a spit and a handshake, much beloved in folk lore, or a legally binding statute with hundreds of clauses.

As such, it is clear that compromise enters into conflict transformation at two distinct phases. The first is during the conflict resolution process itself, where compromise represents a willingness among parties to negotiate a peace agreement that represents a second-best preference in which they give up their first preference (victory) in order to cut a deal. A great deal of literature has been produced in Peace Studies and International Relations on the dynamics of the negotiation process and the institutional and governance structures necessary to consolidate the agreement afterwards. Just as important, however, is compromise in the second phase, when compromise is part of post-conflict reconstruction, in which protagonists come to learn to live together despite their former enmity and in face of the atrocities perpetrated during the conflict itself.

In the first phase, compromise describes reciprocal agreements between parties to the negotiations in order to make political concessions sufficient to end conflict, and in the second phase, compromise involves victims and perpetrators developing ways of living together in which concessions are made as part of shared social life. The first is about compromises between political groups and the state in the process of statebuilding (or re-building) after the political upheavals of communal conflict, and the second is about compromises between individuals and communities in the process of social healing after the cultural trauma provoked by the conflict.

This book series primarily concerns itself with the second process, the often messy and difficult job of reconciliation, restoration and repair in social and cultural relations following communal conflict. Communal conflicts and civil wars tend to suffer from the narcissism of minor differences, to coin Freud's phrase, leaving little to be split halfway and compromise on, and thus are usually especially bitter. The series therefore addresses itself to the meaning, manufacture and management of compromise in one of its most difficult settings. The book series is cross-national and cross-disciplinary, with attention paid to interpersonal reconciliation at the level of everyday life, as well as culturally between social groups, and the many sorts of institutional, interpersonal, psychological, sociological, anthropological and cultural factors that assist and inhibit societal healing in all post-conflict societies, historically and in the present. It focuses on what compromise means when people have to come to terms with past enmity and the memories of the conflict itself, and relate to former protagonists in ways that consolidate the wider political agreement.

This sort of focus has special resonance and significance for peace agreements are usually very fragile. Societies emerging out of conflict are subject to ongoing violence from spoiler groups who are reluctant to give up on first preferences, constant threats from the outbreak of renewed violence, institutional instability, weakened economies and a wealth of problems around transitional justice, memory, truth recovery and victimhood, among others. Not surprisingly therefore, reconciliation and healing in social and cultural relations is difficult to achieve, not least because interpersonal compromise between erstwhile enemies is difficult.

Lay discourse picks up on the ambivalent nature of compromise after conflict. It is talked about in common sense in one of two ways, in which compromise is either a virtue or a vice, taking its place among the angels or in Hades. One form of lay discourse likens concessions to former protagonists with the idea of restoration of broken relationships and societal and cultural reconciliation, in which there is a sense of becoming (or returning) to wholeness and completeness. The other form of lay discourse invokes ideas of appeasement, of being *compromised* by the concessions, which constitute a form of surrender and reproduce (or disguise) continued brokenness and division. People feel they continue to be beaten by the sticks which the concessions have allowed others to keep; with restoration, however, weapons are turned truly in ploughshares. Lay discourse suggests, therefore, that these are issues that the Palgrave Studies in Compromise after Conflict Series must begin to problematize, so that the process of societal healing is better understood and can be assisted and facilitated by public policy and intervention.

One of the features of this Series is its commitment to publish the work of early career researchers (ECRs) who often find it difficult to persuade commercial publishers of their marketability. This allows them to appear alongside the international renowned names who have also contributed to the Series. Some of these ECRs are practitioners or academic independents, who offer a refreshing perspective from outside universities. One such is the current author, Linus Nnabuike Malu, a Nigerian legal practitioner working in international human rights law in Australia.

The role of law in reconciliation is widely disputed. Purists believe the law is free from emotion; indeed, the law designed deliberately to keep emotion out of retributive punishment. Pragmatists recognise the law is infused, even infected, with emotion and is deeply political. The law can serve reconciliation in several ways, the most important of which is to support truth and justice. So important to reconciliation is peace and justice that one of the world's foremost conflict transformation experts, John Paul Lederach, uses a single noun "justpeace" to replace justice and peace as separate terms, signifying their indivisibility in reconciliation. Justice is itself also served in several ways after conflict, such as inquests, truth recovery mechanisms, symbolic reparations, like apologies and criminal prosecutions in domestic and international courts. One of the latter is through the work of the International Criminal Court (ICC). This is the subject of Malu's book.

It poses the supra-legal question of the contribution of the ICC to peace processes through reconciliation. Its focus is upon Africa, a continent ravaged by colonial expropriation and succumbing to significant post-colonial inter-communal violence, specifically addressing the role of the ICC in three case studies of Kenya, Uganda and the Ivory Coast. Based on in-depth qualitative analysis of interview data, Malu offers a damning critique of the ICC that highlights its limitations in contributing to the peace process in the case countries. The failure to assist in reconciliation is linked to its failure to deliver justice, with the lack of criminal prosecutions its most serious fault. Its main contribution has been through its general deterrence effect in preventing even more violence; positive effects on reconciliation are harder to find. The study ends with several policy recommendations to assist the ICC to improve its contribution to reconciliation, such as improving its prosecution rate, increasing the speed of its operations, linking up with political bodies like the African Union and linking its outcomes more closely to transitional justice mechanisms.

Great expectations of the ICC have resulted in little delivery. Legal purists would say this is because the law cannot deal with supra-legal and emotive issues like peace and reconciliation; the law is being asked to do too much and the expectations were wrong. Legal pragmatists would say that its application needs to improve so that justice is delivered; the law has a role in peace, but its practices have been wrong. In charting a course through this debate, Linus's volume is a very welcome addition to the Series.

Belfast, UK
April 2019

John D. Brewer

1
Introduction

> Much early writing on the field of international criminal law focused on its growing body of jurisprudence and its institutional developments, yet less attention has been paid to the effects that international judicial interventions have had upon the communities and state structures where grave crimes have occurred (Introduction to "*Contested Justice: The Politics and Practice of International Criminal Court Interventions*")[1]

This book explores the impacts of the International Criminal Court (ICC or the "Court") on peace processes in Côte d'Ivoire, Kenya and Uganda. It comparatively examines how prosecution of those who bear the greatest responsibility for crimes committed in these countries may have negatively or positively influenced the process of making peace after conflicts. It is concerned with *how* international accountability affects post-conflict countries, and on *what* the ICC brings to the table in a peace process. The central questions are: Does justice spur peace in post-conflict societies? Does justice complicate the peace process? How?

---

[1]De Vos, Christian, Kendall, Sara and Stahn, Carten. 2015. "Introduction". In *Contested Justice: The Politics and Practice of International Criminal Court Interventions*, edited by Christian de Vos, Sara Kendall, and Carsten Stahn, 1–20. Cambridge: Cambridge University Press.

L. N. Malu, *The International Criminal Court and Peace Processes*,
Palgrave Studies in Compromise after Conflict,
https://doi.org/10.1007/978-3-030-19905-0_1

The intervention of the ICC in post-conflict countries is primarily aimed at holding those who played key roles in the conflicts accountable for their crimes. The process of investigating such crimes and prosecuting those who are deemed to have committed international crimes may have affects which could impact on the peace process in the affected countries, and even beyond the borders of such countries (Sikkink 2011). However, the impact of these interventions is not yet well defined or well known (Kersten 2014; Clark 2011). Clearly, the belief that international justice mechanisms contribute to peace processes, though not unfounded, is not fully established or well-settled (Schabas 2011; Nouwen 2012; Wegner 2015). It is still a moot point if and how international accountability contributes to peace (Clark 2011). Thus, this book will contribute to knowledge in this area by, among other things, developing a framework for determining how the ICC contributes to peace processes.

1.1 Rationale for the Study

The Nuremberg and Tokyo trials were defining moments in the history of international accountability (Schabas 2012). With these trials, the world took a firm stand that those who commit atrocities that threaten international peace must be punished. The lull that followed these trials at the international level came to an end after the Cold War with the establishment of the two ad hoc international tribunals for Yugoslavia (1993) and Rwanda (1994), signalling a resurgence in the use of international justice mechanisms to sanction perpetrators of atrocities.

In the last twenty-five years, there has been an increasing reliance on the use of international justice mechanisms, climaxing with the establishment of the ICC (Wegner 2015). This use is justified on several grounds, but mainly on the argument that deployment of international justice mechanisms in conflict and post-conflict situations could assist in ending the wars and in promoting peace. But this belief has not been properly studied to understand whether international justice mechanisms actually contribute positively to the peace process, and if they do, how. There are also few studies on which aspects of the work of international justice mechanisms promote which aspects of the peace process, and how. For instance, it is not certain whether it is the retributive or restorative or the truth-telling functions of the Court that have more impact on a peace process. It is also not certain which aspects of the peace process are influenced by any of these functions of the Court. There are several texts on the impact of international justice mechanisms on conflict and post-conflict situations (Schabas 2012), but there are few on *how* they actually impact on these situations (Kersten 2014; Clark 2011). The central aim of this study is to provide evidence-based answers to some of these questions and to stimulate more discussions that could provide answers to some of the controversies surrounding the involvement of international justice mechanisms in conflict and post-conflict situations.

Since the establishment of the ICC in 2002, the Court has intervened in eight countries in Africa. The involvement of the ICC in Africa will be important in shaping the extent and scope of peace processes in the continent as presently being witnessed in the eight countries where it has intervened. The involvement of the ICC may positively influence peace processes by speeding-up and deepening the judicial process, which may lead to sustainable peace, or alternatively may impede, complicate or stall peace processes. This study hopes to provide a clearer perspective on the impact of the interventions of the ICC on peace processes in three countries in Africa and the circumstances under which it has negative or positive impacts. The researcher hopes that this study will be of value for policymakers working on international accountability and conflict transformation since this study provides valuable insights into how the ICC is impacting on peace and security in Côte d'Ivoire, Kenya and Uganda.

The overarching research question this book will address is whether the interventions of the ICC in Côte d'Ivoire, Kenya and Uganda are contributing positively to the peace processes in the three countries? Drawn from this overarching question are four principal research questions which will also provide answers to the overarching research question. These questions are whether the involvement of the ICC in Côte d'Ivoire, Kenya and Uganda promotes accountability to the law in these countries; whether the involvement of the ICC in Côte d'Ivoire,

Kenya and Uganda promotes reconciliation in these countries; whether the involvement of the ICC in Côte d'Ivoire, Kenya and Uganda promotes respect for victims' rights in these countries; and whether the ICC involvement deters future atrocities in Côte d'Ivoire, Kenya and Uganda.

1.2 Establishment of the International Criminal Court

The 1998 Rome Statute established the ICC. A Diplomatic Conference of Plenipotentiaries of the ICC was held in Rome, Italy, in June/July 1998 to discuss the draft ICC Statute that was prepared by the International Law Commission. The international community, on 17 July 1998, "reached an historic milestone when 120 states adopted the Rome Statute, the legal basis for establishing the ICC" (Williams 2012). Four years later, the Statute obtained the requisite sixty ratifications for its entry into force on 1 July, 2002 (Williams 2012). In October 2018, 123 countries had ratified the Rome Statute of the ICC. Out of these 123 member states, 33 are African states, 19 are Asia-Pacific states, 18 are from Eastern Europe, 28 are from Latin America and Caribbean, and 25 are from Western Europe and other states.[2]

The ICC is the first permanent international criminal Court that was established to help fight impunity for the perpetrators of some international crimes. The ICC is an independent international organisation and is not part of the United Nations system. Although the ICC's expenses are funded primarily by state parties, it also receives voluntary contributions from governments, international organisations, individuals, corporations and other entities. The establishment of the ICC came more than fifty years after the adoption of the Universal Declaration of Human Rights on 10 December 1948 and the 9 December 1948 resolution of the United Nations General Assembly mandating the International Law Commission to commence work on developing a

[2]https://treaties.un.org/Pages/ViewDetails. Accessed 18 October 2018.

draft statute of an International Criminal Court. After many years of work, marked by stoppages due to the Cold War, the final version of the draft statute prepared by the International Law Commission was adopted in 1998 (Schabas 2007). The main objective of the Rome Statute is to establish a permanent international court, complementary to national courts that will prosecute those who commit international crimes (Nouwen 2013).

1.3 The Globalisation of Accountability: The Establishment of the ICC and the Missing Points

The campaign to promote accountability by the international community through international justice mechanisms has a fairly long and tortuous history, stretching back to 1919 after the First World War (Schabas 2012) and taking root in 1945 during the Nuremberg and Tokyo trials. The establishment of international criminal tribunals for Rwanda and the former Yugoslavia in the 1990s and "internationalised" or hybrid Courts in Sierra Leone, Lebanon, East Timor and Cambodia confirmed the global acceptance of international accountability.

The ICC, according to article 1 of the Rome Statute, was established as a permanent institution with power "to exercise its jurisdiction over persons for the most serious crimes of international concern". One of the motivations for establishing the Court is to put an end to impunity for the perpetrators of international crimes and thus to contribute to the prevention of such crimes. Apart from being the first permanent international Court, the Rome Statute also created some features that make the ICC unique. First, the Statute established an independent prosecutor, who is elected for a nine-year term by member states with the freedom to select situations for investigation (Schabas 2012). Secondly, the Statute created the principle of complementarity as a compromise between the legal duty to prosecute international crimes and the principle of state sovereignty (Jurdi 2011). Thirdly, the ICC is a treaty-based international criminal Court, not established as a victor's

Court or by the United Nations Security Council. Fourth, the ICC attempts to focus not just on retributive justice but also adds some elements of restorative justice through its victims' rights protection provisions within the Court and through the Trust Fund for Victims (TFV). Fifth, the ICC is expected to prosecute any person who commits international crimes as defined by the Rome Statute, notwithstanding the person's official status, thus sidetracking the well-established concept of immunity from prosecution for sitting heads of government.

Therefore, by design, the ICC is expected to tackle issues never before undertaken in international criminal law, which has seen the Court entering unchartered murky waters. For instance, the ICC is expected to intervene in both ongoing and terminated conflicts. It has intervened in ongoing conflicts in Libya, Sudan and Northern Uganda. Such interventions pose great challenges with respect to the investigation and arrest of culprits and may also have direct impact, which may raise the peace and justice issue to greater significance (Kersten 2014). Also, the ICC has a much wider jurisdiction than any other international criminal court/ tribunal. It has jurisdiction to try any person who commits international crimes in any of the current 123 member states. The United Nations Security Council can also refer to any situation that poses threats to international peace and security to the ICC, whether the situation arose in a member state or not. These new features and innovations inherently provide both prospects and challenges for the new Court. The positive prospect lies in the establishment of a permanent, international, treaty-based, independent Court with powers to fight impunity. The challenges are numerous and have dogged the Court since its inception.

1.4 The Challenges for the ICC

After the negotiation and the finalising of the Rome Statute in July 1998, expectations were high that the new permanent international Court would end impunity, deter future grave human rights abusers, promote and protect victims' rights and generally promote international accountability. There were also hopes that the ICC could change the dynamics of international relations by being a global body that transcends state interests to enforce an *erga omnes* duty to prosecute international crimes (Jurdi 2011). However, contrary to these expectations the ICC has struggled to deliver. The ICC continues to face significant obstacles in its quest to contribute to an international system premised on respect for human rights, the rule of law and accountability for international crimes (Jurdi 2011). The facts are disturbing: the ICC has only completed few trials after sixteen years of existence; it is also accused of botching some of the investigations and prosecutions; the pace of justice is too slow and trials have been unduly complex; it has been unable to deliver in cases involving sitting presidents and senior government officials; and it has failed in several instances to ensure that those accused of crimes by the Court are brought to The Hague for prosecution. Also, the allegation that a staff member sexually assaulted four witnesses in the ICC protection programme in the Democratic Republic of Congo (DRC) has not helped its image (Independent Review Team Public Report 2014).

Article 25 provides that the Court shall have jurisdiction over natural persons who commit a crime within the jurisdiction of the Court, and such persons shall be individually responsible and liable for punishment. In article 27, it further provides that the Statute shall apply:

> [equally] to all persons without any distinction based on official capacity—in particular, official capacity as a head of state or government, a member of a government or parliament, an elected representative or a government official shall in no case exempt a person from criminal responsibility under this Statute.

It further provides that "immunities or special procedural rules which may attach to the official capacity of a person, whether under national or international law, shall not bar the Court from exercising its jurisdiction over such a person". These provisions make it possible for the Office of the Prosecutor (OTP) to prosecute such state officials (Ladan 2010). The rationale for these provisions is to tackle impunity for heads of state or presidents or any other government officials who hitherto have enjoyed immunity from prosecution when in service. It makes such officials individually responsible for crimes and subject to prosecution even when they are still in office.

In practice, prosecution of sitting heads of state or presidents and even state officials has proved extremely difficult for the ICC. So far, the ICC has failed to execute this aspect of its mandate. In Sudan, Kenya, Uganda and Côte d'Ivoire, the ICC has failed to either prosecute those who are in government or are closely associated with those in government. The failure of the ICC, so far, to successfully prosecute these classes of persons, as originally conceived, gravely undermines the Court, because curbing impunity of those in government is one of the central aims of the ICC. In Sudan, the ICC has been unable to arrest and prosecute Omar Hassan Ahmad al-Bashir (President of Sudan) accused of war crimes, genocides and crimes against humanity and other state officials and those close to the government. Several years after their indictments, these men are still at large. Omar Hassan Ahmad al-Bashir has remained the President of Sudan and has travelled to several African countries, including some that ratified the Rome Statute. In Kenya, the attempt by the ICC to prosecute Uhuru Kenyatta (current president of Kenya), William Samoei Ruto (the current vice-president of Kenya) and Francis Muthaura (former head of civil service/secretary to the cabinet and a close ally of former President Mwai Kibaki) failed. In Uganda and Côte d'Ivoire, the ICC has failed to indict top political and security officers associated with the present governments while there is evidence that they might have committed atrocities. On 5 December 2014, in a press statement, after she dropped charges against Uhuru Kenyatta, Mrs. Fatou Bensouda, the chief prosecutor summarised her frustration with the case thus:

> [today] is a dark day for international criminal justice. Be that as it may, it is my firm belief that today's decision is not the last word on justice and accountability for the crimes that were inflicted on the people of Kenya in 2007 and 2008; crimes that are still crying out for justice.[3]

[3]Statement of the chief prosecutor of the International Criminal Court issued on 5 December 2014, https://www.icc-cpi.int/Pages/item.aspx?name=otp-statement-05-12-2014-2&ln=en. Accessed 18 October 2018.

Article 86 provides that states parties shall, "in accordance with the provisions of the Statute, cooperate fully with the Court in its investigation and prosecution of crimes within the jurisdiction of the Court". Thus, the Statute enjoins state parties to cooperate and assumes that member states will in practice cooperate with the Court. Thus, according to article 87, the Court shall have the authority to make requests to states parties for cooperation. This has proved to be one of the major weaknesses of the ICC (Wegner 2015). Evidence indicates that state parties do not at all times cooperate with the Court. In fact, at times, some state parties seem to have undermined the work of the Court. For example, Cote d'Ivoire has refused to hand over Simone Gbagbo to the ICC, defying the Appeal Chamber's order[4] to transfer her to the ICC. The Office of the Prosecutor (OTP) in the Uhuru Kenyatta case complained of consistent and systematic failure of Kenya to provide necessary information and documents for the prosecution of the case. Kenya is also yet to transfer Messrs Walter Barasa, Paul Gicheru and Philip Bett, accused by the OTP of obstructing the course of justice, to the ICC.[5] After the vacation of charges against Ruto and Sang, the chief prosecutor, while lamenting the failure of the Government of Kenya (GoK) to fully cooperate with the OTP in the case, stated:

> In the ordinary course of events, the Government of Kenya would have been a critical ally and partner of the Office, since the case was about crimes committed against Kenyans, crimes defined and proscribed by a treaty ratified by the Government of Kenya. As a State Party to the Rome Statute, the Government of Kenya has both an international and

---

[4]Situation in the Republic of Côte d'Ivoire in the Case of the Prosecutor V. Simone Gbagbo. Decision on Côte d'Ivoire's challenge to the admissibility of the case against Simone Gbagbo (No.: ICC-02/11-01/12). https://www.icc-cpi.int/CourtRecords/CR2014_10019.PDF. Accessed 18 October 2018.

[5]The Prosecutor v. Walter Osapiri Barasa, ICC-01/09-01/13 (The arrest warrant was issued under seal against Mr. Barasa on 2 August 2013 and unsealed on 2 October 2013). (The case "remains in the Pre-Trial stage, pending the suspect's arrest or voluntary appearance before the Court".); The Prosecutor v. Paul Gicheru and Philip Kipkoech Bett, ICC-01/09-01/15 (The warrant of arrest was issued under "seal against Paul Gicheru and Philip Kipkoech Bett on 10 March 2015 and unsealed on 10 September 2015. Accused are not in the Court's custody. The case remains in the Pre-Trial stage, pending the suspects' arrest or voluntary appearance before the Court".

> constitutional obligation to assist the Office with our investigations. However, despite repeated assurances of cooperation with the Court, the Government of Kenya provided only selective assistance to the Prosecution.[6]

Also, the indicted current President of Sudan has not only defied the ICC's warrant of arrest, but some African states that are member states of the ICC such as Nigeria, South Africa, Uganda and Kenya have allowed him to visit without arresting him. The lesson learnt in the Kenya cases, according to James Goldston, Executive Director of Open Society Foundation, in an article after the charges in the Ruto and Sang case were vacated, is that "if the ICC is going to take on a head of state, it must be at the very top of its game, in respect of the evidence it marshals and the strategic diplomacy it deploys to build legitimacy" (Goldston 2016).

The almost total focus on conflicts in Africa has also attracted severe criticisms, with some accusing it of targeting African states (du Max 2010). In the main, the ICC has been accused of unduly focusing on conflicts in Africa and of not paying attention to conflicts in other parts of the world, even when such conflicts are of equal gravity to those in Africa.

Furthermore, the ICC's methods and procedures put it in the line of fire, with several accusations: that its long and complex trials postpone justice for victims; that the complexities of involving victims are not properly resolved; and that its methodology in some situations of contracting individuals not employed by the ICC to gather evidence to be used in prosecution, infringes on the rights of the accused (Rigney 2014). The limited success of the ICC is also linked to its low budget. Though there are several views on the adequacy of ICC budgets, the dominant opinion is that the ICC is underfunded (Human Rights Watch 2016) and that the Court cannot function optimally when it is grossly underfunded.

[6] Statement of the Chief Prosecutor of the International Criminal Court on 6 April 2016, https://www.icc-cpi.int/Pages/item.aspx?name=otp-stat-160406. Accessed 19 October 2018.

1.5 The Prospects for the ICC

Despite its numerous problems and weak start, the ICC represents a new world order that fights impunity (du Max 2010). The establishment of the ICC after many years of hard negotiations, and the fact that many nations agreed to establish the Court that seemed so improbable, is deemed a success (Rigney 2014). For the first time in human history, a permanent international institution with a wide mandate to sanction those who commit the most heinous of crimes has been established. Thus, the mere existence of the Court, and its Statute, which articulates complex but innovative procedures, strengthens international criminal law and also represents hope for victims of international crimes. Through its innovative concepts and practices, "such as complementarity, victims' participation or 'the interest of justice', the Court actively shapes justice policy, which could be one of its visible traces" (de Vos et al. 2015).

Through its work, based on its complementarity policy, the ICC promotes a global standard of international justice. For instance, some countries have domesticated the ICC Rome Statute, and in some of the countries where the ICC has directly intervened, such as Sudan, Kenya, Côte d'Ivoire, Uganda and the DRC, national authorities have for various reasons enacted/amended laws and establish institutions and agencies modelled after the ICC. According to the website of the Coalition for the International Criminal Court,[7] "currently, 65 countries have enacted legislation containing either complementarity or cooperation provisions, or both, into their domestic law. 35 countries have some form of advanced draft implementing legislation". Based on its *positive* complementarity policy, and as stated by its first chief prosecutor, the ICC legacy could also be judged, not from the cases that appear before it, but from the cases that don't appear before it but are instead tried in impartial domestic settings, ensuring that the rule of law in these countries is strengthened (Rigney 2014).

---

[7] http://www.iccnow.org/index.php?mod=romeimplementation. Accessed 19 October 2018.

The significance of indicting a sitting head of state (Omar al-Bashir), prosecuting a sitting president (Uhuru Kenyatta) and a sitting vice-president (William Ruto) should not, by any account, be underestimated. The indictment of Bashir was the second time a sitting head of state in Africa was indicted by an international court. The first was Charles Taylor, who was on 7 March 2003 indicted by the Special Court for Sierra Leone.[8] The Prosecution of Uhuru Kenyatta was the first-ever attempt to prosecute a sitting head of state from any African country. Thus, despite the failure of the ICC to convict, these actions, seen from an international justice perspective, represent a huge challenge against impunity in Africa. In criminal justice, what is central is not whether a person is found guilty or not, but that the rule of law has taken its course.

Unsurprisingly, these leaders deployed personal and state resources to fight back, and as one respondent in Kenya aptly puts it "if you fight impunity, impunity will also fight back".[9] The resources and political connections of these leaders are enormous and were deployed against the ICC. In Kenya, for instance, the accused employed various antics to ensure that the cases were discontinued, including: lobbying the African Union, African states and members of the UN Security Council to have the matter transferred to a national court or regional court, or for a deferral of the proceedings at the ICC for at least a year (International Crises Group 2012; Mueller 2014); demanding through the East African Legislative Assembly that the cases be transferred to the East African Court of Justice; threatening to withdraw from the Rome Statute; and waging intense legal battles with the OTP. The GoK and the accused have also been accused of intimidating witnesses in attempts to undermine the process. This included attacks, disappearances, enticements to

[8]The Trial Chamber for the Special Court for Sierra Leone on 26 April 2012 found Charles Taylor guilty on all eleven counts, on "the modes of liability of planning of crimes and for aiding and abetting of crimes committed by rebel forces in Sierra Leone", and on 30 May 2012, the former Liberian president was given a single sentence of 50 years in prison. The Appeals Chamber upheld Charles Taylor's conviction and 50-year sentence (The Prosecutor vs. Charles Ghankay Taylor, SCSL-03-01-T). http://rscsl.org/Taylor.html. Accessed 19 October 2018.

[9]Interview with a researcher from Kenya, 2014.

study abroad, harassment by security agents and bribing of witnesses and people who knew much about the PEV (Mueller 2014). The aims of these attacks were to have the cases dropped for lack of evidence and to destroy the credibility of those who remained. The OTP had also complained that the attack against potential and actual witnesses and non-cooperation by GoK had made prosecution difficult. The OTP said it has evidence of intimidation and bribery by politicians, lawyers and businessmen (Mueller 2014). These intimidations contributed to the drying up of key witnesses and to the failure of the cases. In an email interview after the withdrawal of charges, a member of the defence team of Uhuru Kenyatta argues that:

> [no] crimes were committed in Kenya. If such crimes were committed Kenya does not need the ICC since Kenya had an existing effective and independent legal system before the ICC involvement in its affairs… so the ICC does not have anything to teach Kenya about accountability to law, given the failings of the OTP and ICC to present a credible case and how they sought to support a case which was littered with false evidence.[10]

However, the Trial Chamber in the Ruto and Sang cases concluded that the "proceedings are declared a mistrial due to a troubling incidence of witness interference and intolerable political meddling".[11]

Though the contributions of the ICC to international peace and security are contested, it will remain relevant in the coming years despite its dismal performance so far, because there is a continuing need for a legal system to punish international crimes. What is important and needed is to acknowledge the problems of the ICC and also to amend its Statute and Rules of Procedure, where necessary. As shown in the three countries, the Court faces enormous challenges in the field, which were not contemplated during the negotiations of the ICC Statute. Thus, as De Vos et al. (2015) argue "the particular vision of justice

---

[10]E-Interview with a member of the defence team of Uhuru Kenyatta, 2015.

[11]The Prosecutor v. William Samoei Ruto and Joshua Arap Sang, ICC-01/09-01/11.

agreed to in Rome often looks quite different in practice, as it plays out in relation to other sets of priorities and interests that shapes its content as well as its form".

1.6 International Accountability: Setting the Context

The struggle to promote accountability at the national level by the international community through international justice mechanisms stretches back to 1919 after the First World War (Schabas 2012). There is also a domestic dimension to the evolution of international accountability which Sikkink (2011) argues comes from diffusions of accountability practice from country to country, within regions, from region to region and finally flowing into an international system of accountability. As a result of these developments and the new focus of the international community on human security, a new normative order which focuses on protecting people from abuses during conflicts and peace times and which emphasises accountability for such abuses is emerging (Teitel 2011). These developments are concerned with protecting humanity both in the human rights and the criminal law contexts from abusive conduct by states, officials and criminal groups.

Scholars such as Sikkink (2011) and Akhavan (2001) argue that prosecution in transitional societies could lead to improvement in human rights protection. Nevertheless, it is doubtful if the surge in accountability has indeed stirred more respect for the rule of law or prevented conflicts. It is also debatable if accountability has inspired peace. Since the Second World War, for instance, armed conflict continues to confront the world in different regions. The end of the Cold War gave rise to hopes of a new peace based on universal law and the new political order, but these hopes were dashed as conflict rose in Afghanistan, Kosovo, Iraq, Iran, Kuwait, Syria and in different parts of Africa, coupled with the astonishing rise in terrorism and violent religious extremism (Teitel 2011). The international community responded through direct interventions in several of these conflicts and through the deployment of international justice mechanisms in the former Yugoslavia, Rwanda, Sierra Leone, Lebanon and Cambodia, and the establishment of the ICC. The hope was that reliance on law and adherence to law that prohibits aggression and other crimes could ultimately promote peace and reduce conflicts (Schabas 2001). The ICC represents a new order embodying the progress of the international community in combating impunity. This new order frowns on amnesty and requires that the terms of any peace agreement must be in accord with international law, as enshrined in the Rome Statute.

1.7 Justifications for International Accountability

The ICC deals primarily with *people not states* who commit crimes against humanity, genocide, war crimes and aggression in the contexts of the Rome Statute. One of the justifications of an international justice mechanism such as the ICC is that such courts by intervening in conflict or post-conflict situations could facilitate the peace process through deterrence, incapacitation of the main conflicting parties, promotion of reconciliation, promotion of victims' rights, retribution, documentation of the conflict, expression and strengthening of the rule of law.

There is a counter-argument, however, that the intervention of international justice mechanisms in a conflict or post-conflict country may in fact exacerbate the conflict and lead to its prolongation (Ku and Nzeribe 2006). This line of thinking has led to the peace and justice debate, which centres on whether or not it is wise to prosecute those who committed atrocities in a conflict situation during the transition period, or particularly with the use of criminal prosecution as the sole, or one of the transitional justice models in a post-conflict country. The debate boils down to three views: those who argue that the justice mechanism should be part of the entire transition justice process; those who argue that justice should be left out of transitional processes if it will complicate the peace process; and finally, those who argue that there is no conflict between the two, rather that both should be properly integrated.

The determination of the peace-justice issue also affects the type or types of transitional justice mechanism that could be deployed and the timing of the deployment of the mechanism. The timing of the deployment of the justice mechanism could also affect its effectiveness and could be as important as the type of mechanism deployed. The choice of the type of transitional justice mechanism to be deployed in post-conflict countries could be problematic as deployment of ill-fitted mechanisms could impact negatively on the peace process. Also, the engagement of appropriate types of mechanisms could contribute to promoting the peace process. Thus, post-conflict countries have an onerous task of locating appropriate transitional justice mechanisms that will not disrupt the fragile peace, but rather contribute towards the process of establishing sustainable peace. The suitability of the ICC as a mechanism for transitional justice in post-conflict countries is uncertain because the Court's capacity as a mechanism for transitional justice is not yet fully tested and because the impact of prosecution as a sole mechanism of transitional justice is suspect (Malu 2015). There are strong arguments for and against prosecution as a model for transitional justice. Some pro-prosecution arguments are: (a) justice is the foundation for peace and reconciliation; (b) prosecution discharges a country from the pains of collective guilt and pins it on individuals, which is essential for restoration; (c) impunity sets bad examples for the future and undermines the rule of law; and (d) prosecution shares some of the main features of a truth commission as a mechanism for establishing historical records of the conflict. The major anti-prosecution arguments are: (a) a rigorous criminal prosecution of key members of the rebel group could derail or prolong the entire transition programme; (b) the threat of prosecution may stop a dictator or warlord from agreeing to go into exile peacefully; and (c) prosecution could lead to justice but not reconciliation, which is central for successful conflict transformation.

The tensions inherent in the involvement of the ICC in conflict and post-conflict situations and the challenges of deploying an international court in a national setting are discussed by analysing the peace and justice dilemma in Chapter 3 and the situations in particular post-conflict countries in Chapters 4, 5 and 6.

Prosecution by a national or international court of those who committed crimes during an armed conflict, it has been argued, could promote peace because accountability is seen as essential in cases of massive violations of human rights (Akhavan 2001) and is thought to be necessary, through deterrence for conflict prevention, and essential for reconciliation through justice, individualisation of guilt and the establishment of the historical record of the violence (Roht-Arriaza 2006). Accountability and removal of perpetrators of massive human rights atrocities from positions of power are also important for conflict transformation (Roht-Arriaza 2006). However, the effectiveness of prosecution as a means of conflict transformation is not well established since determining the law's effectiveness in conflict transformation is not certain (Amann 2003; Wippman 1999; Nouwen 2012). There are controversies and uncertainties about how international law influences conflicts, how it can be used to transform conflicts and how it can contribute to peacemaking (Lincoln 2011; Meijers and Glasius 2013).

1.8 Complementarity

The principle of complementarity is briefly discussed to highlight its importance in determining if and when the ICC can intervene in a conflict or post-conflict situation. The Rome Statute is based on the principle of complementarity, and paragraph 10 of the Preamble and articles 1 and 17 make references to complementarity. Complementarity means that states shall have primary right to investigate and prosecute cases within their jurisdictions (Nouwen 2013). Thus, the ICC shall determine issues of jurisdiction in all cases and may consider issues of admissibility. In considering the admissibility of a case, the Court shall deal with issues of complementarity and gravity (Schabas 2007). Article 17(1) (d) of the Rome Statute provides that the ICC shall determine that a case is inadmissible if the case is not of sufficient "gravity" to warrant further action by the Court. The "gravity threshold" plays an important role in guiding the prosecutor in selection of both situations and cases. Moreover, in determining the issue of complementarity, it shall consider the provisions of article 17(1), (2) and (3). Article 17(1) provides, among other things, that the ICC shall, having regard to paragraph 10 of the Preamble and article 1, determine that a case is inadmissible where:

> [the] case is being investigated or prosecuted by a state which has jurisdiction over it, unless the state is unwilling or unable genuinely to carry out the investigation or prosecution; the case has been investigated by a state which has jurisdiction over it and the state has decided not to prosecute the person concerned, unless the decision resulted from the unwillingness or inability of the state genuinely to prosecute.

Article 17(2) provides that in order to determine "unwillingness" in a particular case, the Court shall consider, having regard to the principles of due process recognised by international law determine:

> [whether] the national proceeding was being made for the purposes of shielding the person concerned from criminal responsibility; whether there has been an unjustified delay in the proceedings, which is inconsistent with an intent to prosecute; and whether the proceedings were not or are not being conducted independently or impartially.

To determine "inability", according to article 17(3), the Court shall consider whether "due to a total or substantial collapse or unavailability of its national judicial system the state is unable to obtain the accused or the necessary evidence and testimony or otherwise unable to carry out its proceedings". The question of inability to investigate or prosecute will arise when a state cannot obtain the accused or the necessary evidence and testimony, or is otherwise unable to carry out its proceedings, while unwillingness to investigate and prosecute will arise where a state is conducting a sham trial intended to block any other proceeding, and in order to make it look like investigation and prosecution are underway, although it may lack the resolve to see them through (Schabas 2007).

Complementarity is justified on the grounds that it ensures that the ICC does not unduly limit the sovereign rights of states parties

(Nouwen 2013). It is also justified on the grounds that national justice systems are more likely to promote reconciliation in a post-conflict country and assist in establishing a permanent justice system that facilitates conflict prevention. National justice systems are also credited with having better chances of offering a more pertinent sense of justice to the victims of violent conflicts than an international court, which might be sitting in a far-away location, and may try only those who bear the gravest responsibility for the crimes (Bjork and Goebertus 2014; Nouwen 2013). The OTP has developed the concept of positive complementarity which is aimed at encouraging states to investigate and prosecute cases domestically. The focus of this principle is to indirectly assist states to strengthen domestic institutions themselves (and not call for direct intervention) by the ICC to build the capacities of rule of law institutions in state parties (Bjork and Goebertus 2014; Nouwen 2013).

Two decisions of the Pre-Trial Chamber with opposite results illustrate how complementarity can determine whether the ICC will be involved in a situation or not. In *The Prosecutor v Francis Kirimi Muthaura, Uhuru Muigai Kenyatta and Mohammed Hussein Ali*,[12] the GoK challenged the admissibility of the case pursuant to article 17(b) of the Statute. Pre-Trial, Chamber 11, while rejecting one of the requests made by the applicants held, among other things, that in the absence of information, which substantiates the Government of Kenya's challenge, that there are ongoing investigations against the three suspects, the Chamber considers that there remains a situation of inactivity. Thus, the Chamber held that the case is not inadmissible following a plain reading of the first half of article 17(1)(a) of the Statute. The Chamber, therefore, further held there is no need to delve into an examination of the unwillingness or inability of the state, in accordance with article 17(2) and (3) of the Statute. While in *The Prosecutor v. Saif Al-Islam Gaddafi and Abdullah Al-Senussi* (Decision on the admissibility of the case against Abdullah Al-Senussi),[13] Pre-Trial Chamber I held among other

[12]ICC-01/09-02/11-383 of 30 January 2012.

[13]ICC-01/11-01/11-466 of 11 October 2013.

things, that Libya is able to carry out proceedings against Abdullah Al-Senussi and thus the case is inadmissible. According to the Chamber "taking into account all the relevant circumstances, the Chamber considers that Libya is not unable to otherwise carry out the proceedings against Mr. Al-Senussi due to a total or substantial collapse or unavailability of its national judicial system". Thus, the Chamber held that it is "satisfied that Libya is not unable to genuinely carry out the proceedings against Mr. Al-Senussi, within the meaning of article 17(l)(a) and (3) of the Statute".

1.9 Punishment

One of the main distinguishing features of a criminal trial from other types of trials or judicial proceedings is that at the end of a criminal trial, a penalty or punishment is always imposed if a person is found guilty. Punishment is justified on the grounds that it is just and equitable to punish those who commit crimes (retributive theory), that it may deter the offender and others from committing the same offence and other offences (deterrence theory), and that by punishing, the judicial authority will be sending messages to all, that similar acts by any member of the society will be punished (expressive theory). Other aims of punishment in international law may include incapacitation, reconciliation, rehabilitation, restoration and maintenance of peace (International Centre for Transitional Justice 2013; Roht-Arriaza 2006; Turano 2011).

The Rome Statute, however, did not include specific provisions on justifications or purposes of sentencing by the ICC, except for the recognition of the deterrent impact of the Court in the Preamble of the Rome Statute to the effect that putting an end to impunity for the perpetrators of international crimes will contribute to the prevention of such crimes. Expressing the likely deterrent impact of punishment should be distinguished from having a sentencing policy. Rule 145 of the Rules of Procedure and Evidence of the Court provides for factors to be taken into consideration by the Chambers when sentencing. Nonetheless, the purposes of punishment, according to the Trial

Chamber in the Thomas Lubanga Dyilo case,[14] are to punish those who commit international crimes, to put an end to impunity, and to contribute to the prevention of such crimes. This list encompasses both retributive and deterrence values. In its sentence decision, pursuant to article 76 of the Rome Statute, the Trial Chamber states that in considering the purpose of sentencing, the Court has taken note of the Preamble to the Rome Statute, which provides that "most serious crimes of concern to the international community as a whole must not go unpunished". The Court also states that it has taken note of another paragraph of the Preamble which states that state parties are "determined to put an end to impunity for the perpetrators of these crimes, and thus to contribute to the prevention of such crimes". In passing sentence, according to the Court, the Chamber shall also apply articles 23, 76, 78, and 81(2) (a) of the Rome Statute, and rules 143, 145 and 146 of the Rules of Procedure and Evidence of the Court.

Also, according to the OTP 2012–2015 Strategic Plan, the specific mission of the OTP is to impartially and independently strive to bring justice to the victims of the most serious crimes of concern to the international community, to contribute to ending impunity, to promote respect for the rule of law, by investigating and prosecuting to establish the truth, promoting peace by preventing the commission of such crimes, and to protect the safety, well-being, dignity and privacy of victims, witnesses and others at risk.[15] These objectives encompass restitution, deterrence, expressive condemnation, promotion of the rights of victims, promotion of peace and respect for the rule of law.

Article 77(1), which is the main punishment provision, provides that the ICC may impose any of the following penalties on a person convicted by the Court: imprisonment for a specified number of years, which may not exceed "a maximum of thirty years", and "a term of life

[14] Situation in the Democratic Republic of the Congo, The Prosecutor v. Thomas Lubanga Dyilo ICC-01/04-01/06.

[15] Office of the Prosecutor Strategic Plan June, 2012–2015, 9, https://www.icc-cpi.int/iccdocs/otp/OTP-Strategic-Plan-2013.pdf. Accessed 23 October 2018.

imprisonment when justified by the extreme gravity of the crime and the individual circumstances of the convicted person". Article 77(2) provides that in addition to imprisonment, the Court may impose a fine or order a forfeiture of proceeds, property and assets derived directly or indirectly from the crimes. In imposing a sentence, according to article 78(1), the Court is required to take into account such factors as the "gravity of the crimes and the individual circumstances of the convicted person" According to article 78(2), in imposing a sentence the Court is required "to deduct the time, if any, previously spent in detention in accordance with the order of the Court" and may "deduct any time otherwise spent in detention in connection with conduct underlying the crime". The Rome Statute does not provide for trial in absentia, and thus cooperation of state parties is important to enable the Court to perform its duties effectively.

The provisions of article 110 are instructive for the full understanding of the penal regime of the ICC. This article provides that the Court alone shall have the right to decide any reduction of sentence and shall decide on the matter after having heard the person. This review is only possible when the person has served two-thirds of the sentence, or twenty-five years in the case of life imprisonment. The Court shall review the sentence to determine if it should be reduced and shall reduce the sentence if one or more of the following factors are present:

> the early and continuing willingness of the person to cooperate with the Court in its investigations and prosecutions; the voluntary assistance of the person in enabling the enforcement of the judgments and orders of the Court in other cases; and other factors establishing a clear and significant change of circumstances sufficient to justify the reduction of sentence.

If the Court determines that it is not appropriate to reduce the sentence, it shall review the question of reduction of sentence at such intervals and apply such criteria as provided in the Rules of Procedure and Evidence.

On 13 November 2015, a panel of three Judges of the Appeals Chamber, specifically appointed by the Appeals Chamber, reviewed

Germain Katanga's (*The Prosecutor v Germain Katanga*)[16] sentence and decided to reduce it. Accordingly, the date for the completion of his sentence was set to 18 January 2016. The Panel conducted a review concerning the reduction of Mr. Katanga's sentence pursuant to article 110 of the Rome Statute. The Panel found the following factors to support a reduction in Mr. Katanga's sentence:

> (i) an early and continuing willingness by Mr Katanga to cooperate with the Court in its investigations and prosecutions; (ii) a genuine dissociation from his crimes demonstrated by Mr Katanga's conduct while in detention; (iii) the prospect of resocialisation and successful resettlement of Mr Katanga; and (iv) a change in Mr Katanga's individual circumstances.

The Panel also considered that Mr. Katanga's early release would give rise to some "social instability in the DRC", but found no evidence to suggest that it would be of a significant level. Taking into account the number of factors favouring a reduction in sentence and the extent of reduction that those factors supported, the three Judges concluded that it was appropriate to reduce Mr. Katanga's sentence by 3 years and 8 months.

The ICC does not have a prison, as such, according to article 103(1)(a) a sentence of imprisonment shall be served in a state designated by the Court from the list of states which have indicated to the ICC their willingness to accept the sentenced person.

So far the ICC has imposed four sentences. In *The Prosecutor v Thomas Lubanga Dyilo*,[17] Trial Chamber I, on 10 July 2012 sentenced Thomas Lubanga Dyilo to a total period of 14 years of imprisonment. The Appeals Chamber on 1 December 2014 confirmed, by majority, the verdict declaring Mr. Lubanga Dyilo guilty and the decision sentencing him to 14 years of imprisonment.

---

[16] Situation in the Democratic Republic of the Congo The Prosecutor v. Germain Katanga ICC-01/04-01/07.

[17] Decision on Sentence pursuant to article 76 of the Statute, ICC-01/04-01/06-2901, 13 July 2012.

In *The Prosecutor v Germain Katanga*,[18] Trial Chamber II on 23 May 2014 sentenced Germain Katanga to a total of 12 years' imprisonment. The Chamber also ordered that the time spent in detention at the ICC—between 18 September 2007 and 23 May 2014, be deducted from his sentence. Also, on 21 June 2016, the Trial Chamber III of the ICC in *The Prosecutor v. Jean-Pierre Bemba Gombo*[19] sentenced Jean-Pierre Bemba Gombo to 18 years' imprisonment, for war crimes and crimes against humanity committed in CAR. In June, 2018, the Appeal Chamber overturned this conviction and set Jean-Pierre Bemba Gombo free. Trial Chamber II on 27 September 2016 convicted and sentenced Ahmad al-Faqi al-Mahdi[20] to nine years' imprisonment, with time served to be deducted, for intentionally directing attacks against historical monuments or buildings dedicated to religion in Timbuktu, northern Mali.

1.10 Theory

The nexus between international accountability and peace is complex. The study will rely on some theories, among other tools, to discuss this nexus. Prosecution is principally based on the theory of retribution, which posits that those who break the social norm must be punished, and to some extent is based on the theories of deterrence, which states that punishment can deter those who may want to commit crimes. Punishment can also find justification in the expressive theory of justice, which argues that the law, through its actions, can express norms, and this process can lead to changes. These "theories are the most commonly cited underpinnings of international criminal justice despite scepticism about the ability of international criminal mechanisms to actually achieve these goals" (Drumbl 2007). Conflict transformation theories,

---

[18]Decision on Sentence pursuant to article 76 of the Statute, ICC-01/04-01/07-3484-tENG-Corr, 23 May 2014.

[19]Decision on Sentence pursuant to article 76 of the Statute, ICC-01/05-01/08-3399, 21 June 2016.

[20]Judgment and Sentence, The Prosecutor v. Ahmad Al Faqi Al Mahdi, CC-01/12-01/15-171, 27 September 2016.

especially the arguments of leading theorist John Paul Lederach (2003), are relied upon to discuss how the intervention of the ICC may have an impact on a peace process. These theories are discussed in Chapter 2.

1.11 Analytical Framework

One of the major issues in the relationship between international justice and conflict/peace is how to properly evaluate how international justice mechanisms influence peace processes/conflict transformation in conflicts and post-conflict situations (Schabas 2001; Kersten 2014). To address it, the researcher conceptualises that the ICC will be contributing positively to peace processes in Côte d'Ivoire, Kenya and Uganda if the Court promotes reconciliation, accountability to the law, the rights of victims of atrocities, and deters future atrocities or gross human rights violations. The level of influence will depend on the nature, degree and scope of impact on all or some of the variables. On the other hand, the ICC may not be contributing to the peace process in a country by not contributing to, or by complicating efforts to promote accountability to the law or protection of victims' rights or deterrence or reconciliation. Such interventions may also influence peace process in other ways. Thus, the analytical framework for the study is based on this conceptual analysis, the results of previous research, analyses by scholars and judgments of courts. The framework integrates existing findings into a new analytical framework based on four variables, which are considered by many scholars as the major results of the involvement of international justice mechanisms in conflict and post-conflict situations (Akhavan 2001; Nouwen 2012; Fletcher and Weinstein 2002; Sikkink 2011). The variables are: reconciliation, deterrence, victims' rights and accountability to the law. These variables are selected because they are the key aspects of the work of the ICC that could contribute to the peace processes in these countries. The study also explains (in Chapter 7) how these variables could contribute to peace processes in these countries. For instance, it is argued in this book that promotion of accountability to the law will contribute to reducing impunity, and reduction in the level of impunity will contribute to peace through the promotion of the rule of law. The rule of law is based on justice and security, two of the most essential prerequisites for sustainable peace and development (UNDP 2011). Also, incorporation of new laws, amendment of existing ones and judicial reforms will mean that greater pressure will exist for judicial accountability for perpetrators of gross violation of human rights to be initiated at local levels (Freeland 2010).

This study examines how these variables singularly or collectively influence the peace processes in these countries. Thus, in each country, the book examines how the involvement of the ICC stimulates reconciliation; how the ICC promotes victims' rights; how the ICC influences deterrence; and how the ICC promotes accountability to the law. Thus, the research questions were developed to examine how the involvement of the ICC affects the four variables in these countries, which provides a picture of how the involvement of the ICC influences peace processes.

1.12 Key Terms

There are a number of key terms that are central to the development of this study and require clarifications. The first is "Justice", which generally speaking is fairness (Rawls 1971) but it has many other connotations and is also deeply subjective (Clark 2011). It can be "legal" by enforcement of legal rules through the prosecution of those who commit crimes, or "distributive" through the removal of structural or systemic structure that causes inequalities, or "rectificatory" by addressing the direct consequences of injustices on people, or "restorative" which is the restoration of the positions of victims and affected relationships (Nouwen 2012). Justice in this study is seen as "legal" through the enforcement of legal rules by the ICC and "restorative" through the enforcement of legal rules by the ICC to address victims' rights and through direct and indirect involvement of the TFV in protecting victims' rights.

The second term is "Peace". The meaning of peace is disputed; thus, it has several definitions (Francis 2006). The controversies stem from the fact that peace is situational, subjective, a process and relative (Ibeanu 2006). However, there are two main classifications: positive peace and negative peace (Galtung 1996; Faleti 2006). In this negative sense, peace has been defined as: the absence of war, fear, conflict, anxiety and suffering (Francis 2006) or as the absence or reduction of violence of all kinds (Galtung 1996; Jenkins and Branagan 2014). The main criticism against the negative definition of peace is that it is possible not to have peace even in the absence of war or direct violence. Thus, societies that suffer from pervasive poverty, oppression, police brutality and monopolisation of resources by a few cannot be said to have peace or be peaceful, even when there is no direct violence (Ibeanu 2006). Peace is also conceptualised in the positive sense as non-violent and creative conflict transformation (Galtung 1996) or the absence of the causes of war (Nouwen 2012).

Ware (2014) states that there is need for at least four terms to cover various layers of peace. These are: when there is current fighting or armed conflict in the country (0 Peace); negative peace (Peace 1), where there is no mass violence but a risk of renewed fighting; stable peace (Peace 2), where the country has been at peace for a relatively long time, say five years, and looks likely to maintain the status quo for another relatively long time; and peace and justice (Peace 3), in countries that have peace and good institutional structures for realising social justice. In this study, peace is seen from the positive and negative senses. In the positive sense, it means the absence in a society of conditions that make structural violence possible. It includes but is not limited to access to justice, access to basic infrastructures, access to affordable health care, access to resources and access to education. Peace in the negative sense is used in this study as the absence of direct violence or the end of conflict or war. Thus, peace is conceptualised in this study as the absence of direct violence and the presence of basic conditions that make life worth living.

Next is the term "peace process", which like "peace" can be defined in different ways (Burgess 2004; Francis 2006). A peace process is the political process that deals with the obstacles in negotiation (Saunders 2001). The peace process is also seen as involving three or four forms, namely: peacekeeping, peace enforcement, peacemaking, and peacebuilding (Ibeanu 2006; Jenkins and Branagan 2014). The contemporary definition of peace process provided by Ramcharan (2009) will be relied on in this book because it covers major aspects of the contemporary peace process. Ramcharan states that a peace process "entails the efforts of a broad variety, tailored to each situation, to tackle the manifestations and root causes of differences that have led to a dispute or conflict and to help re-establish and sustain peace". The peace process, according to him, includes "the peacemaking phase, the phase at which a peace agreement is being pursued, the implementation phase…as well as the post-conflict peace building phase". Thus, the peace process in this book is the process of making peace and building peace after conflict. It includes all efforts to restore or create sustainable peace, such as re-establishing the rule of law, fostering reconciliation, rebuilding infrastructures, ensuring more access to justice, rebuilding the security sector and the economy. The peace process is, therefore, all efforts to return the society to the path of sustainable peace.

The last concept that requires clarification is conflict transformation. There are many theorists in the field of conflict transformation, such as Galtung, Rupesinghe, Vayrynen and Curle. However, Lederach's (2003) views on conflict transformations will be relied on to discuss the nexus between international justice and peace process. Conflict transformation will be seen as the process of moving a conflict from a destructive to a constructive process, by providing a platform that can creatively address surface problems and change underlying social structures, networks and relationship patterns (Lederach 2003). Lederach sees justice as important to conflict transformation, because transformation must respond to and address issues, challenges and needs of the people on the ground. To him, the central issue in the nexus between peace and justice is how to deal with conflict in ways that reduce violence and at the same time promote justice (Lederach 2003). Lederach is relied upon, because he, unlike most other conflict transformation theorists, provides an extensive discussion of the nexus between conflict transformation and justice.

1.13 Structure of the Book

The evidence presented to support the findings of the study and the analysis explaining how the ICC influences post-conflict situations, including the tensions and challenges inherent in the involvement of the Court in sovereign states, are laid out in eight chapters. Chapter 1 introduced this book by reviewing and explaining the rationale for the study, the research questions, the study's analytical framework and the nexus between international accountability and peace. It provides a brief outline of the development and challenges of the ICC, the major theories of punishment discussed in the book, the structure of the book, the doctrine of complementarity, the punishment provisions of the Rome Statute, the methodology of the study, the main findings of the study and some key terms like: peace, peace process, justice and conflict transformation. Chapter 2 discusses some relevant literature and issues on the relationship between international accountability and peace processes. It explores the nature, scope, challenges and dynamics of this relationship. Also, the chapter highlights the problems, tensions and challenges embedded in the international justice system, and how these issues impede the ability of international justice mechanisms to contribute to peace processes. Some of the issues discussed are: transitional justice, the peace and justice dilemma, the ICC and deterrence, the ICC and reconciliation, the ICC and victims' rights and the ICC and accountability.

Chapter 3 traces the history of violent conflicts in Africa and explores the nature and the types of violent conflicts common in the continent since the last sixty years, the patterns and trends of violent conflicts common in Africa, and the ICC's interventions in conflict situations in Africa. The violent conflicts in Uganda, Kenya and Côte d'Ivoire belong to some of the types identified. The central objective of this chapter is to examine the dynamics of the interaction between violent conflicts in Africa and the ICC.

Chapters 4, 5 and 6 deal with the countries used as case studies. The conflicts in each of the countries are discussed, and the impact of the involvement of the ICC on the peace process in each country is examined and explained. Chapter 4 examines the conflict in Northern Uganda, between the Government of Uganda (GoU) and the Lord's Resistance Army (LRA), the various peace efforts made in managing the conflict and the involvement of the ICC in the conflict. The focus of the chapter is on the nexus between the ICC's involvement and the peace process in the country. In Chapter 5, the causes and scope of the post-election violence (PEV) in Kenya are discussed. The chapter evaluates the nature of the government's responses to recurring election violence. Relying on relevant literature, documents, judgments of courts and field data, this chapter examines the causes and nature of the 2007/2008 PEV, the problems of managing the after-effects of the violence, the struggle for political and legal reforms in Kenya after the violence, the peace process, the politics and intrigues of the ICC's involvement in prosecuting those implicated and the consequences of the ICC's intervention on the peace process in the country.

Chapter 6 examines the political situation in Côte d'Ivoire between 2002 and 2011, and the efforts to resolve the conflicts, particularly the influence of the ICC's prosecutions on the peace process in the country. The chapter is concerned with the armed conflict of 2002/2003 that led to the partitioning of the country between government forces that controlled the South and Forces Nouvelles (FN), the rebel group that controlled the North. Also of special interest is the 2010/2011 PEV between December 2010 and May 2011. The chapter relies on an analysis of data collected from fieldwork in 2014 and 2015 on the situation in Côte d'Ivoire and on a literature review.

Chapter 7 comparatively explores and distils major arguments presented in previous chapters to present a pattern and a coherent account of how the ICC influences the peace processes in each situation. This approach involves comparing patterns and an analysis of impacts. The chapter also comparatively analyses how the intervention of the ICC influences peace processes. Chapter 8 presents the important issues from the discussions of the interventions of the ICC in the three countries, as well as the causes and nature of the violent conflicts, the review of literature and the analysis of the major findings of the study to provide a formal synthesis. It summarises the findings and the major recommendations of the study.

1.14 Methodology

This study is based on qualitative research. Interviews for the study were conducted with respondents in Uganda, Kenya, Ghana, Côte d'Ivoire, Nigeria, Australia, UK, USA and France between 10 November 2013 and 27 February 2015. A total of 48 personal interviews were conducted, 28 questionnaires were completed and received, and 5 interviews were conducted through email correspondence. The nature and objective of a study are some of the issues a researcher takes into consideration in the design of the sampling strategy (Wilmot 2006). Purposive non-random sampling was used to select respondents. Most of the respondents are experts in international accountability, transitional justice, peace/conflicts studies, victims' rights and Africa security studies/development. Others are legal practitioners/law teachers with expertise in national laws, community leaders, youth leaders (some of them victims of violence), government officials, leaders of NGOs and human rights advocates. Purposive sampling is when a researcher chooses specific people within the population to use for a particular research project. The main purpose is to focus on people with certain characteristics who will be very useful for the research (Wilmot 2006; Plooy 1995). The main advantage of purposive sampling is that the respondents are especially qualified to assist in the research (Plooy 1995).

Expert sampling, which is a type of purposive sampling, was used. This kind of sampling is beneficial when a study involves evaluations or opinions of individuals with expertise, high level of skill or knowledge. Expert sampling was used because of the nature and objective of this study, which requires respondents with deep knowledge of international accountability and its impacts on peace processes. Most of the respondents were selected based on their expertise, knowledge of the conflicts, involvement in the peace processes, in victims' redress and in formulating and implementing policies.

The study relies on the responses of respondents, analyses of literature and the situation in each country, and review of other factors, to access how the variables relate to peace processes. For instance, with respect to deterrence the researcher relied on the views of respondents and the situation on ground, as the claim of deterrence can best be substantiated through specific examples (Mendez and Kelly 2015). A practical result of deterrence is conflict prevention.

The countries were selected to serve the purpose of the study and to answer the research questions. Kenya was selected because it represents a case where the chief prosecutor initiated a case *proprio motu*, where top national political leaders were involved in cases before the ICC.

Uganda is the first country that the ICC intervened in, it is also the first example of self-referral by a state party, the first example of an intervention by the ICC in a prolonged armed conflict, a country where an amnesty law was enacted after the intervention of the ICC, and where local reconciliation mechanisms are constantly presented as an alternative to ICC prosecution. Côte d'Ivoire represents a situation where an immediate former head of state is being prosecuted and the first situation from West Africa before the ICC.

1.15 Main Findings

The major finding of the *comparative* analysis of the countries is that the involvement of the ICC has had multiple impacts on the situations across these countries, and that, despite some acknowledged arguments to the contrary, the ICC does contribute positively to peace processes through deterrence and the promotion of accountability to the law. However, there is minimal evidence that the ICC effectively contributes to peace processes in these countries through the promotion of reconciliation and victims' rights. The key findings are highlighted below:

1. The establishment of rule of law institutions and the enactment of laws and regulations that mirror international standards do not automatically result in the promotion of accountability to the law at the national level. Rather these developments are important first steps in the long and tedious process of promoting accountability to the law. Promotion of accountability to the law will contribute to reducing impunity, and reduction in the level of impunity will contribute to peace through the promotion of the rule of law. The rule of law is based on justice and security, two of the most essential prerequisites for sustainable peace and development (UNDP 2011). Also, incorporation of new laws, amendment of existing ones and judicial reforms will mean that greater pressure will exist for judicial accountability for perpetrators of gross violation of human rights to be initiated at local levels (Freeland 2010).

2. The ICC contributes to the promotion of victims' rights in two ways. The first is by influencing some national governments to establish pro-victim rights institutions, to the extent that some pro-victims' rights agencies were established after the ICC got involved. Also, the reparation provisions in the Rome Statute of the ICC are new in international criminal law because they provide victims of conflicts with actual rights to reparation. However, the ICC victims' redress is also symbolic since only a few persons are covered by the mechanism and such persons are only represented by Counsel (Moffett 2014). The ICC, therefore, does not impact on the peace process through its impacts on victims' rights, since these contributions are very minimal and have not concretised to have any significant influence on peace processes.
3. The ICC does not contribute to reconciliation in the short term in Côte d'Ivoire, Kenya and Uganda and to that extent does not contribute to the peace processes in the three countries. In Côte d'Ivoire, the intervention of the ICC was shown to be divisive and to contribute negatively to the process of reconciliation in the country.
4. The practical impact of deterrence is conflict prevention. Some of the aims of conflict prevention are to strengthen likely *preventors*, such as the ICC, and reduce likely causes of war or mass violence (Miall et al. 1999). There are two main aspects of conflict prevention. One is establishing measures for the prevention of violent conflicts. This involves developing short-, medium- and long-term measures for conflict prevention. The second aspect of conflict prevention involves preventing relapses into wars or violent conflicts after peace agreements have been fully executed by the parties. The ICC contributes to conflict prevention in these countries, in the second sense, through deterrence. The practical impact has been an avoidance of relapses to conflicts, which has contributed to de-escalation of conflicts in Kenya, Côte d'Ivoire and Uganda. In this way, the ICC contributes to the peace processes in these countries.

1.16 Conclusion

This chapter introduced the book by reviewing and explaining the rationale for the study, the research questions, the study's analytical framework and the nexus between international accountability and peace. It provided a brief outline of the development and challenges of the ICC, the major theories of punishment discussed in the book, the structure of the book, the doctrine of complementarity, the punishment provisions of the Rome Statute, the methodology of the study, the main findings of the study and some key terms like: peace, peace process, justice, conflict transformation and ICC's intervention. It also highlighted the tensions and challenges of deploying an international Court in a national setting. The next chapter discusses some relevant literature and issues on the relationship between international accountability and peace processes and also explores the nature, scope, challenges and dynamics of this relationship.

References

Akhavan, Payam. 2001. "Beyond Impunity: Can International Criminal Justice Prevent Future Atrocities?" *The American Journal of International Law* 95.7: 7–31.

Amann, Diane Marie. 2003. "Assessing the Criminal Adjudication of Human Rights Atrocities". *Third World Legal Studies* 16: 169–181.

Bjork, Christine and Juanita Goebertus. 2014. "Complementarity in Action: The Role of Civil Society and the ICC in Rule of Law Strengthening in Kenya". *Yale Human Rights Law and Development Journal* 14: 205–230.

Burgess, Heidi. 2004. "Peace Processes: What Are They?" *Beyond Intractability*. Accessed April 15, 2015. http://www.beyondintractability.org/essay/peace-processes.

Clark, Janine. 2011. "Peace, Justice and the International Criminal Court". *Journal of International Criminal Justice* 9: 521–545.

De Vos, Christian, Sara Kendall, and Carten Stahn. 2015. "Introduction". In *Contested Justice: The Politics and Practice of International Criminal Court Interventions*, edited by Christian de Vos, Sara Kendall, and Carten Stahn, 1–20. Cambridge: Cambridge University Press.

Drumbl, Mark. 2007. *Atrocity, Punishment and International Law*. Cambridge: Cambridge University Press.

Du Max, Plessis. 2010. *The International Court Africa Wants*. Pretoria: Institute for Security Studies, Pretoria.

Faleti, Ademola. 2006. "Theories of Social Conflict". In *Introduction to Peace and Conflict Studies in Africa: A Reader*, edited by Shedrack Best, 35–60. Ibadan: Spectrum Books.

Fletcher, Laurel and Harvey Weinstein. 2002. "Violence and Social Repair: Rethinking the Contributions of Justice to Reconciliation". *Human Rights Quarterly* 24: 573–639.

Francis, David. 2006. Peace and Conflict Studies: An African Overview of Basic Concepts. In *Introduction to Peace and Conflict Studies in Africa: A Reader*, edited by Shedrack Best. Ibadan: Spectrum Books.

Freeland, Steven. 2010. "Effectiveness of International Criminal Justice." Accessed September 20, 2015. http://www.austlii.edu.au/au/journals/ALRS/2008/16.html.

Galtung, John. 1996. *Peace by Peaceful Means*. London: Sage.

Goldston, James. 2016. "Three Lessons from the ICC's Kenya Debacle. Open Society Foundation". Open Society Foundation, April 6. Accessed April 15, 2016. https://medium.com/open-society-foundations/three-lessons-from-the-icc-s-kenyadebacle-515df408531b#.fs9dlxwre.

Human Rights Watch. 2016. "To Consolidate This Peace of Ours." Human Rights Watch Report. Accessed February 28, 2016. http://www.hrw.org/report/2015/12/08/consolidate-peace-ours/human-rights-agenda-cotedivoire.

Ibeanu, Okechukwu. 2006. "Conceptualising Peace". In *Introduction to Peace and Conflict Studies in Africa: A Reader*, edited by Shedrack Best. Ibadan: Spectrum Books.

International Centre for Transitional Justice. 2013 "Criminal Justice." International Centre for Transitional Justice Briefing. Accessed May 10, 2013. http://www.ictj.org.

International Crises Group. 2012. "Kenya: Impact of the ICC Proceedings." International Crises Group: Policy Briefing, Africa Briefing No. 84. Accessed April 12, 2016. http://www.crisisgroup.org/en/regions/africa/horn-of-africa/kenya/b084kenya.

Jenkins, Bert and Marty Branagan. 2014. "Introduction". In *Cultivating Peace*, edited by Helen Ware, Bert Jerkins, Marty Branagan, and D.B. Subedi, 1–16. Newcastle upon Tyne: Cambridge Scholars Publishing.

Jurdi, Nidal Nabil. 2011. *The International Criminal Court and National Courts: A Contentious Relationship*. Surry: Ashgate.

Kersten, Mark. 2014. "The ICC and Its Impact: More Known Unknowns". Accessed December 24, 2014. https://justiceinconflict.org/2014/11/05/the-icc-and-its-impactmore-known-unknowns/.

Ku, Julian and Jide Nzeribe. 2006. "Do International Criminal Tribunals Deter or Exacerbate Humanitarian Atrocities?" *Washington University Law Review* 84: 777–833.

Ladan, Muhammed. 2010. "Immunity of Heads of State and the Jurisdiction of ICC Under the Rome Statute". Accessed April 21, 2016. http://mtladan.blogspot.com.au/.

Lederach, John Paul. 2003. *The Little Book of Conflict Transformation*. Intercourse, PA: Good Books.

Lincoln, Jessica. 2011. *Transitional Justice, Peace and Accountability*. Oxon: Routledge.

Malu, Linus. 2015. "The International Criminal Court and Conflict Transformation in Uganda: Views from the Field". *African Journal on Conflict Resolution* 15: 81–102.

Meijers, Tim and Marlies Glasius. 2013. "Expression of Justice or Political Trial? Discursive Battles in the Karadzic Case". *Human Right Quarterly* 35: 720–752.

Mendez, Juan and Jeremy Kelly. 2015. "Peace Making, Justice and the ICC". In *Contested Justice: The Politics and Practice of International Criminal Court Interventions* edited by Christian de Vos, Sara Kendall, and Carsten Stahn, 479–496. Cambridge: Cambridge University Press.

Miall, Huge, Oliver Ramsbotham, and Tom Woodhouse. 1999. *Contemporary Conflict Resolution*. Cambridge: Polity.

Moffett, Luke. 2014. *Victims Before the International Criminal Court*. New York: Routledge.

Mueller, Sussane. 2014. "Kenya and the International Criminal Court: Politics, the Election and the Law". *Journal of East African Studies* 8: 25–42.

Nouwen, Sarah. 2012. "The International Criminal Court: A Peacebuilder in Africa?" In *Peacebuilding, Power, and Politics in Africa*, edited by Devon Curtis and Gwinyayi Dzinesa, 171–192. Athens: Ohio University Press.

Nouwen, Sarah. 2013. *Complementarity in the Line of Fire: The Catalysing Effect of the International Criminal Court in Uganda and Sudan*. Cambridge: Cambridge University Press.

Plooy, G.M., ed. 1995. *Introduction to Communication*. Cape Town: Juta Academic.

Ramcharan, Bertrand. 2009. "Peace Process". In *Post-conflict Peacebuilding: A Lexicon*, edited by Vincent Chetail, 229–245. Oxford: Oxford University Press.

Rawls, John. 1971. *A Theory of Justice*. Oxford: Oxford University Press.

Rigney, Sophie. 2014. "Unsettled Times at The Hague." Accessed November 19, 2014. http://insidestory.org.au/unsettled-times-at-thehague.

Roht-Arriaza, Naomi. 2006. "The New Landscape of Transitional Justice". In *Transitional Justice in the Twenty-First Century: Beyond Truth versus Justice*, edited by Naomi Roht-Arriaza and Javier Mariezcurrena, 1–16. Cambridge: Cambridge University Press.

Saunders, Harold. 2001. "Renegotiation and Circum-negotiation: Arenas of multilevel Peace Process". In *Turbulent Peace: The Challenges of Managing International Conflict*, edited by Chester Croaker, Fen Hampson and Pamela Aall, 483–496. Washington, DC: United States Institute for Peace.

Schabas, William. 2001. "International Law Responses to Conflict". In *Turbulent Peace: The Challenges of Managing International Conflict*, edited by Chester Croaker, Fen Hampson and Pamela Aall, 603–618. Washington, DC: United States Institute for Peace.

Schabas, William. 2007. *An Introduction to the International Criminal Court*. Cambridge: Cambridge University Press.

Schabas, William. 2011. "Transitional Justice and the Norms of International Law". Japanese Society of International Law, Kwansei Gakuin University. Accessed April 2, 2013.www.jsil.jp/annual_documents/2011.

Schabas, Williams. 2012. *Unimaginable Atrocities: Justice, Politics, and Rights at the War Crimes Tribunals*. Oxford: Oxford University Press.

Sikkink, Kathryn. 2011. *The Justice Cascade: How Human Rights Prosecutions are Changing World Politics*. New York: W.W. Norton.

Teitel, Ruti. 2011. *Humanity's Law*. New York: Oxford University Press.

Turano, Laura. 2011. "The Gender Dimension of Transitional Justice". *New York University International Law and Politics* 43:1045–1085.

United Nations Development Program. 2011. "Strengthening the Rule of Law in Crisis-Affected and Fragile Situations". Accessed June 2, 2015 http://www.undp.org/content/dam/undp/library/crisis%20prevention/Global%20Programme%20Phase%20II%20-%20FINAL.pdf.

Ware, Helen. 2014. "What Does the Person on the Street Corner Want? Growing Peace Through Democracy: Issues with Hybridity". In *Cultivating*

Peace, edited by Helen Ware, Bert Jerkins, Marty Branagan, and D.B. Subedi, 17–54. Newcastle upon Tyne: Cambridge Scholars Publishing.

Wegner, Patrick. 2015. *International Criminal Court in Ongoing Conflicts*. Cambridge: Cambridge University Press.

Williams, Sarah. 2012. *Hybrid and Internationalized Criminal Tribunals: Selected Jurisdictional Issues*. Oregon: Hart Publishing.

Wilmot, Amanda. 2006. "Designing Sampling Strategies for Qualitative Social Research: With Particular Reference to the Office for National Statistics' Qualitative Respondent Register". Accessed April 20, 2016. http://www.cdc.gov/qbank/QUest/2005/Paper23.pdf.

Wippman, David. 1999. "Atrocities, Deterrence, and the Limits of International Justice". *Fordman International Law Journal* 23: 473–488.

2

Analysis of Some Background Issues

The trouble with peace and reconciliation is that, unlike warfare and torture, they tend to require time and patience. (Thomas Buergenthal)[1]

2.1 Introduction

The prosecution of war crimes can be traced to the time of ancient Greece, or even before then. These trials were restricted to the vanquished, or to isolated cases of rogue soldiers in the victor's army (Schabas 2007). The trial of Peter von Hagenbach in 1474 for crimes committed during the occupation of Breisach was probably the first genuine international criminal trial (Cryer 2005; Schabas 2007). Contemporary international criminal prosecution has its foundations in the 1648 Peace of Westphalia Treaties and the development of international humanitarian law in the mid-nineteenth century.

[1]Thomas Buergenthal, interviewed by Newsweek, 6 July 2015. https://www.newsweek.com/british-judiciarylord-jannericc-judgeauschwitzjewsholocaustprofessor-law-602725. Accessed 21 January 2019.

L. N. Malu, *The International Criminal Court and Peace Processes*,
Palgrave Studies in Compromise after Conflict,
https://doi.org/10.1007/978-3-030-19905-0_2

The establishment of the ICC in 2002 represents the ultimate example of the modern era evolution of international criminal justice (Kowalski 2011). This chapter examines the literature on the relationship between ICC and peace processes, exploring the nature, scope, challenges and dynamics of this relationship. It also highlights the problems, tensions and challenges embedded in the international justice system and how these influence the ability of the ICC to contribute to peace processes.

2.2 Theoretical Framework for the Study

The subject of this book stands astride two areas: conflict transformation and international criminal justice, and focuses on the impact of law on conflict and post-conflict societies. In between these two areas and subsumed in them are the following: the ICC, peace processes, conflict resolution, international justice, reconciliation and amnesty. The theoretical foundations for this book are therefore located in these above-mentioned fields, but pinned to theories of conflict transformation and international criminal justice. While there is a fast developing theory of conflict transformation, based mainly on reconceptualisation of conflict resolution and conflict management theories to meet the rapidly evolving field of conflict transformation (Botes 2003; Miall 2013), there are few attempts at theorising international criminal law, and a dearth of literature on the theory and philosophy of international criminal law, because it a relatively new field in international law (Gevers 2011; May and Hoskins 2010).

The intriguing question, whether there is a theory of international criminal law, remains largely unanswered (Amann 2003; Gevers 2011; May and Hoskins 2010). Though there has been reliance on some theories relevant to international criminal law, such as expressive, deterrence and retributive theories of punishment, used to explain some aspects of international criminal law, Gevers (2011) and Drumble (2007) argue that international criminal law needs a distinct unifying theory to coherently address some of the difficult challenges facing this field of study and practice. This book relies on three theories of punishment—deterrence, expressive and retribution—to discuss the

ICC's prosecutorial strategies. The ICC may adopt different strategies and methodologies to achieve its objectives depending on the theory or combination of theories used. These theories of punishment are the most commonly cited foundations of international criminal justice (Drumbl 2007). The type of theory or combination of theories adopted by the ICC has practical implications for the Court and its ability to impact on peace processes in the three countries. This book also relies on conflict transformation theory to examine how these interventions by the ICC are impacting on the peace processes in Côte d'Ivoire, Uganda and Kenya.

2.2.1 Conflict Transformation

Conflict transformation is a relatively new and distinct field in the study of conflict and peace. It posits that the existence of conflict is a "valuable and indispensable part of social change and development, but does not see violence as inevitable in the relations and interactions between conflicting parties" (Berghof Foundation 2012). Conflict transformation is the "process of moving from a conflict-habituated system to a peace system" and is different from conflict resolution, because it focuses on "system change" (Botes 2003). According to Botes (2003), *transformationalists* see systemic change as central to conflict transformation, and the "most critical element to be addressed for the transformation process to be completed". Whereas the key question of conflict resolution is: "how do we end something not desired?" that of conflict transformation is: "how do we end something destructive and build something desired?" (Lederach 2003).

Conflict transformation grew out of conflict management and conflict resolution; so also does the theory of conflict transformation, drawing on many of the familiar concepts of conflict management and resolution, and based on the same tradition of theorising conflict (Botes 2003). Conflict transformation theories posit that contemporary conflicts require methodologies for "engaging with and transforming relationships, interests, discourse and if necessary, the very constitution of society that supports the violent conflict". The lenses of conflict transformation focus on the potential for constructive change emergent from and catalysed by the rise of social conflict, and because the potential for broader change is inherent in any episode of conflict, from personal to structural levels, the lenses can easily apply to a wide range of conflicts (Lederach 2003).

The most detailed and perhaps most cited conflict transformation theorist is John Paul Lederach (Botes 2003). Lederach (2003) provides an insightful articulation of the conflict transformation field. He argues that a conflict transformation process begins with two active foundations: a positive orientation towards conflict, and a willingness to engage in the conflict with a desire to produce constructive change or growth. For Lederach, constructive change can be achieved by drawing positive energy out of a conflict and focusing it on the underlying relationships and social structures. Accordingly, the main focus of conflict transformation endeavours is to transform conflict from a destructive to a constructive process. The primary task is to provide a platform that can serve as the basis to creatively address surface problems and change underlying social structures, networks and relationship patterns (Lederach 2003).

Lederach (2003) views justice as important to conflict transformation, because in his view, transformation must respond to and address issues, challenges and needs of the people on the ground. The central issue in the nexus between peace and justice is how to deal with conflict in ways that reduce violence and at the same time promote justice (Lederach 2003). Thus, he posits that peace and justice should be complementary and pursued together, but rejects the argument that there is tension between the two. To reduce violence, the obvious and primary issues such as, content, underlying patterns and root causes must be properly addressed. To promote and ensure justice, opportunities must be created for people to have access to political procedures and a voice in the decision-making processes of the society. Lederach's theory of conflict transformation envisages the deployment of transitional justice institutions such as the ICC in post-conflict situations as part of the peace process.

Lederach (2001) states that the practice of justice in prolonged conflicts addresses how to: "create processes that increase accountability and responsibility for the consequences of past actions that have harmed others in a way that are responsive to victims' needs". Clearly, according to Lederach, justice is important to conflict transformation, because justice ensures accountability, tackles the underlying causes of conflict, and may lead to restoration, if properly pursued with truth and mercy. It is uncertain whether the ICC could ever possess the features that can produce the quality of justice envisaged by Lederach, but the Court can provide the legal mechanism which may contribute to providing short-term responses and long-term strategies that may address some of the root causes of violent conflict such as impunity.

The main weakness of conflict transformation theory is that its definitions and pronouncements are still in flux, constantly in the process of being refined, and somewhat oscillating between conflict resolution and conflict management. Another weakness is that it may not be applicable to all conflicts, since not all conflicts may involve long-term relationships or have shared an extensive past, requiring the exploration of relational and structural patterns or the constructing of new platforms for future relationships. In conflicts where parties need a quick and final solution to a problem, and do not share a deep relationship, such as in hostage-taking, negotiation/mediation may be more appealing. The conflicts in Côte d'Ivoire, Kenya and Uganda involve long-term relationships, share an extensive past and require either exploration of relational and structural patterns or the constructing of new platforms for future relationships, and are suitable for conflict transformation. The third weakness according to Botes (2003) is that it is not always clear how a conflict transformation process can transform conflicts, who should be involved, and how long it takes. Also, conflict transformation processes may take an unduly long time and require great efforts, since it is focused on changing people or societies. Botes (2003) also warns that since changing people and societies rather than the conflicts at hand has become part of the primary purposes of conflict transformation, it may end up achieving neither.

In Chapter 1, it was briefly argued that the ICC's intervention may promote peace process through conflict transformation by promoting reconciliation, addressing impunity, protecting victims' rights and contributing to general deterrence. As discussed in Chapter 1, a peace process involves the efforts of wide-ranging types, to tackle conflicts and its root causes, and the efforts to re-establish and sustain peace. Conflict transformation is the process of moving from a conflict-habituated system to a peace system, and which focuses on how to end something destructive and build something desired. In Chapters 4, 5 and 6, the violent conflicts in Uganda, Kenya and Côte d'Ivoire are discussed, and the impact of the intervention of the ICC on the peace process on each country analysed. In Chapter 7, it is argued that the ICC contributes to the peace processes by contributing to accountability to the law and general deterrence. It is also argued that the ICC does not contribute to reconciliation in the short term, and that the impacts of the ICC on victims' rights are not substantial to contribute to the peace process. It is further argued that the ICC contributes to conflict transformation in the three countries by contributing to the peace process, through its contributions to general deterrence and the promotion of accountability to the law.

As argued in Chapter 7, the ICC does not contribute to reconciliation in the short term, and to that extent, does not contribute to the peace processes in the three countries. The ICC does not contribute to conflict transformation through reconciliation since it does not contribute positively, through reconciliation to the peace process. Also, in furtherance of the argument made in Chapter 7, that the impacts of the ICC on victims' redress is not significant to contribute to the peace process, it is also argued that the ICC does not contribute to conflict transformation through the promotion of the rights of victims since it does not contribute to the peace process through the promotion of the rights of victims. These contributions are very minimal and have not concretised to have any significant impact on conflict transformation.

Further, the failure of the ICC to convict any of those indicted in the three countries, while not negating the peace process does not seems to be promoting peace processes either. In Kenya, the ICC is perceived to be weak, unorganised, and almost as ineffective as national courts by some respondents. This argument cannot be ignored since the Court after over five years has not convicted any of the leaders indicted by the Court. In Uganda, the failure of the ICC to prosecute most of the indicted persons is seen as a sign of weakness, reminiscent of Uganda national courts, and therefore does not promote peace process.

The ICC also seems to be "occupying space" in some cases, and blocking peace processes. In the words of Adam (2011), the ICC may be distracting the international community from using other forms of political organisations and actions that might lead to peace, and reducing international negotiations to criminal justice. In Uganda, the ICC is perceived to have played a significant part in the failure of Juba Peace Talks (Lanz 2007; Nouwen 2012; Tenove 2013). Also, the involvement of the ICC in Uganda is seen to have influenced some leaders of the LRA from taking advantage of the amnesty programme of the government since they were not sure the ICC would respect the amnesty if granted by the GoU. In Côte d'Ivoire, some respondents argue that amnesty for leaders is preferred to prosecution by the ICC, since what the country needed is reconciliation and not prosecution.

2.2.2 Deterrence

The deterrence theory of punishment is linked to the works of classical philosophers such as Thomas Hobbes (1588–1678), Cesare Beccaria (1738–1794) and Jeremy Bentham (1748–1832). These classical deterrence philosophers wrote against the legal policies that had dominated European thought for more than a thousand years and against the spiritual explanation of crime upon which they were founded. They advocated for a social contract between the government and citizens to create a civil society, based on the rule of law, and a criminal justice system founded on deterrence (Onwudiwe et al. 2010).

The principal argument of the deterrence theory of punishment is that people are punished to deter them and others from violating the social contract. It is based on the assumption that people choose to obey or disobey the law after carefully calculating the costs and benefits of their actions. There are basically two main types of deterrence: general and specific. General deterrence aims at crime prevention in the general public, that is, punishment of crimes will serve as an example for others who are not yet offenders. The proposition is that by having a criminal justice regime that can impose sanctions, the populace will be deterred from committing offences (Hopkins Burke 2009; Wood 2012). The goal of general deterrence is for "criminal sanctions to tap into social conditions and social norms to deter criminal activities" (Wood 2012).

In conflict situations, general deterrence may take place when the threats of criminal prosecution deter a person or group of persons in a particular society from committing crimes or deter others, generally from committing crimes, by being aware of the certainty or likelihood of punishment. General deterrence in an international criminal justice context could be achieved through specific legal interventions by an international criminal justice institution such as by: (1) opening investigations, (2) initiating prosecution, (3) issuing public statements/warnings directed at the main conflict parties, and (4) issuing summonses and arrest warrants (Rosenberg 2012).

Specific deterrence is tailored to deter only the specific individual from that crime, and other crimes in the future. It is thought that the sanctioned offender will be deterred from committing the same or other offences because it is certain he/she will be caught and punished. It is based on the assumption that the severity of punishment prevents offenders from committing the same offence again (Hopkins Burke 2009; Wood 2012). A rebel leader, for instance, may be deterred from a criminal action, such as enlisting child soldiers, after calculating the risk of being caught, the cost of committing the crime, (which could be a likelihood of prosecution by the ICC), and benefits, (which could be battlefield gains), and finding that the cost outweighs the benefits (Wood 2012).

The main principles of deterrence theory are: severity, certainty and swiftness (Hopkins Burke 2009; Wright 2010). Severity of punishment arguments state that the more severe a punishment is, the more likely a rational calculating would-be offender will be deterred from committing the crime. Thus, to prevent crimes, the criminal justice system must prescribe severe penalties to deter people from committing crimes and such sanctions must be necessary to deter, as excessive punishments are unjust. Weak punishments will not deter people from committing crimes. The certainty argument posits that punishment has more impact on deterrence if it is certain that punishment will be imposed once an offence is committed. Classical philosophers such as Thomas Hobbes, Cesare Beccaria and Jeremy Bentham maintained that certainty is more effective than severity in preventing crimes (Onwudiwe et al. 2010). Later studies also point in the direction that increasing and ensuring the certainty of punishment is more likely to produce a stronger deterrent impact than increasing the severity of punishment (Wright 2010). Certainty of sanction has been critiqued on the ground that it is based on the assumption that there is a hundred per cent certainty of arrest, while in practice; most crimes do not result in arrest (Wright 2010). Aloyo, Dutton and Heger (2013) assert that the ICC has met or is likely to meet the certainty principle. This assertion is correct to the extent that the ICC is a permanent Court with structures to investigate and prosecute crimes within its jurisdiction, but the Court's inability to execute several arrest warrants for ten accused persons: (Côte d'Ivoire (Simone Gbagbo); DRC (Sylvester Mudacumura); Kenya (Walter Barasa, Paul Gicheru and Philip Bett); Libya (Saif Al-Islam Gaddafi); Sudan (Ahmed Harun, Ali Muhammad Ali Abd-Al-Rahman and Omar al-Bashir) questions its capability to meet this basic requirement of the principle.

Deterrence theorists also contend that for punishment to deter, it must be swift and speedily applied. The closer the punishment is to the time of committing the offence the more likely it will deter (Onwudiwe et al. 2010; Wright 2010). In sum, deterrence theorists posit that if punishment is swift, certain and severe, a rational person will weigh the cost-effectiveness of engaging in a crime and will be deterred if the loss is greater than the gain (Hopkins Burke 2009). Aloyo et al. (2013) also argue that the ICC has met, or has the potential to meet the requirements of the principle of swiftness. While this is so in some conflict situations where the ICC has intervened such as in Libya, Kenya, Sudan, Côte d'Ivoire and Mali, it is doubtful if it is so in some other conflicts such as in DRC, Northern Uganda and Central Africa Republic (CAR).

Deterrence theory has remained an important intellectual foundation for domestic and international criminal justice systems. The Western criminal penal system is essentially based on the idea that sanctions deter criminals, with advocates clamouring for the establishment of more prisons, imposition of harsher sanctions, and a more effective justice system that will ensure certainty of conviction and sentencing, with the hope that these policies will reduce recidivism (Onwudiwe et al. 2010). Despite its merits and wide acceptance, debates on its impact have continued to engage criminologists. The main areas of doubts are in its reliance on the rationality of would-be offenders. It is also not always the case that people will consider the consequences of their actions before committing a crime (Wright 2010). It is also evident that some petty criminals do not engage in cost-benefit analysis before the crime, and that young people who spontaneously engage in street fights do not undertake rational analysis of the consequences of their actions before the fight (Hopkins Burke 2009).

Furthermore, the assumption that people are always deterred by sanctions is highly debatable, with the suicide bomber who is prepared to pay the ultimate price a good example. Yet another problem in assessing deterrence is that in order for sanctions to deter, would-be offenders must be aware of the sanctions that are in place. It is doubtful if most people, especially the uneducated are aware of existing sanctions, amendments of sanctions and the consequences of their actions before committing crimes. In fact, it is highly doubtful, if low-ranked armed fighters in conflict situations in Uganda, DRC, Libya, Darfur and CAR have ever heard of the ICC normative regime.

In Chapter 7, it is argued that the ICC contributes to the peace processes in the three countries through general deterrence. This study argues that without actually convicting any persons from the three countries, the threat of punishment by the ICC still contributes to general deterrence. The ICC's interventions and actions increase the costs of committing crime by increasing the likelihood of punishment. Therefore, according to the cost-benefit model of deterrence, threatening punishment in the three countries contributes to deterrence of crimes by increasing their costs.

However, the application of deterrence theory to mass atrocities faces several problems. One of the problems is that there is little possibility that all those who committed mass atrocities during the conflicts in the three countries will be arrested and prosecuted. Many persons who bear grave responsibility in these conflicts in the countries are yet to be prosecuted for several reasons. The Uganda situation where only one out of five originally accused persons is currently being prosecuted is instructive. It is doubtful if the prosecution of only Dominic Ongwen out of the many that committed atrocities during more than twenty years of armed conflict in Northern Uganda will be sufficient to contribute to deterrence. Also, a state party may refuse to hand over an accused persons to the ICC, as shown in the Simone Gbagbo case where even when Côte d'Ivoire had lost the admissibility application, it still refused to hand over Simone Gbagbo to the ICC. There is also the assumption that perpetrators of mass atrocities are rational in their behaviour, which is not always the case. Despite these difficulties, this study relies on the arguments made in Chapter 7 to conclude that the ICC contributes to general deterrence, which could lead to conflict prevention.

2.2.3 Expressive

The main postulate of expressive theorists such as Richard Pildes, Dan Kahan, Cass Sunstein (Adler 2000) and Elizabeth Anderson (Strudler 2001) is that law "teaches", "educates", "communicates meanings" and "passes messages" or "social meanings". Expressive theorists argue that the law provides a platform for "enunciating societal condemnation of atrocities…and for making an historical record of conflicts" (Amann 2003). It examines the law's potential for changing the meaning of a particular action by changing the social cost of undertaking the behaviour. Expressive theorists also contend that it is what the court expresses, through its case law-judgments, decisions and orders that will over time lead to general deterrence of those considering committing crimes (Rosenberg 2012; Meijers and Glasius 2013). Expressive explanation of punishment in criminal justice states that a sanction is not just meant to punish offenders, but is also a special social convention to indicate moral condemnation. Therefore, the response of the state to criminal offences should convey a message of condemnation of the crime committed (Adler 2000).

Expressive theory discusses the social message of a government action such as a prosecution, sentence or punishment. Expressive theorists are therefore concerned not so much with the message "conveyed or intended" by government officials or institutions, but by the "message that is understood by the people that hear it". Thus, the actions of the government could yield an expressive harm or an expressive good (Amann 2003). Expressive theory has been broken down into descriptive and normative claims about legal meaning. Some of these postulates are that: (1) law has expressive dimensions or sends messages, (2) law's meaning is determined not solely by what legislators intended but also by what the subjects perceive of the law, and (3) legal meaning is not limited to communicative meanings but could extend to those unintentionally communicated (Smith 2012).

International criminal justice could be justified by its expressive role, since "trials can educate people through the spectacle of theatre", which is followed by the imposition of sanctions, and attendant shame and stigma (Meijers and Glasius 2013). Thus, the expressive theory of international law is useful in explaining the roles of international justice institutions in expressing social disproval through the legal process, by a progressive entrenchment of international norms which could lead to self-control among the wider public (Akhavan 2001). The impact of international criminal justice may extend beyond directly affected countries, since the prosecution and political demise of leaders send strong messages that impunity even of political leaders will not be tolerated. Publicly asserting human rights norms and shaming criminal leaders may contribute to conflict prevention through the power of moral persuasion which may transform behaviour. Such impacts may be subtle, long-term, profound and continuing (Akhavan 2001).

The expressive theory could be useful to the ICC, playing a significant role in international criminal justice by expressing global norms as an arrowhead of, and standard setter for international criminal justice. This will free the Court from the controversy of how it selects its cases and enable it to make maximum impact with limited resources. This way, the Court can make more impact on global justice by pursuing illustrative cases, based on the expressive theory, than it could make if it focuses on deterrence and retribution (deGuzman 2012). Though not clearly stated, the ICC may have been adopting an expressive approach in selecting cases, because the prosecutorial strategy of the ICC is focused on selecting a limited number of cases "to allow the Office to carry out short investigations; to limit the number of persons put at risk by reason of their interaction with the Office; and to propose expeditious trials while aiming to represent the entire range of victimisation".[2] However, expressive theory lacks coherence and focus and seems to be positing what is obvious: that the law sends messages, or communicates, educates, or promotes social norms. Also, there is so much diversity and little unity among expressive theorists, to the extent that an "unwieldy variety" is said to characterise the issues that can be expressed (Strudler 2001).

The ICC could make more impact on justice and peace processes by pursuing illustrative cases, based on the expressive theory, than it could make, if it focuses on retribution (deGuzman 2012). The central message is that impunity is no longer acceptable and that those who commit international crimes will be prosecuted. The power of the ICC to name and shame is particularly important for the expressive impact of the Court because political leaders in particular may not want to be shamed by the ICC, as such actions could impact negatively on their political profile in their country and globally.

2.2.4 Retributive Justice

The main objective of retribution is to punish perpetrators of crimes at national and international levels (Drumbl 2007). Retributive justice considers punishment, if proportionate, to be the best response to crime. It has roots in the Mosaic law of the Old Testament that emphasises the idea of "an eye for an eye" and was propagated in the *Metaphysics of Moral* in the nineteenth century by Immanuel Kant. Kant regards punishment as a matter of justice. He argues that punishment

[2] OTP Prosecutorial Strategy, 2009–2012, 2010, 6, https://www.icc-cpi.int/nr/rdonlyres/66A8d-

must be carried out by the state for the sake of the law, not for the sake of the criminal or the victim, and argues that if the guilty is not punished, justice is not done. Further, he avers that if justice is not done, then the idea of law itself is undermined.

The retributive theory of punishment posits that criminal behaviour constitutes a violation of the moral or natural order, and those who violate this order are required to make some kind of payment. Thus, a criminal is sanctioned because he or she deserves it (Aloyo 2012; Starkweather 1992). At the centre of the retributive justice proposition are the notions of merit and punishment; basically that people should receive what they deserve. Therefore, people who break the law deserve to be punished (Brilmayer 1996; Drumbl 2007; Maiese 2004). Retributive theory asserts that there is a moral link between punishment and guilt, so punishment is a matter of responsibility and accountability. Retributivists believe that once the society has decided on a law, it represents the moral code, and those who break it should be punished. They do not query the legitimacy of the law, once it is enacted by the proper rule-making body. Another fundamental pillar of retributive justice is the notion that the offender has gained undue advantage over society by the crime and that punishment will rebalance the relationship between the offender and society. Apart from the natural order and "just dessert" justifications, retributive justice theorists anticipate punishment will lead to deterrence (Maiese 2004).

The classical retributive justice principles of letting the punishment fit the crime which were the foundation of sentencing in many countries in Western Europe in the nineteenth century have been modified to recognise that some offenders are less blameworthy than others, or guilty due to some external factors beyond their control, which ought to mitigate the punishments meted out to them. A new neoclassical thought, embodied in the "just dessert" principle, represents the modified version of retributive justice which places emphasis on the gravity of the offence, more than on the character of the offender (Starkweather 1992).

The goal of the retributive theory of punishment is to restore the rela-
tionship shattered by the crime committed, and this is assumed to b

by the crime he or she committed. Since the goal of retributive justice is to restore relationships, retributive justice theorists insist that an offender should be punished only to the extent necessary to restore the relationships. The level of punishment must be proportional to the seriousness of the crime (Starkweather 1992). The concept of "just dessert", which seeks to preserve human dignity through punishment, arose in response to this criticism. "Just dessert" theorists aver that an offender should be treated with dignity as a human being by responding to his or her conduct in a way that respects his choice to commit a crime (Starkweather 1992).

Retributive justice is one of the theoretical foundations for the imposition of sanctions in national and international justice systems. Thus, in international law those who commit international crimes such as war crimes, crimes against humanity, aggression and genocide are punished because their actions violate international law and deserve to be punished by the Court. Punishment is thought to reinforce the rules of international law and to deny those who have violated these rules any unfair advantage (Maiese 2004). The ICC has a strong foundation in the theory of retributive justice. The Rome Statute of the ICC contains elaborate rules against specified crimes, meant to prevent gross and systemic abuse of human rights. The Statute also contains procedures for enforcing these rules and ensuring that those who violate them are deservedly punished.

One of the main criticisms of retributive justice is that it may degenerate to revenge, which is mere retaliation. Efforts should be made to ensure that revenge is not the principal focus of any retributive justice system, because such emotions are damaging and may lead to overreaction, which may also result in excessive punishments that may lead to further antagonism. Also, punishments "dictated by revenge do not satisfy the principles of proportionality or consistency, and may lead to punishments that vary according to the degree of anger provoked" (Maiese 2004). Another criticism is that retributive justice focuses on only crimes and punishment, not the social causes or social circumstances of crimes, and also does not question the effectiveness of punishment. With retributive theory, it will be irrelevant to ask important questions such as: What is the impact of the fourteen years jail term handed over to Thomas Lubanga Dyilo by the ICC on peace in the DRC? Does it contribute to conflict transformation? Does it satisfy the yearnings and expectations of victims of crimes committed?

Since the ICC has not convicted and sentenced any persons so far in any of the three countries, the impact of the ICC retributive values on peace processes remains at this stage academic, and not yet fully ripe for discussion. Nonetheless, punishing those who committed atrocities in the three countries on the ground that it is just and equitable has the major advantage of removing some of the major actors of the conflicts from the scene which may open the doors for further negotiation. This is evident in Côte d'Ivoire, where the incarceration of former president Laurent Gbagbo, and the former Minister and youth leader Charles Blé Goudé may have contributed to the relative peace in the country. However, considered comparatively, it will have a limited impact on peace processes.

The value of retribution as punishment theory has several constraints that make it problematic and less impactful on peace processes. One of these issues is selectivity, that is, in view of the limited capacity and funds of the ICC, how to determine those to be prosecuted. Selectivity involves prosecutorial discretion, bending towards those cases where there are better chances of securing conviction (Drumbl 2007). The second issue is whether the punishment of just a few in these countries has a significant impact on the ability of the ICC to impact on peace processes. Punishment of the few who bear the greatest responsibility in cases of mass atrocities may lead to justice only for the victims of the offences committed by these few persons, leaving a large number of victims without redress. The third issue is the severity of punishment; that is, what quantum of punishment will adequately punish perpetrators of mass atrocities? Will punishment usually used to punish perpetrators of ordinary crimes, say murder of one person, be sufficient to punish perpetrators of mass atrocities that resulted in the deaths of hundreds or thousands of persons? Aloyo (2012), Drumbl (2007) and Golash (2010) suggest that ordinary punishments may not be adequate or proportional for international crimes because of the vast number of people harmed and the gravity of the offences committed. International justice systems should therefore seek the highest and harshest acceptable punishment for international criminals and need to develop appropriate policies for punishing perpetrators of mass atrocities (Aloyo 2012).

Retributive justice focuses on only crimes and punishment and not the social causes or social circumstances of crimes, which are important for peace processes. Some of the relevant social issues are the systems of governance, the politics of alienation, economic disparities and the scramble for power by elites from major ethnic groups in these countries. Finally, it seems that contingency and selectivity triggered by funding constraints led to situations where culpable individuals in these situations evaded accountability (Drumbl 2007). Thus, in the three countries only a few out of the many that played important roles in the atrocities were prosecuted in The Hague.

Subsequent sections of this chapter examine some attributes of the ICC that may define its interventions in post-conflict situations and influence its ability to contribute to the peace process. It also examines some of the problems, tensions and challenges embedded in the international justice system, and how these problems, tensions and challenges influence the contributes of the ICC to peace processes.

2.3 Peace and Justice Dilemma

One of the most debated issues in transitional justice discourse is the seeming tension between justice and peace, particularly with the use of criminal prosecution as the sole or one of the transitional justice methods in a post-conflict country. The attempt to reinstate the rule of law in transitional societies creates a dilemma (Teitel 2000). The main argument for justice in post-conflict situations is that accountability promotes enduring peace, while impunity distorts the peace process (Chetail 2009; Doswald-Beck 2009; International Centre for Transitional Justice 2009). In the words of Roht-Arriaza (2006), "the past, unaccounted for, does not lie quiet". However, the contention that amnesty does not promote lasting peace has been described as interesting but not yet empirically proved (Schabas 2011). Also, the prospect of prosecution could complicate an ongoing peace process, and some negotiators seem to view the possibility of prosecution as a dangerous impediment to their work (Darehshori and Evenson 2010; Human Rights Watch 2009).

Dealing with the issues of peace and justice when negotiating peace agreements has always been contentious. However, the problem has taken centre stage in recent times because of the tremendous growth of interest in international human rights and international criminal justice (Mallinder 2008). The peace and justice debate has also intensified since the coming into operation of the ICC for two reasons: first, the possibility of national leaders facing the law for human rights abuses is becoming more real than before. Second, the ICC sometimes operates in ongoing armed conflict situations which make the tension acute (Darehshori and Evenson 2010).

The involvement of the ICC in post-conflict situations such as in Sudan, Uganda, DRC and Kenya is making the issue of justice and peace significant, and the question is whether the involvement of the Court in these post-conflict situations is complicating or facilitating conflict transformation (Keller 2008). The establishment of the ICC has been described as one of the results of many years of hard work to link justice with peace. Thus, it is somewhat odd to pit the ICC at the centre of the peace and justice debate, since the ICC is a product of international law which itself evolved from the desire of humanity to connect peace and security with justice (Mendes 2010). Questions regarding the application of international humanitarian law and the establishment of mechanisms to deal with the illegal use of force in armed conflicts have always occupied a central part of the evolution of international law (Mendes 2010; Roht-Arriaza 2006). The inability of the international community to fully develop international humanitarian law and the lack of political will to seriously enforce existing treaties on international humanitarian law and the use of force in the settlement of disputes partially led to the First World War and the Second World War (Mendes 2010).

Mendes further argues that one of several lessons of the early twentieth century is that failure to seriously pursue justice after armed conflicts impairs peace (2010). According to this reasoning, the Allied powers seemed to have realised the importance of linking justice to enduring peace after the Second World War; hence the trials after the war. However, such accounting if not properly managed could complicate the peace process; hence the need to carefully balance the peace and justice tension.

2.4 The International Criminal Court and Reconciliation

Defining reconciliation is difficult (Roht-Arriaza 2006). Even harder is tracing the impact of international criminal trials on reconciliation. The problem of defining reconciliation stems from its varying contexts, and diverse understandings. Reconciliation means different things to different people (Tolbert 2013). Reconciliation for Miall et al. (1999) is the "harmonising of divergent stories, acquiescence in a given situation and the restoration of a friendly situation". It also means the long-time strategic programme of the setting aside disputes between factions that have divided a community; not a strained and hypocritical truce between victims and perpetrators (Mendez 2010). It is a process of enabling victims and perpetrators of crimes in a post-conflict community to move from a divided past to a shared future (Bloomfield et al. 2003). In its broadest meaning, reconciliation could extend to the establishment of strong patterns of social trust and cooperation across ethnic lines in post-conflict societies (Nalepa 2009). The definition of reconciliation can be based on the "thin" and "thick" objectives. When the objective is "thin", it may be understood as simple coexistence, that is, former enemies have agreed to coexist. When the objective is "thick", reconciliation is broadly framed to include forgiveness, mercy, mutual healing and harmony (Skaar 2013).

Reconciliation can also be seen from the context of acknowledgement, contrition, mercy and forgiveness (Fisher 2010) or from the interface between truth and justice (Mendez 2010). However, there seems to be a consensus that reconciliation describes a process rather than an end-state outcome, (Bloomfield et al. 2003; Fisher 2010; Nalepa 2009) with the overall purpose of building relationships between individuals, groups, communities, societies and nations (Fisher 2010).

In this book, reconciliation is viewed as a process of moving from revenge, resentment and bitterness to dialogue, a shared future and a friendly situation.

One of the justifications for an international criminal justice mechanism is that interventions by the mechanism could lead to reconciliation (Fletcher and Weinstein 2002). In fact, criminal trials are seen as critical to enable post-conflict societies to recover from mass violence (United Nations Security Council Resolutions 827 of 1993 and 955 of 1994). Resolution 827 of 1993[3] establishing the ICTY states that "in the particular circumstances of the former Yugoslavia the establishment of an international tribunal and the prosecution of persons responsible for serious violations of international humanitarian law would contribute to the *restoration and maintenance of peace*" (emphasis by author). UNSC Resolution 955 of 1994[4] establishing the ICTR states emphatically: "in the particular circumstances of Rwanda, the prosecution of persons responsible for serious violations of international humanitarian law would contribute to the process of *national reconciliation and the restoration and maintenance of peace*" (italics added).

The above assertions are based on the claim that holding individuals accountable for atrocities will remove the burden of collective guilt from the society and pin it on specific individuals which in the long-run could promote reconciliation (Fletcher and Weinstein 2002). It is also founded on the belief that justice creates enabling conditions for reconciliation and peace (Bensouda 2013). International criminal trials are also thought to be capable of laying the foundation for the rule of law and promoting the transformation of the transition period, with the hope that these developments may somehow contribute to mediating some of the dilemmas of a post-conflict community (Teitel 2000).

---

[3]United Nations Security Council Resolution 827 of 1993, adopted by the Security Council on 25 May 1993, https://documents-dds-ny.un.org/doc/UNDOC/GEN/N93/306/28/IMG/N9330628.pdf?OpenElement. Accessed 28 December 2018.

[4]United Nations Security Council Resolution 955 of 1994, adopted by the Security Council on 8 November 1994, https://documents-dds-ny.un.org/doc/UNDOC/GEN/N95/140/97/PDF/N9514097.pdf?OpenElement. Accessed 28 December 2018.

Criminal trials are also seen to contribute to the process of reconciliation in post-conflict countries by breaking the circle of impunity common in most post-conflict societies, avoiding unbridled revenge and protecting against the return to power of perpetrators (Bloomfield et al. 2003). The involvement of courts in conflict transformation could have negative impacts on reconciliation in the following ways: it may ignore or sideline the feelings of victims of violent conflicts. Political obstacles may make it impossible for criminal trials to connect to victims (Bloomfield et al. 2003). It may also lead to re-victimisation, in the sense that most court trials involve litigious and hostile processes that may expose the victims to another round of humiliation. It is perpetrator oriented, and could lead to the restriction of the free flow of information, to the extent that the flow of information may not be as robust as in a Truth and Reconciliation Commission.

Whether, and to what extent, international accountability can successfully contribute to reconciliation is however difficult to empirically verify (Nalepa 2009; Stahn 2009), because it is hard to measure reconciliation and even more difficult to evaluate the specific contributions of prosecutions to the process. One of the problems of studying the impact of any transitional justice programme on reconciliation is that of "conceptualising" and "operationalizing" reconciliation as a measurable empirical phenomenon (Nalepa 2009). To "conceptualise" is to define reconciliation in the context of each post-conflict situation, while to "operationalize" is to find appropriate empirical indicators of the concept.

Thus, there is very limited empirical data on the contribution of justice to reconciliation (Fletcher and Weinstein 2002). There are also divergent views on the nature, scope and specific impact of criminal prosecutions on reconciliation. Fisher (2010) argue that at best, the impact of the international criminal justice system on reconciliation will be modest, while Fletcher and Weinstein (2002) claim that the impact of the international criminal system on reconciliation is not verifiable, because reconciliation is based on the ability of the individual to forgive or forget, and not an action which the court, or the international community can mandate. The contributions of the ICTY to the processes of reconciliation in the Balkan region have been limited because the court was not equipped to realise such expectations, and more importantly, because there were no existing processes of reconciliation for the court to contribute to (Tolbert 2013). The ICTY disagrees, with claims in its website that:

> Undoubtedly, the Tribunal's work has had a major impact on the states of the former Yugoslavia. Simply by removing some of the most senior and notorious criminals and holding them accountable, the Tribunal has been able to lift the taint of violence, contribute to ending impunity and help pave the way for reconciliation.[5]

The main argument of the proponents of the ICC is that the Court creates conditions which are conducive for reconciliation, which is important for peacebuilding (Bensouda 2013). However, for an international criminal justice mechanism to achieve this objective, it must be part of an integrated process of peacebuilding, not the sole or central transitional justice mechanism (Fletcher and Weinstein 2002). According to Mendez (2010), the appropriate approach should be to devise how best to properly apply different transitional justice programmes to ensure complementarity and compatibility, with the construction of democracy, international law, and the search for reconciliation. The appropriate mix will depend on contexts, circumstances, and the free and rational choices made by local actors, not the international community. This study will contribute to the current state of research on reconciliation and peace by examining how criminal prosecutions by the ICC might either create the necessary environment for reconciliation or might lead directly to reconciliation. In the next section, the nexus between international criminal prosecution and deterrence is discussed.

---

[5]Website of the United Nations International Tribunal for the Former Yugoslavia, http://www.icty.org/en/about. Accessed 14 August 2018.

2.5 The International Criminal Court and Deterrence

The Preamble to the Rome Statute of the ICC provides, *inter alia*, that the Court is established to end impunity for the perpetrators of international crimes and to contribute to the prevention of international crimes. This provision has been interpreted as meaning that deterrence as a fundamental principle of international criminal justice is one of the aims of the ICC (Mendes 2010). Deterrence has also been described as a normal aim of authorities and good legislation (Gallon 2000), and justifiable on the ground that punishments help in building a safer world (Drumbl 2007). Advocates of international criminal justice insist that the involvement of international courts in conflict and post-conflict situations contributes to deterring future atrocities because individual accountability is an important part of a preventive strategy and necessary for sustainable peacebuilding (Akhavan 2001; Grono 2012; Kim and Sikkink 2009; Rosenberg 2012; Scheffer 1999; Whiting 2013). The central argument and goal of international criminal justice are that it serves to deter the commission of future atrocities (Wippman 1999).

As stated in this chapter, deterrence consists of general and specific deterrence. However, prevention in the ICC context is also discussed in terms of immediate deterrence and long-time deterrence (Rosenberg 2012). Immediate deterrence refers to cases when the threat of criminal prosecution will deter a person or group of persons in a particular society from committing a future crime. Long-term deterrence is used to describe the notion that criminal punishment will deter people generally from committing crimes, being aware of the certainty or likelihood of punishment. Immediate deterrence in the international criminal justice context is achieved through specific legal interventions by an international criminal justice institution such as: issuing public statements and warnings directed at the main conflict parties, opening investigations in the midst of ongoing conflicts and issuing indictments and arrest warrants. Long-term deterrence is subdivided into complementarity, which may encourage states to prosecute, and norm proliferation, which is the creation of a normative situation where extraordinary crimes are no longer accepted (Rosenberg 2012). Prosecution is more likely to contribute to norm creation or *norm proliferation* at the national level by reinforcing applicable international norms and contributing to the establishment of a political culture that considers the commission of atrocities unacceptable (Rosenberg 2012).

The central question when discussing the nexus between international criminal justice and deterrence is whether international criminal prosecution deters or exacerbates humanitarian atrocities. Deterrence is a complex phenomenon and its linkages with conflict transformation are questioned because it is intertwined with other variables, and because it is based on the assumption that potential perpetrators of crimes follow rational reasoning before committing or refraining from committing a crime.

Measuring the specific impact of international criminal justice on future warlords or gross human rights violators is difficult, and some say it is impossible, because it is hard to know those who were actually deterred, since only those not deterred come to the notice of the international justice system (Onwudiwe et al. 2010), and also because there are many interrelated factors at play (Whiting 2013). It is also an elusive task especially in countries that are experiencing massive and widespread violence (Akhavan 2001; Rosenberg 2012). The deterrent impact of international criminal justice has also been described as "indeterminate" since it cannot be proved or disproved empirically (Rosenberg 2012). The nature of the task set by the researcher and the particular circumstances or contexts of a post-conflict situation may determine the outcome. For instance, it may well be unrealistic to expect an international criminal justice mechanism to have a positive deterrent impact on a post-conflict situation in the short run, as it may take years before the impact will be felt (Akhavan 2001; Whiting 2013). Also, it may be unrealistic to expect threats of criminal punishment to have an immediate direct impact on human behaviour in a society already intoxicated with hatred and violence (Akhavan 2001), as in Rwanda before the 1994 genocide.

The ICC prides itself as being capable of deterring future crimes. The fundamental questions to pose are: how realistic is this claim? How has the ICC fared so far? The main argument in support of the positive impact of the ICC on future gross human right abusers is that, because of its permanent nature, the possibility of ICC's intervention is one-factor future human rights abusers may now take into consideration when making decisions. There is also anecdotal evidence to suggest that the risk of prosecution by the ICC is one of the few credible threats faced by leaders of militant groups (Grono 2012; Rosenberg 2012). Akhavan (2001, 4), Aloyo et al. (2013), and Grono (2012) also argue, persuasively, that the ICC deters people from committing crimes, reduces support for violent groups and has a peace-enhancing impact. The argument is that since the ICC is a permanent institution it will influence state and individuals' behaviours and will more likely have a deterrent impact.

The focus should rather be on prosecution over the long term, with the hope that the entrenchment of human rights norms could act to deter today's youths and future generations from committing humanitarian atrocities. Effective deterrence depends on normative pressure and material punishment. The ICC has through its investigations and prosecutions contributed and continues to contribute to emerging international criminal norms that act to limit future gross violation of human rights by making them "more costly in terms of a rational public policy choice analysis, and by establishing such crimes as firmly outside the status quo of behaviour accepted on the international scale" (Grono 2012).

2.6 The International Criminal Court and Victims' Redress

International accountability has, as far back as the Nuremberg trials, focused entirely on punishment of perpetrators of international crimes with little attention devoted to the roles and rights of victims and survivors of international crimes (Garkawe 2003; Goetz 2008; McCarthy 2012). Also, the focus of international humanitarian law has been on regulating the methods and materials of war with relatively little interest in the rights of victims (Schabas 2007). The 1945 London Agreements establishing the International Military Tribunals at Nuremberg, and for the Far East[6] made no mention of the rights of victims, but in subsequent years, starting from the 1960s onwards, a *victims' movement* promoting the rights of victims in the criminal justice process sprang up (Garkawe 2003), climaxing in the 1990s with the establishment of the ICTY, the ICTR, and the ICC.

The most common forms of victims' redress are: compensation, rehabilitation, restitution and satisfaction/guarantee of non-repetition (REDRESS 2013). Victims' redress under the Rome Statute covers victims' participation in proceedings, restitution, compensation and rehabilitation (Goetz 2008; Schabas 2007). The Rome Statute introduced innovative measures for the protection of victims' rights; namely, pursuant to Article 68 (2) of the Rome Statute, special measures may be implemented in cases of victims of sexual violence or a child who is a victim or a witness, and under Article 68 (3), victims of crimes before the Court are allowed to have their own legal representation during the trial of alleged offenders (Garkawe 2003). The most challenging and significant innovation is the right to participate in the proceedings of the ICC as independent parties with legal representation, as such moral and legal recognition can be more satisfying than financial compensation (Goetz 2008).

The Rome Statute represents a turning point in the campaign for victims' protection in international criminal justice (Schabas 2007; REDRESS 2013) because it makes several references to the roles and interests of victims, including the right of victims to intervene in proceedings (Articles 15 (3), 19 (3) and 82 (4)), the establishment of a Victims and Witnesses Unit within the Registry (Articles 43 (6) and 68 (4), the recognition of the entitlement of victims to reparations (Schabas 2007), the establishment of the Trust Fund for Victims (TFV) (Article 79), and the right to be informed or notified by the Registrar or Prosecutor of key decisions of the Court in all stages of the proceedings (Goetz 2008). The Rome Statute provides for two distinct

[6] The 1945 Charter of the International Military Tribunal, http://legal.un.org/ilc/documentation/english/a_cn4_5.pdf. Accessed 29 December 2018.

forms of victims' redress, to wit: reparation by the Court, pursuant to Article 75(2) of the Rome Statute empowering the Court to make reparation orders against a convicted person, specifying reparations to, or in respect of victims. The second is support provided to victims by the TFV, independent of the Court's order. The TFV plays important roles in the victims' regime of the ICC by providing resources for physical and psychological support to victims of physical and psychological harm as a result of violations of international crimes covered by the Statute of the ICC (McCarthy 2012).

The thorny issue is the relevance of victims' rights and redress as a distinct aspect in international justice processes, the principle role of which is the prosecution and punishment of offenders. UNGA Resolution 60/147, (which established the Basic Principles and Guidelines on the Right to a Remedy and Reparation for Victims of Gross Violations of International Human Rights Law and Serious Violations of International Humanitarian Law) in its Preamble, provides a glimpse of the importance of victims' rights. It states: "in honouring the victims' rights to benefit from remedies and reparation, the international community keeps faith with the plight of victims, survivors and future human generations and reaffirms international law in the field[7]". The Preamble to the Basic Principles and Guidelines on the Right to Remedy and Reparations for Victims amplifies this relevance. It states that "in adopting the document the international community affirms its human solidarity with victims of violations of international law[8]".

Though restorative justice theory is useful in understanding the role of victims' redress mechanisms in the international justice system, on its own it is inadequate in providing convincing justifications for the

[7]UNGA Resolution 60/147 of 16 December 2005, http://legal.un.org/avl/pdf/ha/ga_60-147/ga_60-147_ph_e.pdf. Accessed 29 December 2018.

[8]The Basic Principles and Guidelines on the Right to a Remedy and Reparation for Victims of Gross Violations of International Human Rights Law and Serious Violations of International Humanitarian Law, https://www.un.org/ruleoflaw/blog/document/basic-principles-and-guidelines-on-the-right-to-a-remedy-and-reparation-for-victims-of-gross-violations-of-international-human-rights-law-and-serious-violations-of-international-humanitarian-law/. Accessed 29 December 2018.

creation of the ICC victims' redress mechanism (McCarthy 2012). Also, it should be noted that a criminal justice system with mechanisms for providing reparations, may not even be restorative unless it produces restorative results, that is, transforms relationships among victims, offenders and society.

Victims' redress mechanisms can also be justified on the ground that criminal prosecution is focused on incapacitation and deterrence to the detriment of redressing harm suffered by victims; thus criminal prosecution is deemed inadequate to account for, and respond to "the needs of victims, the character of the harm done to the victims and the complexity of the harm done to the wider social bonds by the transgressor's conduct" (McCarthy 2012). However, the judicial process, if properly managed, treating victims with respect and dignity, may contribute to victims' healing (Goetz 2008). To protect victims' rights, a crime should not be treated merely as a "wrong against an abstract community requiring societal sanction, but should also be dealt with as a dispute between transgressors and victims as part of a process in which the relationships among victims, offenders, and society are restored through the criminal justice system" (McCarthy 2012). It is important to note that not all victims may wish to claim reparation, however victims' redress may have a healing impact on victims, while sustained dialogue with victims and the affected population generally could help reduce frustration and disappointment (Goetz 2008).

The weaknesses of criminal prosecution as a sole mechanism in the international criminal justice system also highlight the importance, relevance and functions of reparative justice. Some of these weaknesses, as pointed out by McCarthy (2012), are: (1) the staggering number of persons implicated in atrocities committed during armed conflicts which makes it difficult for criminal prosecution to have a serious impact on addressing the problem, (2) a lack of cooperation from certain states may make it difficult for an international court to prosecute certain perpetrators, (3) the need to move forward and promote reconciliation after an armed conflict may make criminal prosecution undesirable, (4) the large number of victims usually excluded from the court's prosecutorial system, (5) the trial of leaders, most times is in far removed places from the locations of crimes, and (6) prosecution which lacks immediacy may become irrelevant to victims. It is also doubtful if the reparative justice regime created by the ICC can play the sort of transformative roles which are important for the system to satisfy the principles of reparative justice theory. Some of these weaknesses, as notes McCarthy (2012), are the limited funds of the Court, and the inadequacy of the ICC mechanisms to assess and remedy the harm done by armed conflicts.

Nonetheless, the ICC victims' redress system, particularly the TFV mechanism, has the potential to provide justice to a wider range of victims, beyond those covered by the retributive justice mechanism of the Court. In contrast to prosecution, reparation or victim support provides a "potentially more tangible and concrete form of justice" and one that can be localised to a much wider range of victims than is possible with criminal prosecution (McCarthy 2012). The next section examines the nexus between the ICC and the promotion of accountability to the law.

2.7 The International Criminal Court and Accountability to the Law

The rule of law has varied meanings (Williams et al. 2014; Ogbu 1999). The concept of the rule of law incorporates the following ideas or concepts: "accountability to the law, respect for the law, supremacy of the law, equality before the law, fairness in the application of the law, separation of power, participation in decision-making, legal certainty, avoidance of arbitrariness, and procedural and legal transparency" (Nouwen 2012). In this book, for clarity, and to create a definitional boundary required for empirical study, the rule of law is taken to mean accountability to the law. The Rome Status in paragraph 4 provides that "the most serious crimes of concern to the international community as a whole must not go unpunished and that their effective prosecution must be ensured by taking measures at the national level and by enhancing international cooperation". To a large extent, this paragraph incorporates the concept of accountability to the law. In this context, accountability to the law is conceptualised as "processes, norms, and structures that hold the population and public officials legally responsible for their actions and that impose sanctions if they violate the law" (United States Institute for Peace 2015). It is "operationalised" by all efforts, programmes and activities that promote, or could promote accountability to the law. The intention of the ICC to contribute to accountability to the law is clearly stated in paragraph 4 of the Preamble to the Rome Statute. Thus, the provision in paragraph 5 of the Preamble states that state parties are "determined to put an end to impunity for the perpetrators of these crimes and thus contribute to the prevention of these crimes".

The nexus between the promotion of accountability to the law and peace is thought to exist by the power of the law to incapacitate, discredit and delegitimise powerful personalities that participate in conflict, and therefore open the space for peaceful resolution of the conflict (Human Rights Watch 2009). Accountability could also promote justice, reconciliation (Bensouda 2013) and the rule of law (Teitel 2000), which could assist in promoting peace. International criminal investigations and trials are also thought to be capable of laying the foundations for the rule of law which may promote peace in post-conflict community (Teitel 2000). Criminal trials could also contribute to the process of reconciliation by breaking the cycle of impunity common in post-conflict countries, avoiding unbridled revenge, and protecting against the return to power of perpetrators (Bloomfield et al. 2003).

Thus, in the pursuit of its complementarity principles, and other objectives, the ICC may spur national activities that may contribute to establishing, re-establishing or strengthening accountability to the law, and thus contribute to peace (Nouwen 2012). Prosecution is more likely to contribute to norm creation or *norm proliferation* at the national level by reinforcing applicable international norms and contributing to the establishment of a political culture that considers the commission of atrocities unacceptable (Rosenberg 2012). Even so, the establishment of institutions for the promotion of accountability to the law, and enactment of laws for the same purpose often does not in practice amount to effective promotion of accountability to the law, since the problem of accountability to the law, in some countries, is connected with the limited enforcement of existing laws, not the absence of laws and legal institutions (Nouwen 2012). Still these developments are first steps in the long journey towards the promotion of accountability to the law in post-conflict countries.

2.8 Conclusion

This chapter discussed some relevant literature and issues on the relationship between international accountability and peace processes, and some theories and principles relevant to this study. It has also examined the application of these theories and principles to conflict and post-conflict situations. It explored the nature, scope, challenges and dynamics of this relationship. Also, the chapter highlighted the problems, tensions and challenges embedded in the international justice system, and how these issues impede the ability of international justice mechanisms to contribute to peace processes. Some of the issues discussed are: the peace and justice dilemma, the ICC and deterrence, the ICC and reconciliation, the ICC and victims' rights and the ICC and accountability.

Using relevant literature, the chapter explored how the ICC relates with the four variables, and whether it has the capacity to achieve any of the objectives of criminal prosecution as specifically stated in the Preamble to the Rome Statute. The chapter also explored the nexus between these objectives and peace processes. The overall aim therefore is to examine the nexus between the ICC and the four variables, and the likely results of the relationship on the peace processes in Côte d'Ivoire, Kenya and Uganda.

References

Adam, Branch. 2011. "Neither Liberal Nor Peace: Practices of Global Justice by the ICC". In *The Problems and Practice of Peace-Building*, edited by Susanna Campbell, David Chandler, and Meera Sabaratnam, 121–137. London: Zed Books.

Adler, Matthew. 2000. "Expressive Theory of Law: A Skeptical Overview". *University of Pennsylvania Law Review* 148: 1364–1493.

Akhavan, Payam. 2001. "Beyond Impunity: Can International Criminal Justice Prevent Future Atrocities?" *The American Journal of International Law* 95.7: 7–31.
Aloyo, Eamon. 2012. "To Indict or Not to Indict? The ICC, Deterrence, and Nonviolent and Subordinate International Criminals". Accessed June 20, 2013. https://wpsa.research.pdx.edu/meet/2012/aloyo.pdf.
Aloyo, Eamon, Yvonne Dutton, and Lindsay Heger. 2013. "Does the International Criminal Court Deter Torture?" One Earth Future Foundation. Accessed May 30, 2013. http://oneearthfuture.org/research/publications/does-international-criminalcourt-deter-torture.
Amann, Diane Marie. 2003. "Assessing the Criminal Adjudication of Human Rights Atrocities". *Third World Legal Studies* 16: 169–181.
Bensouda, Fatou. 2013. "Justice, Reconciliation and the Role of the ICC, 2008". Accessed April 15, 2013. www.idea.net/resources/analysis/.
Berghof Foundation. 2012. "Berghof Glossary of Conflict Transformation". Berghof Foundation. Accessed May 28, 2013. http://www.berghof-foundation.org/.
Bloomfield, David, Teresa Barnes, and Luc Huyse, eds. 2003. "Reconciliation After Violent Conflict, International Institute of Electoral Assistance and Democracy". Accessed February 11, 2016. http://www.un.org/en/peacebuilding.
Botes, Johannes. 2003. "Conflict Transformation: A Debate Over Semantics or a Crucial Shift in the Theory and Practice of Peace and Conflict Studies". *The International Journal of Peace Studies* 8: 1–30. http://www.gmu.edu/pro#grams/icar/ijps/vol8_2/botes.htm.
Brilmayer, Lea. 1996. "International Justice and International Law". Faculty Scholarship Series, Paper 2441. Accessed June 10, 2013. http://digitalcommons.law.yale.edu/fss_paper/2441.
Chetail, Vincent. 2009. "Introduction: Post-conflict Peacebuilding-Ambiguity and Identity". In *Post-conflict Peacebuilding: A Lexicon*, edited by Vincent Chetail, 1–33. Oxford: Oxford University Press.
Cryer, Robert. 2005. *Prosecuting International Crimes*. Cambridge: Cambridge University Press.
Darehshori, Sara, and Elizabeth Everson. 2010. "Peace, Justice and the International Criminal Court". Oxford Transitional Justice Research Working Papers Series. Accessed May 1, 2013. http://www.otjr.csls.ox.ac.uk.
deGuzman, Margaret. 2012. "Choosing to Prosecute: Expressive Selection at the International Criminal Court". *Michigan Journal of International Law* 33: 265–319.

Doswald-Beck, Louise. 2009. "International Crimes". In *Post-conflict Peacebuilding: A Lexicon*, edited by Vincent Chetail, 158–173. Oxford: Oxford University Press.

Drumbl, Mark. 2007. *Atrocity, Punishment and International Law*. Cambridge: Cambridge University Press.

Fisher, Martina. 2010. "Transitional Justice and Reconciliation: Theory and Practice". Accessed April 12, 2013. http://www.berghof-handbook.net/documents/publications/fisher_tj_and_rec_%20handbook.

Fletcher, Laurel, and Harvey Weinstein. 2002. "Violence and Social Repair: Rethinking the Contributions of Justice to Reconciliation". *Human Rights Quarterly* 24: 573–639.

Gallon, Gustavo. 2000. "Deterrence: A Difficult Challenge for the International Criminal Court". The Helen Kellog Institute for International Studies. Volume 275 of Working Papers. Accessed March 31, 2013. http://www.kllogg.nd.edu.

Garkawe, Sam. 2003. "Victims and the International Criminal Court: Three Major Issues". *International Criminal Law Review* 3: 345–367.

Gever, Christopher. 2011. "A Theory of International Criminal Law?" Accessed June 9, 2013. http://www.warandlaw.blogspot.com.au.

Goetz, Mariana. 2008. "The International Criminal Court and Its Relevance to Affected Communities". In *Courting Conflict? Peace and the ICC*, edited by Nicholas Waddel and Phil Clark. Royal African Society. Accessed May 20, 2013. http://www.royalafrican/society.org.

Golash, Deirdre. 2010. "The Justification of Punishment in the International Context". In *International Criminal Law and Philosophy*, edited by Larry May and Zachary Hoskins. Cambridge: Cambridge University Press.

Grono, Nick. 2012. "The Deterrent Effect of the ICC on the Commission of International Crimes by Government Leaders". Accessed April 23, 2014. http://www.crisesgroup.org/en/publication.

Hopkins-Burke, Roger. 2009. *An Introduction to Criminology*. Devon: Willan Publishing.

Human Rights Watch. 2009. "Selling Justice Short: Why Accountability Matters for Peace." Human Rights Watch Report. Accessed May 2, 2013. https://www.hrw.org/sites/default/files/reports/ij0709webwcover_1.pdf.

International Centre for Transitional Justice. 2009. "Pursuing Peace, Justice or Both?" International Centre for Transitional Justice Report. Accessed April 29, 2013. www.ictj.org.

Keller, Linda. 2008. "Achieving Peace with Justice: The International Criminal Court and Uganda Alternative Justice Mechanisms". *Connecticut Journal of International Law* 23: 210–278.

Kim, Hunjoon, and Kathryn Sikkink. 2009. "Explaining the Deterrence Effect of Human Rights Prosecutions for Transitional Countries". *International Studies Quarterly* 54: 1–46.

Kowalski, Mateus. 2011. "The International Criminal Court: Reflections for a Stress Test on Its Foundations". *JANUS.NET e-Journal of International Relations* 2: 110–124. Accessed June 12, 2014. http://observare.ual.pt/janus.net/en/home-eng/54-englishen/vol-2,-n-º2-autumn-2011/articles/8-the-international-crimina.

Lanz, David. 2007. "The ICC's Intervention in Northern Uganda: Beyond the Simplicity of Peace vs. Justice". Accessed September 4, 2014. http://www.reliefweb.int/sites/reliefweb.int/files/resources/EC66215A0071F156C12573910051D06D-Full_Report.pdf.htm.

Lederach, John Paul. 2001. "Civil Society and Reconciliation." In *Turbulent Peace: The Challenges of Managing International Conflict*, edited by Chester Croaker, Fen Hampson, and Pamela Aall, 603–618. Washington, DC: United States Institute for Peace.

Lederach, John Paul. 2003. *The Little Book of Conflict Transformation*. Intercourse, PA: Good Books.

Maiese, Michelle. 2004. "Retributive Justice". *Beyond Intractability*. https://www.beyondintractability.org/essay/retributive.justice.

Mallinder, Louise. 2008. *Amnesty, Human Rights and Political Transitions: Building the Peace and Justice Divide*. Oxford: Hart Publishing.

May, Larry, and Zachary Hoskins. 2010. *International Criminal Law and Philosophy*. Cambridge: Cambridge University Press.

McCarthy, Conor. 2012. "Victims' Redress and International Criminal Justice". *Journal of International Criminal Justice* 10: 352–372.

Meijers, Tim, and Marlies Glasius. 2013. "Expression of Justice or Political Trial? Discursive Battles in the Karadzic Case". *Human Right Quarterly* 35: 720–752.

Mendes, Errol. 2010. *Peace and Justice at the International Criminal Court: A Court of Last Resort*. Cheltenham: Edward Elgar.

Mendez, Juan. 2010. "National Reconciliation, Transitional Justice, and the International Criminal Court". *Ethics and International Affairs* 15: 25–44.

Miall, Hugh. 2013. "Conflict Transformation: A Multi-Dimensional Task". Berghof Research Centre for Constructive Conflict Management. Accessed May 12, 2013. http://www.berghof-handbook.net/.

Miall, Huge, Oliver Ramsbotham, and Tom Woodhouse. 1999. *Contemporary Conflict Resolution*. Cambridge: Polity.

Nalepa, Monika. 2009. "Reconciliation, Refuge Returns, and International Criminal Justice: The Case of Bosnia and Herzegovina". In *Transitional Justice*, edited by Melissa Williams, Rosemary Nagy Williams, and Jon Elster, 316–361. New York: New York University Press.

Newsweek. 2015. "Former International Court of Justice Judge: Dick Cheney Should Face Prosecution". *Newsweek*. July 6. Accessed January 21, 2019. https://www.newsweek.com/british-judiciarylord-jannericc-judgeauschwitz-jewsholocaustprofessor-law-602725.

Nouwen, Sarah. 2012. "The International Criminal Court: A Peacebuilder in Africa?" In *Peacebuilding, Power, and Politics in Africa*, edited by Curtis Devon and Dzinesa Gwinyayi, 171–192. Athens: Ohio University Press.

Ogbu, Osita. 1999. *Human Rights, Law and Practice in Nigeria: An Introduction*. Enugu: CIDJAP Press.

Onwudiwe, Ihekwoaba, Jonathan Odo, and Emmanuel Onyeozil. 2010. "Deterrence Theory." Accessed April 30, 2013. http://marisluste.files.wordpress.com/.

REDRESS. 2013. "Justice for Victims: The ICC's Reparation Mandate." Accessed May 3, 2013. http://www.redress.org/downloads/publications/REDRESS_ICC_Reparations_May2011.pdf.

Roht-Arriaza, Naomi. 2006. "The New Landscape of Transitional Justice". In *Transitional Justice in the Twenty-First Century: Beyond Truth Versus Justice*, edited by Naomi Roht-Arriaza and Javier Mariezcurrena, 1–16. Cambridge: Cambridge University Press.

Rosenberg, Sheri. 2012. "The Relationship Between the International Criminal Court and the Prevention of Mass Atrocities." Accessed April 24, 2014. http://www.genocidepreventionnow.org/Portals/0/docs/Relationship_ICC_Prevention_HU.pdf.

Schabas, William. 2007. *An Introduction to the International Criminal Court*. Cambridge: Cambridge University Press.

Schabas, William. 2011. "Transitional Justice and the Norms of International Law". Japanese Society of International Law, Kwansei Gakun University. Accessed April 2, 2013. www.jsil.jp/annual_documents/2011.

Scheffer, David 1999. "War Crimes and Crimes Against Humanity". *Pace International Law Review* 112: 319–340.

Skaar, Elin. 2013. "Reconciliation in a Transitional Justice Perspective". *Transitional Justice Review* 1: 54–103.
Smith, Steven. 2012. "Expressive Jurisprudence and the Depletion of Meaning". *Maryland Law Review* 60: 507–539.
Stahn, Carsten. 2009. "The Future of International Criminal Justice". *The Hague Justice Portal*. Accessed April 12, 2013. http://www.haguejusticeportal.net/index.php?id=11106.
Starkweather, David. 1992. "The Retributive Theory of 'Just Desserts' and Victims' Participation in Plea Bargaining". *Indiana Law Journal* 67: 853–878.
Strudler, Alan. 2001. "The Power of Expressive Theories of Law". *Maryland Law Review* 60: 492–505.
Teitel, Ruti. 2000. *Transitional Justice*. Oxford: Oxford University Press.
Tenove, Chris. 2013. "Uganda and the International Criminal Court: Debates and Developments". Accessed July 17, 2014. http://www.africaportal.org.htm.
Tolbert, David. 2013. "Can International Justice Foster Reconciliation?" Accessed April 16, 2013. http://www.aljazeera.com/indepth/opinion/2013/04/201341074354441 90.htm.
United States Institute for Peace. 2015. "Accountability to Law". Accessed March 23, 2016.
Whiting, Alex. 2013. "The International Criminal Court Impact". Accessed April 22, 2013. http://today.law.harvard.edu/whiting-offers-views-on-the-international-criminal-courts-impact/.
Williams, George, Sean Brennan, and Andrew Lynch. 2014. *Australian Constitutional Law: Commentary and Materials*. Sydney: The Federation Press.
Wippman, David. 1999. "Atrocities, Deterrence, and the Limits of International Justice". *Fordman International Law Journal* 23: 473–488.
Wood, Andrew. 2012. "Moral Judgment and International Crimes: The Disutility of Desert". *Virginia Journal of International Law* 52: 634–681.
Wright, Valerie. 2010. "Deterrence in Criminal Justice: Evaluating Certainty vs. Severity of Punishment". The Sentencing Project. Accessed May 20, 2013. http://www.sentencingproject.org/wp-content/uploads/2016/01/Deterrence-inCriminal-Justice.pdf.

3

Violent Conflicts in Africa: Types, Trends, Challenges and the International Criminal Court

3.1 Introduction

Africa has had numerous cases of violent conflicts (Meredith 2005) and is often viewed as a continent wrecked by intractable violent conflicts (Furley and May 2006). During the last sixty years, many countries in the continent have witnessed various types of violent conflicts, wars and mass killings. This has been described as unsurprising because of the difficult and challenging pasts of most countries in Africa and the problems of development/governance, such as the high level of poverty, corruption, illiteracy and at times natural catastrophes (Cilliers and Schunemann 2013). This chapter examines violent conflicts in Africa. It explores the nature and types of violent conflicts common in Africa in the last sixty years. The violent conflicts in Uganda, Kenya and Côte d'Ivoire belong to some of the types identified. The central objective of this chapter is to examine the dynamics of the interaction between conflicts in Africa and the involvement of the ICC. The term "violent conflict" is used to encompass all types of armed conflicts. Violent conflict is similar to armed conflict but also includes one-sided violence such as genocide (Miall et al. 1999).

L. N. Malu, *The International Criminal Court and Peace Processes*,
Palgrave Studies in Compromise after Conflict,
https://doi.org/10.1007/978-3-030-19905-0_3

3.2 History of Violent Conflicts in Africa

Many African states gained political independence in the 1960s. By 1950, only three countries in sub-Saharan Africa were independent states: Ethiopia, Liberia and South Africa (Marshall 2005). For many of these newly independent states, colonialism had been a period of social unrest, political agitation for independence and the struggle for identity. By the late 1950s, the struggle for independence reached its peak in most African states, and by the 1960s, many attained political independence in rapid succession. Some gained independence after long and protracted wars, civil conflicts or rebellions, while others attained independence after long and hard constitutional and political negotiations. However, the post-independent era posed numerous challenges to the newly independent states. Some of these challenges were: governance problems, non-inclusive polity, natural catastrophes, divisive boundary demarcations, poverty, poor economies and violent antecedents from colonial rule. Also, these newly independent states had to grapple with the then bipolar world that presented limited policy options, beyond those linked to the West and those of the members of the Warsaw Pact, and the historic slumping of GDP growth rates in many African states in the 1970s (Cilliers and Schunemann 2013).

African states responded to these challenges in different ways: often in the form of struggles for political powers and social changes which manifested in political upheavals, coups, rebellions, armed conflicts and civil wars. Also, this era witnessed the founding of different armed groups and entities, which have played significant roles in the political violence that has severely undermined human security and the capacity of the state to deal with the situation. Thus, a major feature of the political development of many African states in the 1960s and 1970s was the presence of a multiplicity of armed groups, such as armed bands, vigilantes, cultist groups, private armies, rebel groups, Islamists groups, armed wings of political parties, private security companies and armed criminal groups (Ikelegbe and Okumu 2010). These armed groups also played major roles in the ethnic, regional, religious, political and resource conflicts that have plagued some African states. Between 1980 and 1994, nearly half of the world's war-ravaged countries were in Africa, and not less than 28 of sub-Saharan African states had experienced at least one form of violent conflict (Jackson 2007). There have been 19 civil wars and one interstate war in 16 African countries and numerous internal conflicts in which these armed groups were involved within 1990 and 2000 (Ikelegbe and Okumu 2010), and between 1960 and the 1990s, there have been 80 violent changes of government in sub-Saharan Africa (Bujra 2002).

Thus, during the sixty years of independence, Africa has become engulfed in armed conflicts of various types, to the extent that Africa was long-rated the world's most conflict-prone region and the region with the highest number of civil conflicts (Arnold 2009; Furley and May 2006). For instance, between 1945 and 1995, out of 295 violent conflicts in the world, 79 originated in Africa (Jackson 2000), while between 1970 to the present, Africa has witnessed a total of 30 wars (Baker 2007). Also, Africa's violent conflicts tend to be more severe and more costly in terms of the number of lives lost. For instance, a third of Africa's conflicts are said to have involved more than 10,000 deaths, and an estimated 17 million people died from violent conflicts in Africa from 1945 to 2000 (Jackson 2000) (Table 3.1).

Most of these violent conflicts grew out of failures of the decolonisation experiment (Clapham 1998; Jackson 2007). They are also the results of varied structural, economic, political, cultural and historical factors (Jackson 2007). The decolonisation failures manifested because: (a) some governments that took over power after independence were not truly representative of the people, and (b) some of the political systems that evolved out of the decolonisation experiment were alien to the governance history of the people (Clapham 1998; Jackson 2007). Some of these conflicts were also direct and indirect responses to the failures of governments and leaders that took over from the colonial governments to meet the minimum aspirations of the people, in terms of providing basic amenities and ensuring representative government which was the bedrock of the independent agitations or movements (Meredith 2005). Insurgencies and rebellions in Nigeria, Sierra Leone, Ethiopia, Chad, Uganda, Sudan, Senegal and Liberia could be traceable to these causes. Most of the violent conflicts in post-colonial Africa were

Table 3.1 Africa's major wars and violent conflicts, from 1960 till date

S/no	Nature of conflicts	Dates	Estimated fatalities
1	Congo Conflict	1960–1965	110,000
2	Eritrean Secession War	1961–1975	450,000–1 million
3	Nigerian Civil War	1967–1970	2–3 million
4	Uganda Internal Repression	1971–1979	500,000
5	Burundi Ethnic Massacre	1972	100,000–150,000
6	Western Sahara/Morocco Secession War	1975–Present	21,000
7	Angola Civil War	1975–2002	300,000–500,000
8	Mozambique Civil War	1976–1992	450,000–1 million
9	Uganda Civil War and Insurgency	1981–Present	100,000–500,000
10	Sudan Civil War	1983–2005	500,000–1.5 million
11	Somali Civil War	1983–Present	300,000–400,000
12	Burundi Ethnic Conflict	1988	100,000+
13	Zaire Civil War	1996–1997	200,000+
14	Liberian Civil War	1989–2003	200,000+
15	Sierra Leone Civil War	1991–2002	100,000+
16	Rwanda Civil War and Genocide	1990–1994	800,000+
17	Algerian Civil Conflict	1992–2000	1 million
18	DRC	1998–Present	3.5 million+
19	Eritrean/Ethiopia Border War	1998–2000	85,000+
20	CAR Civil Conflicts	2001–Present	1500+
21	Côte d'Ivoire Civil War/Post-election Violence	2002–2010	5500+
22	Guinea-Bissau Civil war and Internal Conflict	1998–Present	3000+
23	Niger Delta Conflict in Nigeria	1999–2012	5000+
24	Post-election Violence in Kenya	2008	1000+
25	Tunisia Civil Conflict	2010–2011	50,000+
26	Egypt Civil Conflict	2010–2014	50,000+
27	Libya Civil War	2011–2012	40,000+
28	Mali Civil War	2012–2013	1555+
29	South Sudan Civil War	2013–2015	10,000+
30	Boko Haram Conflicts in Nigeria	2008–Present	5000+

Source Initial data from Furley, Oliver and May, Roy (2006). *Ending Africa's Wars: Progressing to Peace*, with updates by the Author

generally a result of "blocked political aspirations, exploitative exaction of statehood, and reactive desperation" (Clapham 1998).

By the 1990s, most of the post-independent governments had been removed through rebellions, military coups, insurgencies, popular uprisings, or peaceful democratic means and replaced by new governments

(Bujra 2002). The characters of these new governments were mostly influenced by factors, such as the manner in which the previous government was removed and the particular context of each country (Clapham 1998). These new governments did not fare much better than the ones they replaced (Meredith 2005). New faces in government in several African countries, such as Nigeria, Ethiopia, Ghana, Burundi, Sudan, Gabon, Rwanda, Kenya, Egypt, Somali, Senegal, Gambia, Malawi, Zambia, Liberia, Sierra Leone and Uganda, did little to significantly transform their societies (Meredith 2005). The dire economic situation of the period which necessitated the introduction of Structural Adjustment Programs (SAP) in some African states exacerbated the fragile economic, social and political conditions of these states, frequently undermined the ability of governments to control the sources of economic patronage and fuelled more conflicts in many African states (Clapham 1998). Thus, armed conflicts remained a recurring issue during the 1990s and the 2000s with violent conflicts recorded in Rwanda, Somali, Senegal, Uganda, Sudan, Libya, Côte d'Ivoire, Kenya, Nigeria, CAR, DRC, Mali and Guinea-Bissau.

However, the twenty-first century ushered in a better economic and political outlook and Africa presents a better and more optimistic outlook which contrasts sharply with the previous position as a continent with deep chronic instability, poverty and of marginal importance to the global economy. The African Futures Project, which is a collaboration between the Institute for Security Studies and the Frederick S. Pardee Centre for International Futures, claims that there is potential for positive changes to the development trajectory of Africa; that these include benefits from investments in education, water, sanitation, health and agriculture; and that collectively these changes and investments present the potential for longer life expectancy, better quality education and higher income in most countries. Some of the factors driving the positive changes are the growth of south-south trade, especially with China and India, improvements in the capacity of African governments, impressive progress on developing regional and African Union conflict management capabilities, and the jump in the number of democracies in the continent (Cilliers and Schunemann 2013).

In contrast, the 2016 UNDP Human Development Index[1] shows that most African countries still fall into or under the Low Human Development Category (the lowest rating). The Index also confirms that none of the 51 countries in the Very High Human Development Category (the highest rating) is from Africa, and that 38 out of the 45 countries in the Low Development Category are from Africa. Thus, while African states may be showing potential for growth, they still lag behind other countries in standards for measuring economic growth and standard of living.

What is evident from this period of political transition is that African political elites which took over power from the colonial governments proved to be bad managers, despite the heroic intentions of some of them to transform their societies (Meredith 2005). The causes of economic and political stagnation and underdevelopment in most Africa states have been the subject of intense debate and a vast literature, and are not simple. However, the positive developments on the economic and political fronts seem to be impacting positively on conflict management in the continent. Cilliers and Schunemann (2013) and Furley and May (2006) suggest that the number of violent conflict-related deaths has been declining steadily in Africa, and that the reduction in a country's incidence of armed violence corresponds with improved development outcomes. According to Cilliers and Schunemann (2013), rapid economic growth and improvements in standard of living are expected to continue to impact positively on violent conflicts, and are more likely to lead to declining levels of violent conflicts in Africa. They caution, however, that in some instances instability and violence will persist and even increase. Scott (2012) agrees that large-scale armed violence is declining in Africa, but argues that Africa may continue to witness such violence in the future.

[1]The UNDP Human Development Index comparatively measures life expectancy, literacy, education, standards of living and quality of life for countries worldwide. http://10.150.35.18:6510/hdr.undp.org/sites/default/files/2016_human_development_report.pdf. Accessed 20 August 2018.

3.3 Types of Violent Conflicts

Violent conflicts in Africa come in various forms and types, and may not be easily classified (Clapham 1998). However, civil wars and internal conflicts are the most common types of violent conflict (Bujra 2002; Cilliers and Schunemann 2013). Arnold (2009) identifies three types of civil wars as: racial, ideological and political. These types can as well be identified as causes of civil wars rather than types of civil wars, and Arnold (2009) further notes that these motivations for civil wars could overlap with dangerous consequences. Marshall (2005) states that the vast majority of violent conflicts in Africa are what he called "societal", comprising: communal, ethnic and revolutionary types. Bujra (2002) opines that the two broad categories of violent conflicts in Africa are interstate and internal conflicts. He identifies seven types of internal conflicts: rebellion to overthrow a government, secessionist's rebellion, coup d'état, Cold-War sustained conflicts, many-sided conflicts to seize state power, rural conflicts over resources, and urban violence and conflicts.

Clapham (1998) identifies four types of African insurgencies as: liberation insurgencies, which are insurgencies that set out to achieve independence from colonial or minority rule as in Algeria, Angola, Guinea-Bissau, Namibia, South Africa, Zambia and Zimbabwe. Separatist insurgencies represent ethnic groups that seek to represent the aspirations and identities of groups from an existing entity, by either seceding or securing greater autonomy. Such groups can be found in Southern Sudan, Nigeria, Eretria and Senegal. The reform insurgencies pursue radical changes to the existing central or national government. They seek to change the status quo or the mode of governance. Examples of such insurgencies can be found in Uganda (LRA), CAR (Sėlėka), Sudan (SPLA) and Liberia (Liberians United for Reconciliation and Democracy, LURD). The fourth type is warlord insurgencies, which arise where the insurgents seek to change leadership, but do not seek to create another state different from the one it seeks to lead.

It has also been argued that the nature of actors in conflicts in Africa determines the types of conflicts, and that such actors rarely conform to the conventional conception of an organised, hierarchical and disciplined army that fights in identifiable uniforms. Rather, most fighters in violent conflict situations in Africa are non-military actors, such as rebels, insurgents, private militias, warlords, criminal gangs, mercenaries and child soldiers (Jackson 2007). However, these groups are often organised actors, who may appear from the outside to be disorganised but also have had internal command mechanisms and structures, such as the LRA (Uganda), Boko Haram, MEND (Nigeria) and SPLA (Sudan). Also, many insurgent/secessionist groups had organised structures with defined command systems, such as the Biafra Army (Nigeria), UNITA and MPLA (Angola), and RENAMO (Mozambique).

3.4 Patterns and Trends of Violent Conflicts Common in Africa

Patterns of violent conflict in Africa since the end of the Cold War in 1990 appear to be changing from the typical types—civil wars or internal armed conflicts to fragmented and low-level violent conflicts. They are becoming difficult to compartmentalise, but are typically fought at the peripheries of states by weak and factionalised insurgencies. They are smaller in scale, scope and intensity than the violent conflict of previous decades, and are mainly fought by fragmented armed groups (Jackson 2007; Scott 2012). These conflicts are difficult to end because of the mobile and fractionalised nature of the armed groups, and the abilities of the groups to operate across international borders, and to have access to funds acquired through illicit trades. Some of these illicit transactions/criminal activities are: trade in raw materials, kidnapping, oil bunkering, drug trade, illegal cigarette trade, and illegal trading in small arms and light weapons.

Scott (2012) describes this development as the decline of big wars that were fought for state control, which involved rebel groups that have firm control of a part or parts of the territory of the state for a long time, and pitted against well-structured armies, like the Nigeria-Biafra War, the Ethiopian Civil War and the Civil Wars in Angola and Mozambique. Wars of the twenty-first century are smaller, mostly fought by fractionalised rebel groups, tend to take place in the periphery of the state, have a strong trans-border dimension and have connections with international terrorist networks. The networked nature of these conflicts creates regional conflicts (For instance, Al-Qaeda in the Maghreb, El-Shabab, Boko Haram) and distorts the previous divide between internal and international conflicts (Jackson 2007).

In the twenty-first century, both the volume and character of civil wars have changed in significant ways. Civil wars that used to be dominant have declined and given way to other types of violent conflicts (Scott 2012). Some of the discernible patterns of armed conflicts are that: violent conflicts in Africa are becoming fragmentised with the involvement of several non-state actors, as witnessed in the 2012–2013 conflict in Mali where several rebel/Islamists groups fought against each other and also against the central government. Darfur, Sudan, where several rebels groups were involved in the fight for the political autonomy of the region. CAR, where the Sėlėka Coalition (Union of Democratic Force for Unity, Convention of Patriot for Justice and Peace, Patriotic Convention for Saving the Country), after protracted battles in 2013 recently overran the government of Francois Bozizė in Bangui; and DRC, where the M23 rebel movement split into different factions.

Election violence, which is associated with the conduct of elections (Ladan 2005; Ogbu 2005), is becoming common in Africa. The African Electoral Violence Database shows that between 1990 and 2008, 60% of African elections witnessed low-level violence, and 20% involved high-level violence. This has been attributed to the increasing popularity of democracy in Africa, and common in African countries with fragile democracies or settings where democracy has not been fully entrenched, or where governments have been fractionalised or based on ethnic ideologies (Scott 2012). Cilliers and Schunemann (2013) also argue that the era of democracy and elections has inevitably shifted competition for political advantages from armed oppositions in rural areas to election conflicts, and that in future, elections will remain latent sources of conflicts in some

African states, until equitable power-sharing arrangements evolve. The post-election violence in Zimbabwe (2005), Kenya (2008), Côte d'Ivoire (2010) and Nigeria (2011) are typical examples.

Another discernible trend is that most insurgent groups in Africa seem to have strong transnational characteristics, with the tendency to move across international borders (Scott 2012), but limited military capability to pose serious threats to the central government or to hold part of the territory of a state. Some of these groups exploit the gains of weak central governments as in DRC, while others operate at the periphery of well-established states like Nigeria (Boko Haram), Mali (National Movement for the Liberation of Azawad, Movement for Oneness and Jihad in West Africa, and Ansar Dine), Senegal (Movement of Democratic Forces of Casamance) and Uganda (The LRA). Closely related to this trend is that "mobile insurgent groups that move back and forth across national borders engage the security of multiple states, and inflict harm on civilian populations across borders" (Scott 2012). Good examples of this type are the LRA that has moved soldiers from Northern Uganda to Sudan, CAR and DRC. Al-Qaeda in the Maghreb operates across Algeria, Mali, Niger and Mauritania, while the Al-Shabab with bases in Somali has attacked targets in Kenya and Uganda.

Religious violence has remained a recurring type of violent conflict which has claimed thousands of lives in Africa, mainly in Nigeria, but also in other countries of Africa, such as in Kenya, CAR and Egypt. Over the last three decades, religious violence has occurred in many northern cities in Nigeria and has claimed over 40,000 lives and led to the destruction of property worth millions of dollars (Imobighe 2003). Africa has also witnessed a large number of resource-based conflicts (Cater 2003; Ross 2003). Resource-based conflicts, such as the conflicts over land and water and between farmers and herders, are common, salient and likely persist in many parts of Africa (Jackson 2007; Scott 2012). In such conflicts, the possession of natural resources or raw materials and the profit derived from them become determining factors in the conflicts. This may also include what is commonly called "indigenes/settlers" or "sons of the soil" conflicts where a group that considers itself indigenous clashes with a migrant group over political, natural or economic resources. Competition over resources at the community level is the major cause of ethnic and community conflicts. The conflicts in Angola, the Niger Delta region of Nigeria, Sudan, DRC, CAR, Côte d'Ivoire and Sierra Leone are resource related (Ross 2003). Between 2000 and 2010, conflict over resources accounted for approximately thirty-five per cent of all conflicts in sub-Saharan Africa (Cilliers and Schunemann 2013).

Ethnic-based community conflicts, which are conflicts involving people from different ethnic groups mainly over resources, political power and boundaries, are also common in Nigeria, Kenya, Ethiopia, Somali, Burundi, Rwanda, Liberia, Côte d'Ivoire, Ghana, Morocco, Mauritania, Senegal, Kenya, Tanzania, Zaire, Zimbabwe and Benin (Nnoli 1998; Imobighe 2003). The causes of ethnic conflicts are many, varied and complex: such as struggles over scarce resources, the divide and rule policy of the colonial regimes which pitted ethnic groups against each other, capitalism which introduced and reinforced an unsustainable appetite for wealth among ethnic groups, poor governance at the centre, poverty, and limited or no mechanisms for conflict resolution by governments.

Climate change has been identified as capable of posing a significant threat to peace and security in most countries in Africa in future. Climate change is likely to increase competition over resources, leads to drought and flooding, and increases global warming. These may lead to a reduction in food production, water shortages, severe competition over scarce natural resources, displacements, migration and an increase in conflicts, mostly in African states with low capacity and resources to adapt to these changes (Cilliers and Schunemann 2013).

3.5 International Criminal Court's Interventions in Conflict Situations in Africa

The ICC is currently prosecuting persons from eight situations—all in Africa: CAR, Uganda, DRC, Kenya, Libya, Côte d'Ivoire, Mali and Sudan. The ICC is also currently investigating the situations in Georgia and CAR(11) and conducting preliminary examinations in Honduras,

Afghanistan, Colombia, Nigeria, Guinea, Burundi, Palestine, Iraq/UK, Ukraine, and the Registered Vessel of Comoros, Greece and Cambodia.

The interventions of the ICC in conflict and post-conflict situations have been praised as being capable of contributing to post-conflict reconstruction. However, the ICC's choice of cases and the perception that the Court has disproportionately focused on Africa is controversial (Arieff et al. 2011). The ICC has also been accused of restricting the space for global justice in Africa, distracting the international community from using other forms of political organisations and actions that might lead to peace and reducing international negotiations to criminal justice (Adam 2011). Clarke (2009) argues that one consequence of the growing power of the ICC is its ability to use the law to establish new terms of engagement within which defendants, lawyers and prosecutors re-classify evidence and articulate crimes in legally relevant terms. This re-classification of terms has had the effect of sublimating the root causes of violence and reassigning accountability to leaders in sub-Saharan Africa who are then seen as responsible for mass violence, while the causes of such mass violence are much deeper than the roles of leaders who perpetrated international crimes. The new face of justice, according to Clark, is "the convergence of the guilt of key leaders and the defence of the victims", which may be having unintended consequences that may not promote the peace process. Nonetheless, the roles played by top actors in the conflicts in Angola, Liberia, Sierra Leone, South Sudan and Côte d'Ivoire should not be underestimated and do not wholly amount to "sublimating the root causes of conflicts and reassigning accountability to leaders". According to Miall et al. (1999), "armed conflicts often arise from the juxtaposition and combination of events—what matters most is not the juxtaposition in times of different chains of events, but the meaning these events have for those who are responsible for taking decisions". Therefore, leaders who led wars and armed conflict are often an obvious part of the problem. Indicting, incarcerating and sanctioning them could, in some cases, be useful in conflict prevention.

In spite of these complexities of international justice mechanisims interventions in conflict and post-conflict situations, what is indisputable is that the involvement of the ICC in these situations provides another platform or mechanism to deal with these conflicts. The ICC, according to articles 13, 14 and 15 of the Rome Statute, may exercise jurisdiction with respect to any of the crimes provided by its Statute only if a situation in which one or more of such crimes appears to have been committed is referred to the chief prosecutor by a state party in accordance with article 14 of the Statute, or a situation in which one or more of such crimes appears to have been committed is referred to the chief prosecutor by the UNSC, acting under Chapter VIII of the United Nations Charter or the OTP has initiated an investigation in respect of such a crime in accordance with article 15. The situations in Libya and Sudan were referred to the chief prosecutor by the UNSC, while those in Uganda, CAR, DRC and Mali were referred to the chief prosecutor by the state parties. The situations in Kenya and Côte d'Ivoire were initiated by the chief prosecutor *propriomotu* on the basis of information on the crimes committed in both countries. The OTP has already opened 48 cases against individuals in Africa who are accused of committing different international crimes in eight conflict situations in Africa.

3.6 The International Criminal Court and Africa: Is the Court Targeting Africa?

The ICC has been accused of unduly focusing on conflicts in Africa and of not paying attention to conflicts in other parts of the world, even when such conflicts are of high or higher gravity than those in Africa. The African Union (AU) and some African leaders have accused the ICC of targeting Africa and its leaders, and of undermining AU's efforts to peacefully resolve some of the violent conflicts. The ICC has been branded an agent of imperialism and a tool of Western powers (du Max 2010). The AU on the other hand has been accused of blocking accountability. But this allegation has been rebutted, with the AU stating that its primary concern is with the timing of ICC's investigations and prosecutions in some countries in Africa. The AU also states that ICC's investigations and prosecutions in Africa need to take cognisance of the complex humanitarian and security realities on the ground, and done with the consultation of the AU (Jalloh 2014). In view of the initial strong backing the ICC received from African states, the misunderstanding between the ICC and AU is ironical. Africa, with 34 state parties, has the highest regional block membership of the ICC. Senegal was the first country to ratify the Rome Statute, and this was followed by ratifications by more than half of the member states of the AU. African NGOs and scholars have also shown strong respect and backing for the Court (Jalloh 2009). The relationship between Africa and the ICC began to sour in 2009 when the ICC issued an arrest warrant for President Omar al-Bashir of Sudan for allegedly committing international crimes in Darfur (du Max 2010), and nosedived to its worst level in 2011 with the prosecutions of Uhuru Kenyatta and William Ruto of Kenya at the ICC. One of the consequences of the ICC-AU feud was seen in the disarray at the AU summit held in Johannesburg from 13 June 2015 to 15 June 2015. The meeting had several important issues before it such as women's empowerment, terrorism, Ebola, peace and security, but it was "the dramatic arrival and stealthy departure of President Al Bashir" that became the "singular defining characteristic" of the summit (Makinwa 2015).

The ICC involvement in some countries of Africa is justifiable on the grounds that the ICC is responding to the invitations of African countries to intervene and also to the unduly high number of violent conflicts in the continent. To a good extent, these lines of argument are in line with facts about the court and conflicts in Africa. The proposition that the ICC is focusing only on Africa and ignoring conflicts in other parts of the world, thereby creating an impression of bias, is also tenable and in line with the facts. However, the controversy is not good for conflict transformation in Africa, as it distracts the ICC from its primary tasks and erodes the confidence some important stakeholders have in the ICC. The situation calls for more collaborations and discussions between the ICC and the AU to address areas of differences. The ICC should also consider taking more cases from other parts of the world. Issues that could lead to allegations of bias or likelihood of bias should be urgently dealt with.

3.7 Conclusion

This chapter examined the nature, types and trends of violent conflicts in Africa. It also examined the mechanisms for conflict transformation, the nature of ICC interventions in some conflicts in Africa and the likely impact of these interventions on conflicts. The objective of the chapter was to examine the nature, types and causes of violent conflicts in Africa, and to highlight some of the reasons why the ICC is involved in these violent conflicts. The chapter concludes that the ICC could play significant roles in conflict management in Africa by contributing to conflict prevention and by assisting in ending impunity. Though it is difficult to properly assess the impact of any court on conflict transformation, the hope is that by establishing strong legal institutions, such as the ICC, which has the potential to enforce the rule of law, it could assist in ending impunity in Africa. The next three Chapters (4, 5, and 7) discuss the violent conflicts in Uganda, Kenya and Côte d'Ivoire, respectively, as well as the impact of the interventions of the ICC on the peace processes in these countries.

References

Adam, Branch. 2011. "Neither Liberal nor Peace: Practices of Global Justice by the ICC". In *The Problems and Practice of Peace-Building*, edited by Susanna Campbell, David Chandler, and Meera Sabaratnam, 121–137. London: Zed Books.

Arieff, Alexis, Rhoda Margesson, Marjorie Ann Browne, and Matthew Weed. 2011. "International Criminal Court Cases in Africa: Status and Policy Issues". Accessed September 24, 2013.

Arnold, Guy. 2009. *A to Z of Civil Wars in Africa*. Playmouth: Scarecrow Press.

Baker, Bruce. 2007. "Post-Settlement Governance Programs: What Is Being Built in Africa". In *Ending Africa's Wars*, edited by Oliver Furley and Roy May, 31–35. Burlington: Ashgate.

Bujra, Abdalla. 2002. "African Conflicts: Their Causes and Their Political and Social Environment". DPMF Occasional Paper, No. 4. Development Policy Management Forum, Addis Ababa. Accessed October 20, 2013. http://www.uneca.org.

Cater, Charles. 2003. "The Political Economy of Conflicts and UN Intervention: Rethinking the Critical Cases of Africa". In *The Political Economy of Armed Conflict: Beyond Greed and Grievance*, edited by Karen Ballentine and Jake Sherman, 19–45. London: Lynne Rienner.

Cilliers, Jakkie, and Julia Schunemann. 2013. "The Future of Interstate Conflict in Africa: More Violence or Greater Peace?" Institute for Security Studies Paper. Accessed April 30, 2013.

Clapham, Christopher, ed. 1998. *African Guerrillas*. Bloomington: Indiana University Press.

Clarke, Kamari Maxine. 2009. *Fictions of Justice: The International Criminal Court and the Challenges of Legal Pluralism in Sub-Saharan Africa*. Cambridge: Cambridge University Press.

du Max, Plessis. 2010. *The International Court Africa Wants*. Pretoria: Institute for Security Studies, Pretoria.

Furley, Oliver, and Roy May. 2006. "Introduction". In *Ending Africa's Wars: Progressing to Peace*, edited by Oliver Furley and Roy May, 1–14. Burlington: Ashgate Publishing.

Ikelegbe, Augustine, and Wafula Okumu. 2010. "Introduction: Towards Conceptualisation and Understanding of the Threats of Armed Non-state Groups to Human Security and the State in Africa". In *Militias, Rebels and Islamist Militants*, edited by Augustine Ikelegbe and Wafula Okumu. Institute for Security Studies. Accessed September 4, 2013.

Imobighe, Thomas, ed. 2003. *Civil Society and Ethnic Conflict Management in Nigeria*. Lagos: Spectrum Books.

Jackson, Richard. 2000. "Managing Africa's Violent Conflicts". *Peace and Change* 25: 208–224. Accessed March 11, 2015. http://onlinelibrary.wiley.com/doi/10.1111/0149-0508.00151/abstract.

Jackson, Richard. 2007. "African Wars: Overview, Causes and the Challenges of Conflict Transformation". In *Ending Africa's Wars: Progressing to Peace*, edited by Oliver Furley and Roy May, 15–31. Burlington: Ashgate.

Jalloh, Charles Chernor. 2009. "Kenya's Dangerous Dance with Impunity". JURIST—Forum. Accessed August 13, 2014. http://jurist.law.pitt.edu/forumy/2009/08/kenyas.

Jalloh, Charles. 2014. "Reflections on the Indictment of Sitting Heads of State and Government and Its Consequences for Peace and Stability and Reconciliation in Africa". *African Journal of Legal Studies* 7: 43–59.

Ladan, Muhammed. 2005. "Causes of Election Violence in Nigeria: Analysis of Public Perception". In *Election Violence in Nigeria*, edited by Muhammed Ladan and Aisha Kiru, 27–66. Zaria: Ahmadu Bello University Press.

Makinwa, Bunmi. 2015. "The Lingering ICC-African Union Feud". *The Guardian Newspaper*. Accessed January 2016.

Marshall, Monty. 2005. "Conflict Trends in Africa: 1946–2004". Center for Global Policy George Mason University. Accessed August 12, 2013. http://www.globalpolicy.gmu.edu.

Meredith, Martin. 2005. *The State of Africa: A History of Fifty Years of Independence*. London: Free Press.

Miall, Huge, Oliver Ramsbotham, and Tom Woodhouse. 1999. *Contemporary Conflict Resolution*. Cambridge: Polity.

Nnoli, Okwudiba, ed. 1998. *Ethnic Conflict in Africa*. Nottingham: CODESTRIA.

Ogbu, Osita. 2005. "Legal, Constitutional and Institutional Mechanisms Against Electoral Violence in Nigeria". In *Election Violence in Nigeria*, edited by Muhammed Ladan and Aisha Kiru, 71–95, Zaria: Ahmadu Bello University Press.

Ross, Michael. 2003. "Oil, Drugs and Diamond: The Varying Roles of Natural Resources in Civil War". In *The Political Economy of Armed Conflict: Beyond Greed and Grievance*, edited by Karen Ballentine and Jake Sherman, 47–63. London: Lynne Rienner.

Scott, Straus. 2012. "Wars Do End! Changing Patterns of Political Violence in Sub-Saharan Africa". *African Affairs* 111: 179–201.

4

The International Criminal Court and the Peace Process in Uganda

4.1 Introduction

This chapter examines the conflict in Northern Uganda between the Government of Uganda (GoU) and the Lord's Resistance Army (LRA), the various peace efforts made in managing the conflict, and the involvement of the ICC in the conflict. The focus of the chapter is on the impact of the ICC on the peace process in the country. Hence, the central issue examined is whether the ICC is facilitating the peace process or stalling or complicating it, or having little or no effect on it. It examines this question by exploring the impact of the Court's involvement on the following issues: reconciliation, promotion of accountability to the law, deterrence and protection of victims' rights. Relying on data from field study in Uganda in November 2013, analysis of the involvement of ICC in Uganda, analysis of relevant developments in the country, like, the Juba Peace Talk, the Amnesty programme, the interface between the ICC and traditional justice mechanisms, and the review of relevant literature, this chapter assesses how the ICC influences the peace process in Uganda.

L. N. Malu, *The International Criminal Court and Peace Processes*,
Palgrave Studies in Compromise after Conflict,
https://doi.org/10.1007/978-3-030-19905-0_4

4.2 Synopsis of the Conflict in Northern Uganda

The conflict in Northern Uganda erupted after the National Resistance Army/Movement (NRA/M) took over the Government of Uganda in January 1986 (Human Rights Watch 2005), and the subsequent NRA/M's attacks on Acholis after the regime change (Otunnu 2002; Royo 2008). Economic and political divisions and disparities between the North and South, which were partly created by the colonial government and exacerbated by the post-independence governments, are frequently cited as some of the main causes of the conflict (Happold 2007; Mallinder 2009; Royo 2008).

After the overthrow of General Tito Lutwa Okello in January 1986 by the NRA/M, "embattled government soldiers from the deposed regime fled to the North, and to neighbouring countries" (Royo 2008). In subsequent months, these soldiers, "who were mainly from Northern Uganda, re-grouped under different armed organisations (the most significant among them being the Uganda People's Democratic Army (UPDA)) to fight the NRA and to protect the interests of the North" (Human Rights Watch 2005). The crisis in the North also "led to the emergence of political and military leaders who claimed to be spirit mediums. One such leader was Alice Auma Lakwena, who established the Holy Spirit Movement (HSM) and led armed campaigns against the NRA" (Mallinder 2009).

These Northern resistance groups soon disappeared: "the HSM was crushed in Jinja as its soldiers marched toward Kampala in late 1986, while the UPDA signed a peace agreement in 1988 with the GoU" (O'Kadameri 2002). The demise of the two groups created a vacuum which was filled by the former members of these groups, who later formed two other new groups: The Lord's Army (also called the Holy Spirit Movement 11), led by Alice Aluma Lakwena's father, Savarino Lukoya, and the LRA led by Joseph Kony (O'Kadameri 2002). The Lord's Army quickly disintegrated because the leader could not provide charismatic leadership reminiscent of the Alice Lakwena era. The LRA led by the charismatic Joseph Kony combined spiritual elements and military powers to become the de facto fighters for the Acholi cause (Lanz 2007).

The LRA enjoyed the support of the Sudanese government, but this was said to have stopped after the signing of the Nairobi Peace Agreement in 2005 (Human Rights Watch 2005). Between 1989 and 1991, the group killed hundreds of people and abducted thousands in villages in Northern Uganda, and also tortured and mutilated civilians by cutting off their hands, ears or lips (Nyeko and Okello 2002; UN High Commissioner for Human Rights and Uganda Human Rights Commission 2011). Over 66,000 persons were said to have been abducted in Acholiland between 1998 and 2005, with 20% of male abductees and 5% of female abductees believed to have been killed (UN High Commissioner for Human Rights and Uganda Human Rights Commission 2011).

In 2002, the Ugandan Army, (also called the Uganda People's Defence Forces (UPDF)), with the Sudanese government's consent, launched "Operation Iron Fist I", and in 2004 "Operation Iron Fist II" against the LRA inside Sudan. In response, the LRA fled to Northern Uganda where it expanded its operations to areas previously untouched by the war such as Lira and Teso subregions and territories in the DRC (Lanz 2007). The LRA also began larger-scale abduction, killing, looting and general attacks on civilians, thus causing an upsurge in the number of people leaving their homes, and significantly exacerbating the humanitarian situation. The government responded by ordering people in villages that were attacked to move to government camps. According to a Human Rights Watch's account (2005), in early 2002, there were more than 500,000 internally displaced persons. By late 2002, as a result of LRA's return to Northern Uganda, and the UPDF order, the number increased to about 800,000. The LRA has since 2005 been driven out of Northern Uganda. Its operations have also decreased substantially and are now limited to the DRC and CAR.

4.3 The International Criminal Court's Involvement in the Conflict

Uganda signed the Rome Statute in 1998 and later ratified it in June 2002. The conflict in Northern Uganda was subsequently referred by the GoU to the ICC in December 2003. In July 2004, the chief prosecutor decided that there was a reasonable basis to open an investigation into the "situation concerning Northern Uganda". The chief prosecutor later filed an application for warrants of arrest for five leaders of the LRA. No member of the UPDF was indicted because, according to the OTP, the crimes committed by the LRA were of higher gravity than those allegedly committed by the Ugandan Army (Lanz 2007). In July 2005, Pre-Trial Chamber II of the ICC granted the chief prosecutor's application and issued warrants of arrest for five LRA leaders, namely: Joseph Kony, Vincent Otti, Okot Odhiambo, Raska Lukwiya, and Dominic Ongwen. The warrants of arrest were unsealed in October 2005. The cases against Raska Lukwiya and Okot Odhiambo were terminated after their deaths were confirmed. In 2014, Dominic Ongwen surrendered and is currently in the custody of the ICC, charged with seventy counts of crimes against humanity and war crimes. Joseph Kony and Vincent Otti are still at large.

The involvement of the ICC in Uganda was received with mixed reactions (Tenove 2013). While the intervention was welcomed by most international human rights and justice non-governmental organisations (Allen 2006), it received a hostile reception from many local groups in the North such as Acholi leaders, local nongovernmental organisations, the Amnesty Commission of Uganda and religious groups under the auspices of Acholi Religious Leaders' Peace Initiative (ARLPI). The main concerns about the ICC's involvement are that: the timing of the arrest warrant was ill-conceived; the chief prosecutor did not make public the results of his investigations into the crimes committed by the UPDF (Human Rights Watch 2009); the Court is biased (Mallinder 2009), and the ICC will exacerbate the conflict or complicate the peace process.

Another concern about the ICC in Uganda is that it sidelines traditional mechanisms for conflict resolution and reconciliation, thereby allegedly complicating the peace process. The ICC is perceived as an inappropriate imposition that dispenses a foreign concept of justice, without the capacity to heal psychological wounds, establish individual responsibility, or to reconcile parties to the conflict. The proposition for the use of a traditional transitional justice mechanism for the conflict came from various groups, including human rights activists, peace activists, aid workers, religious groups, traditional leaders and representatives of the LRA. The GoU is also in support of the use of traditional mechanisms for resolving the conflict. Though it referred the situation to the ICC in 2003, in 2007 however, following the peace talks in Juba, it also signed an agreement on accountability and reconciliation with the LRA, which proposed (among other things), that local measures drawn from the customs of the Acholis and their neighbours should be recognised and incorporated into Ugandan law.

4.4 The ICC and Traditional Justice Mechanisms in Northern Uganda

Traditional justice mechanisms, particularly those from Acholiland are presented as an alternative to the ICC in resolving the Northern Uganda conflict. The central argument is that criminal prosecution is not a universally recognised method of justice and may not work in Northern Uganda, where there are traditional mechanisms that emphasise forgiveness and reconciliation (Nakayi 2008; Hovil and Lomo 2005). Nonetheless, there seem to be doubts whether there is an established, time-tested, Acholi system of conflict resolution or reconciliation or whether the Acholi traditional system of justice is being propagated as an established truth by those who are opposed to the ICC (Allen 2006; Forgotten Voices 2005). This view was corroborated by a respondent who claims that: "The local system is not very developed to meet the needs of modern conflict resolution; those who peddle it do so as a matter of pride and ownership, and not because of its efficiency".[1] However, some argue that although there is evidence of decline because of the influence of colonialism, western education, other religions and urbanisation, still, there is a common knowledge and understanding of these mechanisms, even when they are rarely used (Hovil and Lomo 2005).

[1]Interview with a Human Right Activist in Uganda, 2013.

Discussion on traditional justice mechanisms in Northern Uganda has centred mainly on the Acholi traditional justice mechanisms despite the existence of similar mechanisms in other ethnic groups affected by the conflict in the region. The term "traditional justice mechanism" in Northern Uganda in this study is used to refer to the Acholi mechanism. It is restorative in nature, involving processes that include a community, during which the community deliberates over past crimes, allowing victims and perpetrators to take centre-stage in a process which aims to restore dignity and empowerment to the victims (Nakayi 2008). Traditional justice practice in Acholiland is based on the principle that "Acholi survival depends on unity" (Forgotten Voices 2005). It is, however, fragmented (Allen 2006) and differs from clan to clan, but with common features shared across the clans such as the voluntary nature of the process, mediation of truth, acknowledgement of wrongdoing and reconciliation through symbolic acts and spiritual appeasement (Nakayi 2008; Forgotten Voices 2005). Some of the basic traditional mechanisms, according to Nakayi (2008), are the ceremony of "stepping on the egg" (*Nyono tong gweno*) and the "drinking of bitter root" (*Mato oput*). The ritual of "stepping on the egg" is normally used as a cleansing mechanism intended to welcome a member who has been away for a long time, to ensure that the person does not bring back a foreign spirit into the community and thus, bring misfortunes. It is usually used before *mato oput* (Hovil and Lomo 2005; Nakayi 2008; Allen 2006).

The ritual of "stepping on the egg" is traditionally used when a person has done some immoral or amoral thing such as having a child outside the ancestral home (Nakayi 2008; Allen 2006). This ritual has been adapted in the LRA context as a ceremony to forgive LRA returnees. The ritual is at times followed by the "washing away the tears" ceremony. During the ceremony, the parents of a returnee kill a goat, and water is poured on the roof of the homestead where the child will stay. This is to indicate the washing away of the tears shed over the child while living outside the ancestral home (Hovil and Lomo 2005). The ritual or ceremony of *mato oput* or "drinking of the bitter root" takes place within a clan, and in cases of wrongful killings or murder, between clans with strong relationships (Hovil and Lomo 2005).

Mato oput encompasses the killing of animals, the killer admits committing the offence, accepts responsibility, and asks for forgiveness. This is followed by the wrongdoer and the next of kin of the victim drinking an alcoholic drink mixed with the bitter powder of the *oput* tree. Other members of the family join to drink from the same calabash. A bull brought by the wrongdoer is killed and shared by the two families. The principal goal of *mato oput* is reconciliation between enemies, and restoration of bonds between the clans of the perpetrator and that of the victim. This is achieved through the processes of acknowledgement of guilt, compensation by the offender, and participation of the victim (Nakayi 2008).

The importance of these mechanisms is that they are home-grown systems which may promote reintegration and reconciliation (Nakayi 2008). However, their viability, relevance to the current conflict, acceptability and widespread usage is also in doubt (Allen 2006; Nakayi 2008). *Mato oput* is also dismissed on the ground that it is not documented; it is overestimated, and only applicable to the Acholi people—not to other ethnic groups directly affected by the conflicts in Northern Uganda such as the Langi, Madi and Itesot.

4.5 The Amnesty Programme in Uganda

The current amnesty was introduced in Uganda in January 2000 as part of Ugandan government's efforts to implement its policy of reconciliation in order to establish peace and security in the country. The programme was introduced after years of violent conflicts and disastrous attempts by the government to end these conflicts through the use of force (Hovil and Lomo 2005). Thus, the Amnesty Act was enacted in 2000 to provide amnesty to Ugandans involved in armed conflicts in various parts of the country. The central objective is to entice people to abandon insurgency without fear of prosecution, with the aim of ending the conflicts (International Centre for Transitional Justice and Human Rights Centre, University of California 2005). Since the enactment of the Act, over 26,000 persons have benefited from the Amnesty Programme,[2] but only 5000 have been resettled. Out of this number, only 55% were from the LRA (Mallinder 2009).

The Amnesty programme introduced by the 2000 Act is however popular as there seems to be widespread support for it as one of the mechanisms of conflict transformation in Northern Uganda (Hovil and Lomo 2005, 1; International Centre for Transitional Justice and Human Rights Centre, University of California 2005). Despite a number of "challenges in its implementation, the Amnesty Law is perceived as a vital tool for conflict resolution, and for long-term reconciliation and peace within the specific context in which it is operating" (Hovil and Lomo 2005). The programme has also been praised for its ability to promote the peace process and encouraging combatants to surrender. The programme is one path toward peace in Northern Uganda, because "if the rebels all come out from the bush, including their commanders and leaders, then peace can also prevail, all the killings and atrocities will reduce, and justice can follow. First, it is important to stop the fighting before justice".[3]

Most of the respondents interviewed in Uganda state that amnesty is important for the resolution of the conflict in the North because the majority of the people who participated in the war were former abductees who deserve amnesty,[4] and because amnesty will assist in settling the conflicts since it facilitates reconciliation and resettlement.[5] Other respondents argue that the amnesty programme supports the peace process "by enabling people to abandon the rebellion and return to their homes",[6] and that African culture and processes of peace support amnesty, forgiveness, reconciliation, and performance of rituals to

[2]Interview with a staff of Ugandan Amnesty Commission, 2013.

[3]Interview with a member of Acholi Religious Leaders' Peace Initiative, 2014.

[4]Interviews with a human rights advocate in Uganda, a lecturer in peace and conflict studies in Uganda, and the director and the project coordinator of a peace and conflict NGO in Uganda, 2013.

[5]Interview with a legal practitioner in Uganda, 2013.

[6]Interview with a youth leader from Northern Uganda, 2013.

cleanse the society.[7] Another view is that in conflict transformation all mechanisms, including amnesty should be explored.[8] However, several respondents objected to granting of amnesty to senior members of the LRA who allegedly committed grave international crimes. They argue that such persons should be punished. The views of respondents in support of the Amnesty programme are captured by one interviewee, who states:

> Amnesty helped the peace process in Uganda. First, in the amnesty programme, there is a perspective for peace and reconciliation, because of the nature of the conflict; since we were dealing with our children, amnesty was important. Second, there is no contradiction in the ICC interventions and the amnesty programme of the government.[9]

The amnesty programme in Uganda, despite its procedural, legal, financial and implementation challenges is good for the peace process in Uganda since it has facilitated the return of over 26,000 persons, some of them from the LRA. The ICC's involvement does not stop the rank-and-file LRA fighters from taking advantage of the amnesty programme, but, as alleged by the LRA leaders during the Juba Peace Talks, the ICC may be blocking the leaders of the LRA from taking advantage of the amnesty programme, and to that extent may be complicating the peaceful resolution of the conflict.

4.6 The Juba Peace Talks

One of the main initiatives to end the conflict in Northern Uganda was the Juba Peace Talks (JPT) held in Juba, South Sudan, between the GoU and the LRA from July 2006 to April 2008. The JPT was mediated by the then South Sudan Vice-President, Riek Machar

---

[7]Interview with a lecturer in peace and conflict studies in Uganda, 2013.

[8]Interview with a former chairman of the Human Rights Commission of Uganda, 2013.

[9]Interview with a lecturer in peace and conflict studies in Uganda, 2013.

(Wijeyaratne 2008). The negotiation produced six main documents or agreements signed by the GoU and the LRA. The Final Peace Agreement (FPA) signing ceremony was arranged for April 2008 at Ri-Kwangba, but Kony failed to arrive for the ceremony. The failure of the LRA to sign the FPA was a big disappointment to many (Wijeyaratne 2008). However, some of the agreements are already being implemented by the GoU. For instance, the establishment of the International Crimes Division of the High Court of Uganda in 2008 is a result of the agreement on accountability and reconciliation. The JPT is also credited with promoting the peace process, improving security in Northern Uganda and embedding international accountability standards into the negotiation agenda. The ICC has been criticised for obstructing the Peace Talks by refusing to withdraw the arrest warrants for five LRA leaders and for supposedly being directly responsible for the refusal of the LRA to sign the FPA as Kony was said to fear being apprehended and taken to The Hague (Nouwen 2012; Tenove 2013). The ICC was also hailed for propelling the Peace Talks because the threat of international prosecution by the ICC helped in bringing the LRA to the negotiation table, and for making accountability one of the core issues during the negotiation. Thus, the ICC is seen to have positively and negatively influenced the peace process in Uganda.

The preponderance of the opinion of respondents is that the involvement of the ICC propelled the peace process by influencing the LRA to join the JPT. This view was canvased by some of the respondents who opine that it is doubtful if the LRA would have joined the JPT if the ICC had not indicted its leaders. They argue that the LRA leadership calculated that they could neutralise the ICC's intervention and arrest warrants by seeking peace. One such respondent is a legal practitioner in Uganda who argues that "the ICC was a driver to the JPT and promoted the peace process in Uganda positively by indicting leaders of the LRA, which forced them to negotiate for peace".[10] The ICC was one of the key factors that "influenced the LRA to the negotiating table, and the JPT were very useful as it led to discussions about the Ugandan

[10]Interview with a legal practitioner in Uganda, 2013.

conflict, and eventually to the withdrawal of the LRA from Northern Uganda. Without the ICC, Kony would have hesitated to join the peace talk".[11] However, there is a minority view that the ICC's intervention stalled the JPT and frustrated the peace process, because "the ICC negatively impacted on the peace process in Uganda as it was clear the ICC disrupted the Juba peace deal, because Kony was about to sign the peace agreement, but refused because of the intervention of the ICC".[12]

4.7 The Impact of the ICC's Involvement on the Peace Process in Uganda

This section examines the contributions of the ICC to the restoration of peace in Northern Uganda. It goes beyond the most cited impact of the ICC to the peace process, which is its contribution in propelling the LRA to the JPT (Akhavan 2005) and its influence on Kony that made him refuse to sign the Final Peace Agreement (Schabas 2007). It will rather examine how the ICC has contributed to the peace process in much deeper and fundamental ways. It also explores the nature of these contributions and examines which aspects of the work of the ICC contributes to which aspects of the peace process. The chapter assumes that these contributions could be positive or negative, and thus examines these issues from multiple perspectives, by exploring the impact of the ICC on accountability to the law, promotion of victims' rights, promotion of reconciliation and deterrence.

4.7.1 The ICC and the Promotion of Accountability to the Law in Uganda

Accountability to the law suffered during the years of conflict in Uganda. In the North, where the LRA held sway, there was almost a

[11] Interview with the director and the project coordinator of a peace and conflict NGO in Uganda, 2013.

[12] Interview with a project coordinator of a peace and conflict NGO in Uganda, 2013.

total collapse of justice institutions. In the South, the rule of law also suffered as neither the LRA nor government forces that committed grave human rights abuses against civilians during the years of conflict in the North were prosecuted (Human Rights Watch 2012). Since the end of the conflict in the North, the GoU says it has made restoration of the rule of law and accountability to the law one of the cardinal points of the administration. The GoU embarked on the process of reopening justice institutions in the North, which were closed during the conflict, building new courts, establishing the International War Crimes Division of the High Court of Uganda (Tadeo 2012), and publishing a comprehensive transitional justice policy.

The ICC's influence on accountability to the law in Uganda is assessed by examining: (a) the nexus between the ICC's involvement and enactment of accountability laws, (b) the link between ICC's involvement and establishment of justice institutions, and (c) the link between the ICC's involvement and prosecution of offenders. These issues are explored by eliciting information from respondents and by analysis of relevant publications.

The findings are that there are some connections between the involvement of the ICC in Uganda and the creation of more justice institutions, or the introduction of reforms in some existing justice institutions. It is not clear to what extent the ICC influenced the establishment of these institutions or the introduction of these reforms. However, it is clear that these developments took place after the ICC intervened in Uganda, and secondly, that these reforms and institutions that were established, attempt to mirror international standards or models. The GoU established the International Crimes Division of the High Court of Uganda in 2008 to try those who committed international and other crimes. The International Crimes Division is modelled after international tribunals, comprising a Bench of at least three Judges, a Registry, an Office of the Prosecutor and Office of the Defence Counsel. Another important development is the establishment of the Justice, Law and Order Sector which works on justice reforms, law and order. These developments were linked to the involvement of the ICC in Uganda by several respondents in Uganda. The ICC has promoted the establishment of the International Crimes Court in Uganda and has entrenched the rule of law in the area of international crimes, because right now, "there is a full court dealing with international crimes operating in the country. The point is not on the functionality of the court but on the fact that the court is there already. Much will however depend on what the government makes of it".[13] The whole discussion of establishing the Uganda International Crimes Court was "because of the ICC. The whole debate about establishing the transitional justice system in Uganda was because of the ICC's intervention". Also, "the intervention of the ICC has helped in promoting access to justice in Uganda, as there are now more mechanisms for promoting the rule of law and accessing the courts in Uganda".[14]

The ICC influenced the enactment of accountability laws, to the extent that some accountability to the law legislations were enacted/amended after the ICC became involved. Some of these laws mimic international laws while others introduced reforms. The ICC has contributed to accountability to the law in Uganda "by promoting democracy, enactment of new laws, such as the 2010 ICC Act, and by promoting more respect for the international legal system, through the establishment of the Ugandan International Criminal Court".[15] The ICC has also contributed to the rule of law and accountability, because Ugandan leaders are now more conscious about international criminal law/human rights and this has contributed to accountability.[16] A law teacher at Makerere University thinks that the ICC has promoted the establishment of the International Crimes Court in Uganda and has "entrenched the rule of law in the area of international crimes because right now Uganda has a court dealing with international crimes, and that is prosecuting Mr Thomas Kwoyelo. The Court can also be seen as being used by Uganda to show that it is willing and capable of dealing with international crimes".[17] She notes, however, that:

---

[13]Interview with a staff of an intergovernmental organisation in Uganda, 2013.

[14]Interview with a former chairman of the Human Rights Commission of Uganda, 2013.

[15]Interview with a project coordinator of a peace and conflict NGO in Uganda, 2013.

[16]Interview with a youth leader and security expert in Uganda, 2013.

[17]Interview with a human rights advocate and lecturer in law in Uganda, 2013.

> The lack of seriousness of the new court is evidenced by the fact that it has dealt with only one person, who is not actually a leader of the conflict, and it has focused on issues like discrimination and not substantive issues of international crimes. Also, it should be noted that knowing the rule of law does not necessarily mean promoting the rule of law, which has to do with enforcement, and with people being willing to litigate.[18]

The GoU enacted the International Criminal Court Act, 2010, signed the Accountability and Reconciliation Agreement with the LRA and published a comprehensive Transitional Justice Policy. The Prevention of Genocide Bill was introduced in the Ugandan Parliament in 2015. The bill seeks to establish an Independent National Committee to spearhead the fight against genocide.

Many respondents in Uganda argue that the involvement of the ICC in Uganda may have influenced the decision of the GoU to take these steps. There are many positive contributions of the ICC to the rule of law. Some are: "it led to the enactment of the Ugandan ICC Act; it led to the establishment of the War Crimes Court, within the High Court; and the last, government now has embarked in the development of a transitional justice policy".[19] The argument is not that the ICC directly facilitated the enactment of these laws and regulations, but that since these laws and regulations came into place after the ICC involvement, and some of the provisions mirror their international counterparts, there is a likelihood that the ICC involvement may have influenced the decisions to enact these laws and regulations.

However, the enactment of these laws and the establishment of justice institutions have not led to the prosecution of more people for crimes committed during the armed conflict in Northern Uganda. Presently, only Thomas Kwoyelo is being prosecuted in the International War Crime Division of the High Court of Uganda. The case is still pending because the Supreme Court of Uganda has only recently ruled that the Thomas Kwoyelo trial before the International

---

[18] Interview with a human rights advocate and lecturer in law in Uganda, 2013.

[19] Interview with a legal practitioner in Uganda, 2013.

Crimes Division of the High Court of Uganda must resume.[20] This is an appeal by GoU against the decision of the Constitution Court of Uganda which directed the International Crimes Division of the High Court to cease the trial of Thomas Kowyelo (International Centre for Transitional Justice 2015, 4). Thus, the establishment of rule of law institutions and the enactment of laws and regulations that mirror international standards does not automatically lead to the promotion of accountability to the law at national level.

4.7.2 Promoting Victims' Rights in Uganda

The Rome Statute makes several references to the roles and interests of victims, including the right of victims to intervene in proceedings, the establishment of a Victims and Witnesses Unit within the Registry, the recognition of entitlement of victims to reparation (Schabas 2007), and the establishment of the TFV. The Rules of Procedure and Evidence of the ICC also provide that a Chamber in "making any direction or order, and other organs of the Court in performing their functions under the Statute or the Rules, shall take into account the needs of all victims and witnesses in accordance with article 68, in particular, children, elderly persons, persons with disabilities and victims of sexual or gender violence".[21] Article 75 provides that the court shall establish principles relating to reparations to, or in respect of, victims which shall include restitution, compensation and rehabilitation. Thus, the Court may, either upon request or, in exceptional circumstances, in its own motion determine the scope and extent of any damage, loss and injury to, or in respect of victims. The order may be made directly against a convicted person stating appropriate reparation to or in respect of victims, or the court may order that the award be made through the TFV.

The Rome Statute also established the TFV to cater for the often forgotten victims of international crimes in conflict situations the ICC

[20] Uganda v Thomas Kwoyelo, Constitutional Appeal No.01 of 2012.

[21] Rule 86 of the Rules of Procedure and Evidence of the ICC, 2nd Edition, 2013. https://www.icc-cpi.int/iccdocs/PIDS/legal-texts/RulesProcedureEvidenceEng.pdf. Accessed 5 January 2019.

is involved in. The TFV has two mandates: (i) to implement court-ordered reparations; and (ii) to provide physical and psychosocial rehabilitation or material support to victims of crimes within the jurisdiction of the ICC.[22] The TFV supports activities which address the harm resulting from crimes under the jurisdiction of the ICC by assisting victims to return to a dignified and contributory life within their communities. The TFV develops its activities with the victims themselves as partners, helping them rebuild their families and communities and regain their place as fully contributing members of their societies.

According to information on the website of the TFV,[23] "the TFV has established about eighteen projects designed to assist an estimated number of 39,750 victims of crimes against humanity and war in the following categories: survivors of sexual violence & child mothers, former abductees & former child soldiers, returnee communities, acutely impacted communities, surviving family members, disabled persons & amputees, disfigured and tortured persons, orphans, elderly, and child-headed households" (McCleary-Sills and Mukasa 2013).

Some of the projects are "Counselling, Materia Support and Village Savings for Victims of War in Northern Uganda", where the TFV is working with an international NGO to help manage seven Ugandan sub-grantees implementing a broad range of services for about 950 victims in Northern Uganda. The North-East Chili Producers Association (NECPA) has been working with the TFV since 2008 in the Lira and Teso subregions of Northern Uganda, supporting an estimated 2700 victims from communities who suffered deeply from displacement, massacre, torture and abduction. Healing of memory sessions for about 50 victims of torture and mutilation to express their trauma in small groups and help each other reach a point of forgiveness and reconciliation. Vocational training and school fees for about 100 victims of torture or mutilation. Other projects are: prosthetic limbs and orthopaedics support for about 140 amputees and other victims of torture

[22]Website of the Trust Fund for Victims, https://trustfundforvictims.org/en/what-we-do/projects. Accessed 5 January 2019.

[23]https://trustfundforvictims.org/. Accessed 5 March 2015.

or mutilation. Construction of ramps at health centres to allow access for disabled victims, and reconstructive surgery for about 160 victims of mutilation, including nose, ear and lip reconstruction.

The ICC's victims redress mandate provides exceptional opportunities for the ICC to contribute to the process of post-conflict peacebuilding and facilitating sustainable peace in the countries in which the Court investigates and prosecutes (Nester 2006, 9). Thus, the TFV considers its assistance to victims a key step toward ending impunity for human rights abusers, establishing durable peace and reconciliation in conflict settings. TFV projects in physical rehabilitation have provided some victim some degree of physical healing, which promotes reintegration of victims into their communities by allowing them to function as normally as possible and to participate in regular community-based activities. The projects in these areas have led to increased ability of victims effected by the projects to live "a normal life again, to make plans for the future, to resume school and work, and to develop the confidence to participate in community gatherings again, social independence and self-reliance" (McCleary-Sills and Mukasa 2013).

The TFV projects in promoting psychological rehabilitation, according the 2013 evaluation report[24] also achieved a high degree of effectiveness. According to this report, the project may have led to victims taking a more positive outlook to life and some had gained the confidence to reengage in community activities, and being better able to deal with their problems because of their increased sense of self-confidence and social cohesion (McCleary-Sills and Mukasa 2013). The TFV in providing material supports has supported "communal savings group and/or vocational training or literacy programmes" that resulted in increased ability of victims "to borrow, save, invest, pay school fees and afford emergency medical care" (McCleary-Sills and Mukasa 2013).

The ICC has not approved reparations for victims of the armed conflict, since the Court commenced the trial of Dominic Ongwen in

[24]McCleary-Sills, Jennifer, and Stella Mukasa. 2013. "External Evaluation of the Trust Fund for Victims' Programs in Northern Uganda and the Democratic Republic of Congo: Towards a Perspective for Upcoming Interventions". http://www.icrw.org. Accessed September 10, 2014.

December 2016, the first case from the country. Pre-Trial Chamber II of the ICC on 23 March 2016, in a confirmation of charges decision, in *The Prosecutor v. Dominic Ongwen*, issued a decision confirming 70 charges brought by the OTP against Dominic Ongwen and committed him to trial before a Trial Chamber. According to information on the website[25] of the ICC, a total of 4107 victims have been granted the right to participate in the proceeding. These are alleged victims of the offences Dominic Ongwen was charged with, and not all the victims of the conflict. Dominic Ongwen is alleged, in his capacity as Brigade Commander of the Sinia Brigade of the LRA, to have ordered the commission of crimes within the jurisdiction of the Court in the context of the attack on Lukodi IDP Camp on or about 20 May 2004. The Camp was attacked by an armed group which first attacked the local defence forces and then started "shooting and beating civilian residents, burning huts and looting"; that resulted in 41 people killed, 6 abducted, 13 injured and approximately 210 civilian houses being burnt. On 21 December 2015, the prosecutor amended the charge bringing the total number of offences to seventy. The additional charges relate to attacks on the Pajule IDP camp, the Odek IDP camp and the Abok IDP camp. The expanded charges against Dominic Ongwen also include sexual and gender-based crimes committed from 2002 to 2005 in Sinia Brigade. For now, the victims of other offences committed by Ongwen and other persons are not represented.

The TFV considers its assistance to victims a key step toward establishing durable peace and reconciliation in conflict settings such as Northern Uganda. The TFV's projects will hopefully have a long-lasting impact on victims and on conflict transformation, by promoting reconciliation and rehabilitation, which could indeed assist such victims in rebuilding their lives and their communities.[26] The TFV projects are capable of promoting sustainable peace in these communities[27] because

[25]https://www.icc-cpi.int/CaseInformationSheets/ongwenEng.pdf. Accessed 5 January 2019.

[26]Interviews with a project coordinator of a peace and conflict NGO in Uganda, and the director and the project coordinator of a peace and conflict NGO in Uganda, 2013.

[27]Interviews with a community leader in Uganda and an international accountability expert in Uganda, 2013.

they will assist victims to return to a dignified community life. These TFV projects are very useful to individuals and communities that suffered from the brutality of the LRA and government forces, during the armed conflict in the North. Victims' protection projects will assist people to "resettle after several years of living in camps and being exposed to diseases and danger, and will contribute to peace, reconciliation, and conflict transformation since it will facilitate reintegration and return to normal life".[28] It seems that victims are happy that people who committed atrocities against them are being held "accountable for crimes against humanity by the ICC. But victims need much more than justice. They need food on their tables, and also shelter. They want their kids back to school".[29]

However, it seems that the ICC and the Government of Uganda are simply not doing enough for victims. Victims are being "neglected by the ICC and the government. The ICC projects are few and do not have serious impacts on many victims, while the government is still undecided on what to do with victims".[30] Victims are struggling to "succeed, to survive and rebuild and do not see much hope in the ICC system of justice".[31] Also, "there are many victims and the ICC cannot cope with the numbers of victims in the country".

The proceedings at the ICC and activities of the ICC in Uganda through the TFV projects are helpful in promoting victims' rights in Uganda. The involvement of 4107 victims through lawyers indicates that the victims of the crimes committed are not forgotten. Though reparations may take time to materialise, and the number of victims involved does not represent the thousands that are direct and indirect victims of the Northern Uganda conflict, but the involvement of 4107 victims and the projects executed by the TVC show that victims' rights are on the agenda of the ICC. These actions are however few and do not have any significant impact on many of the victims.

[28]Interviews with a community leader in Uganda and a human rights activist in Uganda, 2013.

[29]Interview with a member of Acholi Religious Leaders' Peace Initiative, 2015.

[30]Interview with an executive director of a Victims' NGO in Uganda, 2013.

[31]Interview with a human rights advocate and lecturer in law in Uganda, 2013.

4.7.3 Promoting Reconciliation in Uganda

As discussed in Chapter 2, defining reconciliation is complex because of its varying contexts, diverse understandings, and because it means different things to different people (Tolbert 2013). The main argument of the proponents of the ICC is that the Court creates conditions which are conducive for reconciliation, which is important for peacebuilding (Fisher 2010). There is another view that there is insufficient evidence to conclude that international justice contributes to national reconciliation (Drumbl 2007; Tolbert 2013).

Uganda is already divided along ethnic and political lines. These divisions are deep and longstanding, and as a result of many factors, such as economic and political divisions and disparities between the North and South, allegedly created by the colonial government, and aggravated by the post-independent governments. The Civil Society National Conference on Reconciliation held in Uganda in 2007 noted, among other things, that reconciliation consists of addressing mistrust, prejudice and marginalisation and may require the healing of wounds of conflict, and other measures (Civil Society National Conference on Reconciliation 2007). Some think that there is structural injustice, which requires structural reconciliation by promoting economic activities in Northern Uganda, to reduce the political and economic marginalisation of the region.[32] Also, many in the North think that the ICC is against the region since the Court has not indicted any person from the Ugandan Army but has focused on the LRA.[33]

The central issue examined is whether the ICC's involvement in Uganda promotes reconciliation. The majority of those interviewed think the ICC does not contribute to reconciliation in Uganda for several reasons such as: "it is not the work of the ICC to reconcile", the "ICC does not have the capacity to reconcile", "the problem of Uganda is complex" and "the ICC cannot reconcile them". For instance, a respondent argues that "Uganda is divided, there is structural injustice,

---

[32]Interview with a lecturer in peace and conflict studies in Uganda, 2013.

[33]Interviews with a youth leader and security expert in Uganda, 2013.

so the country need structural reconciliation".[34] The best reconciliation will be for the government to "promote economic activities in Northern Uganda, reduce the political and economic marginalisation of the North, and promote inclusive governance".[35] Thus, unless these fundamental issues are tackled there "may be no reconciliation in Uganda. The government must address the factors that made Kony to come up. So, the ICC cannot contribute to any reconciliation in Uganda because the issue goes beyond them".[36] The ICC is perceived as incapable of bringing reconciliation between the North and South, because "the problem of reconciliation in Uganda is deep, multifaceted, goes back to colonial rule, and the so-called un-answered questions of Uganda. The ICC cannot provide answers to these questions".[37] The "North/South divide" in Uganda is "central to the problem of reconciliation. People in the South do not care about the conflict in the North, while people in the North, do not think it is the ICC that brought about the peace in Uganda, so the ICC cannot claim credit for any link between the outcomes of the peace in Northern Uganda, such as reconciliation, if at all there is any".[38]

The indictment of leaders of the LRA who are from the North and the failure of the ICC to prosecute leaders of Uganda security forces who are thought to have committed atrocities are seen to be dividing the country instead of reconciling it. In the views of the director and project coordinator of a peace and conflict NGO in Uganda:

> The ICC intervention in Uganda may not lead to reconciliation because the North feels that the ICC is biased against them, because only LRA leaders are being prosecuted while nobody from the Uganda security forces and government is prosecuted. Also, we should not expect much from the ICC on the issue of reconciliation, because its mandate is to try very few leaders of the rebellion, and one should be very careful to link

---

[34]Interview with a lecturer in peace and conflict studies in Uganda, 2013.

[35]Interview with a human rights advocate and lecturer in law in Uganda, 2013.

[36]Interview with a lecturer in peace and conflict studies in Uganda, 2013.

[37]Interview with a project coordinator of a peace and conflict NGO in Uganda, 2013.

[38]Interview with a human rights advocate and lecturer in law in Uganda, 2013.

> such intervention to reconciliation. Let the ICC do its work of trying, and leave the issue of reconciliation, because it is not cut out for reconciliation. Reconciliation is about a win-win process, while prosecution is win-lose, and the two may not meet.[39]

Some interviewees also think that retributive justice in Uganda may not lead to reconciliation but emphasis should be placed on restorative justice mechanisms[40] such as the traditional justice mechanisms and the amnesty programme of the government. The ICC in Uganda is seen to be engaged in selective prosecutions which have polarised the country further along the North-South divide[41] and also blamed for contributing to prolonging the war as a result of the arrest warrants on leaders of the LRA.[42]

On the other hand, the involvement of the ICC in Uganda could contribute to reconciliation in the long run in Uganda, by creating the necessary environment for reconciliation. The ICC's intervention has some impacts on reconciliation, since it has helped the society to stabilise and to promote the peace process. This may help the country "to move forward. This may help in promoting the rule of law. This may help the government to respect human rights. All these could help in entrenching democracy and reconciliation".[43] Also, it is important to note that the intervention of the ICC made Ugandans start thinking about reconciliation. The government has "established institutions that somehow deal with reconciliation. Many NGOs now work on reconciliation, and some have held conferences, workshops and seminars on reconciliation. Before the ICC intervention, reconciliation was not on the agenda".[44] Despite obvious setbacks, the ICC and the government are contributing to reconciliation in several ways. For instance, in the

[39]Interview with the director and the project coordinator of a peace and conflict NGO in Uganda, 2013.

[40]Interview with a member of Acholi Religious Leaders' Peace Initiative, 2015.

[41]Interview with a human rights advocate and lecturer in law in Uganda, 2013.

[42]Interview with a project coordinator of a peace and conflict NGO in Uganda, 2013.

[43]Interview with a youth leader and security expert in Uganda, 2013.

[44]Interview with an international accountability expert in Uganda, 2013.

North the ICC has had an impact on reconciliation, because the "ICC brought lots of discussions and reflections on ways of bringing peace to the North. So the intervention by the ICC helped the North to consolidate its positions and move forward".[45] There are also lots of efforts by the "government to promote peace, reconciliation and economic activities under the office of the Prime Minister".[46]

In conclusion, the involvement of the ICC does not contribute to reconciliation in the short term, but could create conditions which are necessary for reconciliation in Uganda, by investigating the conflict in Northern Uganda, prosecuting one of the main actors in the violent conflict, influencing the GoU to focus more on transitional justice and accountability to the law, encouraging discussions on the violent conflict and challenging the culture of impunity in Uganda. Whether these conditions will facilitate reconciliation in the medium and long terms is debatable and not certain.

4.7.4 Deterring Atrocities in Uganda

The main argument in support of the positive impact of the ICC on future gross human right abusers is that, because of the presence of the ICC and its permanent nature, the possibility of ICC intervention is one factor future human rights violators now take into consideration when making decisions (Grono 2012; Kim and Sikkink 2009). Some scholars argue, however, that the deterrent impact of international justice mechanisms such as the ICC is not yet established (Wippman 1999; Ku and Nzeribe 2006).

In Uganda, the debate is whether the intervention of the ICC since 2004 has contributed to deterrence. The majority of those interviewed think the ICC contributes to general deterrence in Uganda by threatening punishment, which could deter people from offending by increasing the costs of committing grave human rights offences. They argue that

[45] Interview with a former chairman of the Human Rights Commission of Uganda, 2013.

[46] Interview with a former chairman of the Human Rights Commission of Uganda, 2013.

through the possibility of imposition of sanction by the ICC, and by "simply being there" the ICC contributes to deterrence. The ICC has the potential and even capability to deter. Its mere presence in Uganda has led to deterrence. Before the ICC, those in government and government security officers behaved as if they were above the law. With the ICC's intervention, "politicians now taunt themselves about sending each other to The Hague".[47] However, to be an effective deterrent, the "ICC should prosecute more persons from both the LRA and the government security agencies".[48] The ICC has deterred military and political leaders from committing atrocities, because the ICC has the power to "touch the untouchables".[49] It seems that "politicians and other top business leaders in Uganda are now afraid of the ICC, so they are likely to be more cautious about human right abuses".[50] The ICC may not have any deterrent influence on fighters because they do not know the law as represented by the ICC, "but for heads of states, political leaders and elites—those that know the law and understand it—the ICC may deter them from committing atrocities, since the ICC has the power to touch the untouchables, the ICC may deter them from committing atrocities".[51] The ICC has also "promoted respect for the law in Uganda, and people are conscious of the power of the ICC to prosecute".[52] An international justice expert in Uganda opines that from the "totality of the actions of the ICC in Uganda, it has shown clearly that it has the capability to deter, since it has the power to sanction".[53]

Some respondents however doubt that the ICC deters anybody in Uganda. The point is that the ICC does not have the capability to deter since it has not sanctioned many people that participated in the war, and that the deterrence debate is theoretical. In practical terms, "the failure of the ICC to arrest and prosecute the leaders of LRA, the

---

[47]Interview with an executive director of a Victims' NGO in Uganda, 2013.

[48]Interview with an executive director of a Victims' NGO in Uganda, 2013.

[49]Interview with a project coordinator of a peace and conflict NGO in Uganda, 2013.

[50]Interview with a former chairman of the Human Rights Commission of Uganda, 2013.

[51]Interview with a human rights advocate and lecturer in law in Uganda, 2013.

[52]Interview with a human rights activist in Uganda, 2013.

[53]Interview with an international accountability expert in Uganda, 2013.

failure of the ICC to prosecute sitting presidents emboldens the belief that the Court is powerless, and does not help its deterrence roles".[54] Also, examples of ongoing conflicts abound in many parts of the world despite the ICC's intervention in some countries. There are other factors that "drive conflicts; thus, there is a need for a holistic approach to conflict management. The ICC cannot do it alone, since it is concerned with punishment only, which may not deter some of the LRA rebels".[55]

Effective deterrence contributes to conflict prevention, and in the Ugandan situation, preventing the escalation of the conflict in Northern Uganda. Evidence shows that the Northern Uganda conflict has not been escalating, but rather has been de-escalating since the ICC intervention. The LRA has since 2005 virtually left Uganda and is operating minimally in some neighbouring countries, and life is gradually returning to normal in Northern Uganda. Thus, it is plausible to argue that, based on the opinions of majority of the respondents, and the situation on ground in Northern Uganda, that the ICC is contributing to conflict prevention and deterrence in Uganda through its various activities in country.

Such actions include the prosecution of Dominic Ongwen, the ICC's numerous public comments on the situation in Uganda, its investigations in Uganda, and the issue of arrest warrants for five leaders of the LRA. Also, as a permanent international Court, the ICC is a constant reminder to all would-be violators of international norms in Uganda, that their conduct can be punished. These conclusions are in line with the main argument proffered by deterrence theorists that an increase in the likelihood of imposition of sanctions will lead to a decrease in violations. The "likelihood of imposition of sanctions" by the ICC is real in Uganda, as the ICC is a permanent Court which has established its capability to prosecute some of those who committed international crimes in Uganda. Before the intervention of the ICC, a system of impunity for political leaders was evident in the country's justice system as those who committed atrocities during previous armed conflicts in

[54]Interview with a legal practitioner in Uganda, 2013.

[55]Interview with the project coordinator of Uganda Youth Network, 2013.

Uganda were not prosecuted. Since the ICC's intervention, the prosecution of some of those who committed international crimes is a possibility since the ICC initially indicted five persons. The cost of committing international crimes has evidently increased in the country and the benefits have remained relatively constant.

4.8 Conclusion

This chapter examined the conflict in Northern Uganda, the efforts made at different periods in bringing peace to the region, and the impact of the ICC's intervention in ending the conflict and preventing a relapse to conflict. It briefly discussed the impact of the ICC on the Juba Peace Talks, the Amnesty Programme, the roles of traditional justice mechanism in resolving the conflict and focused on the impact of the ICC on reconciliation, accountability, deterrence and victim's redress. These four issues were used to assess the impact of the ICC on the peace process in Uganda. The conclusions are that the ICC is contributing to the peace process in Uganda by promoting accountability to the law and by contributing to deterrence through its actions and activities in Uganda. The study also found that the ICC is not making much positive impact on reconciliation. This is because the problems that led to the conflict are deep-rooted and linked to the political and economic development of the country, and need to be tackled from many perspectives, and with the concerted efforts of Ugandans led by their government. The impact of the ICC's involvement on victims' rights is deemed too minimal to have any significant impact on the peace process in Uganda. The next chapter discusses the 2007/2008 post-election violence in Kenya, the efforts to manage the violent conflict and the impacts of the ICC's intervention on the peace process in Kenya.

References

Akhavan, Payam. 2005. "The Lord's Resistance Army Case: Uganda's Submission of the First Referral to the International Criminal Court". *The American Journal of International Law* 99: 403–421.

Allen, Tim. 2006. *Trial Justice: The International Criminal Court and the Lord's Resistance Army*. London: Zed Books.
Civil Society Consultative Conference. 2007. "Report of the Civil Society Consultative Conference on Paving the Way for a Sustainable Reconciliation Process in Uganda". Kampala, Uganda. Accessed September 20, 2014.
Drumbl, Mark. 2007. *Atrocity, Punishment and International Law*. Cambridge: Cambridge University Press.
Fisher, Martina. 2010. "Transitional Justice and Reconciliation: Theory and Practice". Accessed April 12, 2013. http://www.berghofhandbook.net/documents/publications/fisher_tj_and_rec_handbook.
Forgotten Voices. 2005. "A Perception-Based Survey on Altitudes and About Peace and Justice in Northern Uganda". Accessed May 5, 2014.
Grono, Nick. 2012. "The Deterrent Effect of the ICC on the Commission of International Crimes by Government Leaders". Accessed April 23, 2014. http://www.crisesgroup.org/en/publication.
Happold, Mathew. 2007. "The International Criminal Court and the Lord's Resistance Army". *Melbourne Journal of International Law* 8: 1–26.
Hovil, Lucy, and Zachary Lomo. 2005. "Whose Justice? Perception of Uganda's Amnesty Act 2000: The Potential for Conflict Resolution and Long Term Reconciliation". Accessed September 8, 2014. http://www.refugeelawproject.org.
Human Rights Watch. 2005. "Uprooted and Forgotten: Impunity and Human Rights Abuses in Northern Uganda". Human Rights Watch Report. Accessed October 16, 2014. https://www.hrw.org/reports/2005/uganda0905/uganda0905.pdf.
Human Rights Watch. 2009. "Selling Justice Short: Why Accountability Matters for Peace". Human Rights Watch Report. Accessed May 2, 2013. https://www.hrw.org/sites/default/files/reports/ij0709webwcover_1.pdf.
Human Rights Watch. 2012. "Justice for Serious Crimes Before National Courts: Uganda's International Crimes Division". Human Rights Watch Report. Accessed August 9, 2014.
International Centre for Transitional Justice and Human Rights Centre, University of California, Berkeley. 2005. "Forgotten Vices. A Population-Based Survey on Attitudes About Peace and Justice in Northern Uganda". Accessed January 12, 2014. https://ictj.org/sites/default/files/ICTJ "https://ictj.org/sites/default/files/ICTJ-HRC-Uganda-Voices-2005-English.pdf".
International Centre for Transitional Justice. 2015. "Pursuing Accountability for Serious Crimes in Uganda's Courts". *International Centre for Transitional Justice*

Briefing. Accessed August 13, 2015. https://www.ictj.org/sites/default/files/ICTJ "https://www.ictj.org/sites/default/files/ICTJ-Briefing-Uganda-Kwoyelo-2015".

Kim, Hunjoon, and Kathryn Sikkink. 2009. "Explaining the Deterrence Effect of Human Rights Prosecutions for Transitional Countries". *International Studies Quaterly* 54: 1–46.

Ku, Julian, and Jide Nzeribe. 2006. "Do International Criminal Tribunals Deter or Exacerbate Humanitarian Atrocities?" *Washington University Law Review* 84: 777–833.

Lanz, David. 2007. "The ICC's Intervention in Northern Uganda: Beyond the Simplicity of Peace vs. Justice". Accessed September 4, 2014. http://www.reliefweb.int/sites/reliefweb.int/files/resources/EC66215A0071F156C12573910051D06D-Full_Report.pdf.htm.

Mallinder, Loiuse. 2009. "Uganda at a Crossroads: Narrowing the Amnesty?" Accessed September 7, 2014. http://www.academia.edu/205946/Uganda_at_a_Crossroads_Narrowing_the_Amnesty.htm.

McCleary-Sills, Jennifer, and Stella Mukasa. 2013. "External Evaluation of the Trust Fund for Victims' Programs in Northern Uganda and the Democratic Republic of Congo: Towards a Perspective for Upcoming Interventions". Accessed September 10, 2014. http://www.icrw.org.

Nakayi, Rose. 2008. "Reaching Out for Justice and Reconciliation in Northern Uganda: The Proposed War Crimes Court and Traditional Justice". University of Notre Dame, Centre for Human Rights, Working Paper No. 5, Winter 2008. Accessed August 12, 2014. http://www3.nd.edu/~ndlaw/cchr/papers/rose_uganda.pdf.

Nester, Adam. 2006. "Victims Issues, Multi-track Diplomacy and the International Criminal Court". Accessed September 30, 2014. http://www.imtd.imtdeast.org/papers/OP-17.pdf.htm.

Nouwen, Sarah. 2012. "The ICC's Intervention in Uganda: Which Rule of Law Does It Promote?" In *Rule of Law Dynamics*, edited by A. Nollkaemper, R. Peereboom, and M. Zürn, 278–394. New York: Cambridge University Press.

Nyeko, Balam, and Lucima Okello. 2002. "Profile of the Parties to the Conflict". In *Protracted Conflicts, Elusive Peace: Initiatives to End the Violence in Northern Uganda*, edited by Lucima Okello, 16–23. Accessed July 12, 2014. http://www.cr.org/downloads/11_Uganda_2002_ENG_F.pdf.

O'Kadameri, Billie. 2002. "LRA/Government Negotiations, 1993–94". In *Protracted Conflicts, Elusive Peace: Initiatives to End the Violence in Northern Uganda*, edited by Lucima Okello, 34–41. Accessed July 12, 2014. http://www.c-r.org/downloads/11_Uganda_2002_ENG_F.pdf.

Otunnu, Ogenga. 2002. "Causes and Consequences of the War in Acholiland". In *Protracted Conflicts, Elusive Peace: Initiatives to End the Violence in Northern Uganda*, edited by Lucima Okello, 10–15. Accessed July 12, 2014. http://www.cr.org/downloads/11_Uganda_2002_ENG_F.pdf.

Royo, Josep Maria. 2008. "War and Peace Scenarios in Northern Uganda". *Quaderns de Construccio de Pau* 6. Accessed June 12, 2015. http://escolapau.uab.cat/img/qcp/war_peace_uganda.pdf.

Schabas, William. 2007. *An Introduction to the International Criminal Court.* Cambridge: Cambridge University Press.

Tadeo, Asiimwe. 2012. "Effecting Complementarity: Challenges and Opportunities: A Case Study of the International Crimes Division of Uganda". Accessed August 13, 2014. http://www.asf.be.htm.

Tenove, Chris. 2013. "Uganda and the International Criminal Court: Debates and Developments". Accessed July 17, 2014. http://www.africaportal.org.htm.

Tolbert, David. 2013. "Can International Justice Foster Reconciliation?" Accessed April 16, 2013. http://www.aljazeera.com/indepth/opinion/2013/04/2013410743544190.htm.

United Nations High Commissioner for Human Rights and Uganda Human Rights Commission. 2011. "The Dust Has Not Yet Settled: Victims' Views on the Right to Remedy and Reparation: A Report from the Greater North of Uganda". Accessed July 13, 2014. http://www.uganda.ohchr.org.htm.

Wijeyaratne, Surendrini. 2008. "Promoting an Inclusive Peace: A Call to Strengthen Canada's Peace-Making Capacity". Accessed May 24, 2014. http://www.ccic.ca/_files/en/what_we_do/002_peace_200811_inclusive_peace_drc.pdf.

Wippman, David. 1999. "Atrocities, Deterrence, and the Limits of International Justice". *Fordman International Law Journal* 23: 473–488.

5
The International Criminal Court and the Peace Process in Kenya

The Kenya cases offered perhaps the paradigmatic example of why an international criminal court was created–James Goldston.[1]

5.1 Introduction

Kenya's reputation as one of the most peaceful countries in Africa was dented by the 2007/2008 post-election violence (PEV). Mediation efforts by African leaders produced a national government, which led to a truce, but efforts to prosecute those responsible for the violence have been stonewalled at both national and international levels.

This chapter examines the causes and nature of the 2007/2008 PEV, the problems of managing the after-effects of the violence, the struggle for political and legal reforms in Kenya after the violence, the peace

[1]Goldston, James. 2016. "Three Lessons from the ICC's Kenya Debacle. Open Society Foundation". Open Society Foundation, April 6. https://medium.com/open-society-foundations/three-lessons-from-the-icc-s-kenyadebacle-515df408531b#.fs9dlxwre. Accessed 15 April 2016.

L. N. Malu, *The International Criminal Court and Peace Processes*,
Palgrave Studies in Compromise after Conflict,
https://doi.org/10.1007/978-3-030-19905-0_5

process, the politics and intrigues of the ICC's involvement in prosecuting those implicated and the impact of the ICC's intervention on the peace process in the country. The chapter focuses on how the ICC's involvement in the situation contributes to national and international efforts at building a stronger Kenya after the PEV.

The first part of the chapter discusses the 2007/2008 PEV, and the efforts at building peace in Kenya, while the second part uses data collected during field research to analyse the impact of the ICC's involvement in Kenya. This is examined through the lenses of its impact on: reconciliation in Kenya, deterrence, protection of the rights of victims of the violence and promotion of accountability to the rule of law.

5.2 A History of Election Violence

Kenya has a history of election-related violence (Human Rights Watch 2013; Commission of Inquiry into Post-election Violence (CIPEV) 2008). Almost all elections held in Kenya since 1991 when multi-party democracy was re-introduced were marred by various types of electoral violence or violence associated with party politics (Human Rights Watch 2013; International Crisis Group 2012; Kenya National Commission on Human Rights 2008; CIPEV 2008). However, the 2007/2008 PEV was unprecedented because it was by far the most deadly, the most destructive and the most widespread of election violence ever experienced in Kenya. Also, "unlike previous election-related violence, much of it followed, rather than preceded the elections" (CIPEV 2008).

The Kenya National Commission on Human Rights account of election violence in Kenya states that election-related violence was recorded in the Rift Valley Province in the early 1990s (Kenya National Commission on Human Rights 2008). The violence targeted opposition supporters from the Luo, Kikuyu, Luhyia and Kisii communities with an estimated 1500 deaths and 300,000 internally displaced when it ended in 1994. The 1997 elections also witnessed election violence, mostly in the Coast Province. The main targets were members of ethnic groups perceived to be hostile to Arap Moi and his Kenyan African

National Union (KANU). Pre-election violence was also recorded in 2006 and early 2007 in several regions, with over 600 deaths recorded.

Kenya also has a reputation for impunity for perpetrators of election violence. No recognisable efforts have been made by the Government of Kenya (GoK) to try those who finance, mastermind and participate in this violence; thus the culture of impunity has facilitated the recurrence of violence in subsequent elections (International Crisis Group 2012). Kenya's past efforts at combating impunity had been through isolated and uncoordinated attempts by the judiciary to prosecute perpetrators, and the establishment of commissions of inquiry to determine the causes of the violence. These commissions were mostly ineffective and seen as ploys by those in power to "deflect public pressure and achieve little", as some were disbanded even before they commenced their work, and the recommendations of others were never implemented (International Crisis Group 2012). What has become evident through these years is a manifest lack of political will at high levels to genuinely address election violence, as well as a widespread fear of prosecuting powerful people who perpetrated or financed violence, resulting in a culture of impunity and the withering of the rule of law (Jalloh 2009). The CIPEV or Waki Commission concluded that "elements of systemic and institutional deficiencies, corruption, entrenched negative socio-political culture have...caused and promoted impunity" in Kenya (CIPEV 2008).

Multi-party general elections were held in Kenya in 1992, 1997, 2002, 2007, 2013 and 2017. The 2007 general elections in Kenya were the fourth since multi-party politics was re-introduced in 1991. The 2007 elections were highly anticipated and witnessed a record turnout particularly of young voters (International Crisis Group 2012). The build-up to the 2007 elections was characterised by intense and intriguing political alignments and wrangling by the Orange Democratic Party (ODM), led by Raila Odinga and the Party of National Unity (PNU), led by Mwai Kibaki. The build-up to the elections followed years of political bickering between the Mwai Kibaki's National Alliance Party (NAK) and Raila Odinga's Liberal Democratic Party (LDP), the two main parties that formed the National Rainbow Coalition (NARC). NARC had defeated the Kenya African National Union (KANU) in the

December 2002 general elections after KANU had dominated Kenya's politics since independence in 1963. The bickering between NAK and LDP covered many issues wherein the two parties had divergent views and could not agree.

In many ways, the 2007 elections were platforms to settle political scores between President Mwai Kibaki and Raila Odinga. The parties ran a tight race, with the ODM maintaining a slight lead before the election. However, the campaigns which were fierce and extensive but generally peaceful were also characterised by ethnic prejudice and stereotyping (Wanyeki 2012) and obvious tension between the supporters of the two main parties.

5.3 The 2007 General Election and the Post-election Violence

The 2007 elections were held on 27 December 2007 against the backdrop of ethnic tension, intense bitterness and suspicion between the main parties. Voting was relatively quiet and uneventful, generally running smoothly across the country. Initial results gave ODM the lead, but on the second day, counting and tallying slowed and eventually stopped, mostly in constituencies believed to be the strongholds of PNU. As the ODM advantage began slowly to dwindle, there were allegations and counter-allegations of vote rigging.

Tension soared even higher when the Chairman of the Electoral Commission of Kenya (ECK), said he was unable to locate some Electoral Officers, and that he feared the result may have been manipulated (International Crisis Group 2012). The ODM also alleged that there were serious discrepancies in the number of votes already counted (International Crisis Group 2012). In the confusion that followed, the ECK announced Mwai Kibaki the winner on 30 December 2007. He was subsequently sworn-in on the same day. The ODM rejected the results of the elections and refused to go to Court, alleging that the judiciary would be biased. Instead, the party called for a national protest (International Crisis Group 2012).

The violence that followed these events, according to the CIPEV (2008), was "spontaneous in some geographic areas and a result of planning and organisation in other areas, often with the involvement of politicians and business leaders". Angry demonstrators from both the ODM and the PNU and from different ethnic groups fought each other, destroyed property and killed. The violence, which lasted about seven weeks, caused the death over 1000 persons, and 3561 were injured. There were about 1,117,216 instances of property destruction (CIPEV 2008) and about 350,000 displaced persons (Kenya National Commission on Human Rights 2008).

Active mediation commenced with the setting-up, by the African Union, of a Panel of Eminent African Personalities, headed by Kofi Annan as the chief mediator. After days of mediation, the main parties agreed with the Panel on the following agenda: (1) immediate actions to stop the violence and restore fundamental human rights and liberties, (2) immediate measures to address the humanitarian crisis and promote reconciliation, healing and restoration, (3) measures to overcome the current political crisis, and (4) long-term issues and solutions. Some of the results of the mediation were the establishment of a grand coalition government of national unity that included the PNU and ODM, the signing of the National Accord on 28 February 2008, and an agreement to establish the CIPEV to deal with consequences of the violence and prevent recurrences.

The CIPEV's final report was released on 15 October 2008. The major findings of the report were that the violence was spontaneous, widespread and carefully planned in many areas. The report also stated that "the police were overwhelmed by the massive numbers of attackers and the relatively effective coordination of the attacks". In order to break the cycle of impunity which was described as being at the centre of election violence in Kenya, the report recommended "the creation of a Special Tribunal with the mandate to prosecute crimes committed as a result of post-election violence".

The government, however, abandoned the idea of establishing the Tribunal despite earlier endorsing it and opted to prioritise national healing and reconciliation (Jalloh 2009). Even before the Government of Kenya's action, the Parliament had failed to enact an Act establishing the Tribunal. As time went on, it became clear that both the Executive and the Parliament were not keen on prosecuting those suspected of perpetrating the violence in which numerous politicians had themselves been involved (Wanyeki 2012).

5.3.1 The International Criminal Court Involvement and Kenya's Response

Following the recommendation of CIPEV on prosecuting those who were allegedly responsible for the violence and the failure of Kenya to establish a Tribunal, a sealed envelope containing the names of the suspects was handed over to the chief prosecutor of the ICC by the lead mediator on 9 July 2009. The ICC chief prosecutor in November 2009 commenced preliminary examination of the situation in Kenya. On 31 March 2010, Pre-Trial Chamber II, upon the chief prosecutor's application, pursuant to article 15 of the Rome Statute, authorised the commencement of an investigation into the situation. Pre-Trial Chamber II held, among other things, that cases from Kenya will be admissible before the Court because the country was not investigating or prosecuting those who allegedly bore the greatest responsibility for crimes committed during the PEV (Jalloh 2012). However, the suitability of the ICC to deal with the post-election violence has remained uncertain, since the issues involved are mostly political.

The ICC initially indicted six persons for being responsible for the crimes. This number was reduced to four as the indictments of two persons were not confirmed. The four indicted persons are William Samoei Ruto, Joshua Arap Sang, Uhuru Muigai Kenyatta and Francis Muthaura. The charges against Francis Muthaura and Uhuru Kenyatta were subsequently dropped because there was insufficient evidence to sustain them (Mueller 2014).[2] Also, the charges against William Samoei Ruto and Joshua Arap Sang were, on the 5 April 2016, vacated by the

[2] Decision on the withdrawal of charges against Mr. Kenyatta, ICC-01/09-02/11-1005, 13 March 2015.

Trial Chamber.[3] In separate cases, warrants of arrest were also issued against Walter Osapiri Barasa, Paul Gicheru and Philip Kipkoech Bett (*The Prosecutor v. Walter Osapiri Barasa*,[4] and *The Prosecutor v. Paul Gicheru and Philip Kipkoech Bett*[5]) for offences against the administration of justice, consisting of corruptly or attempting to corruptly influence the ICC's witnesses.

Kenya's responses to the involvement of the ICC in prosecuting the violence have been a mixture of official cooperation, rejection of ICC involvement, campaigns/lobbying against the ICC (Wrong 2014), threats to withdraw from the ICC and legal defence (Jalloh 2012). These responses have resulted in practical actions, such as visits of top government officials to the ICC, mobilisation of African states through the AU against the ICC (Wrong 2014), lobbying at the United Nations Security Council to have the matters deferred, intimidating and lobbying witnesses, and challenging the admissibility of the cases from Kenya in the ICC. The election of Kenyatta and Ruto as President and Vice-President, respectively, became a turning point in the relationship between the government and the ICC. It became clear after the election of the duo that the government was not ready to cooperate with the ICC (Hoehn 2013).

Kenya cooperated with the ICC in 2008 and 2009 before the unsealing of the names of those suspected to bear the greatest responsibility for the PEV. The GoK responses changed after the OTP released the names of the six suspects in December 2010. Kenya began lobbying the African Union, African states and members of the UN Security Council to have the matter transferred to a national court, or a regional court, or for a deferral of the proceedings at the ICC for at least a year (Mueller 2014; Rigney 2014). The African Union backed Kenya's intention to have the cases deferred but the motion was defeated at the United Nations Security Council (Mueller 2014). In the same vein, the East

[3]Public redacted version of Decision on Defence Applications for Judgments of Acquittal, ICC-01/09-01/11-2027-Red-Corr, 5 April 2016.

[4]The Prosecutor v. Walter Osapiri Barasa, ICC-01/09-01/13.

[5]The Prosecutor v. Paul Gicheru and Philip Kipkoech Bett, ICC-01/09-01/15.

African Legislative Assembly also requested that the cases be transferred to the East African Court of Justice. Pursuant to these requests, the East African Community Summit of 28 April 2012 moved to extend the mandate of the court to include crimes against humanity (Mueller 2014).

In continuation of the GoK's campaign against the ICC, Kenya's Parliament on 6 September 2013 voted to withdraw from the Rome Statute. This action makes Kenya, the first state party to renounce its ratification (Hoehn 2013; Mueller 2014). The GoK and those accused have also waged legal battles with the OTP. The GoK challenged the admissibility of the cases before the ICC and the jurisdiction of the ICC to try the cases.[6] The suspects had moved the Court to transfer the cases to a regional court in order to accommodate the busy schedules of the president and the vice-president. Also, the accused persons have moved applications for a staggered schedule of hearings and for the parties to be absent from the trials.[7]

The GoK and the accused have been accused of intimidating witnesses in attempts to undermine the process. Accusations included attacks, killings, disappearances and enticements to study abroad, harassment by security agents and bribing of witnesses and people who knew about the PEV (Mueller 2014; Rigney 2014). The OTP had also complained that the attacks against potential and actual witnesses, and non-cooperation by GoK had made prosecution difficult (Rigney 2014). The OTP said it has evidence of intimidation and bribery by politicians, lawyers and businessmen, thus it brought charges against some persons for offences against the administration of justice consisting in corruptly or attempting to corruptly influencing three ICC witnesses (Mueller 2014).

---

[6]Decision on the Presiding Judge of the Appeals Chamber in the appeal of the Republic of Kenya against the decision of Pre-Trial Chamber II entitled "Decision on the Application by the Government of Kenya Challenging the Admissibility of the Case Pursu", ICC-01/09-01/11-114, 7 June 2011.

[7]Judgment on the appeal of the Prosecutor against the decision of Trial Chamber V(a) of 18 June 2013 entitled "Decision on Mr Ruto's Request for Excusal from Continuous Presence at Trial", ICC-01/09-01/11-1066, 25 October 2013.

5.3.2 The 2013 General Elections in Kenya and the International Criminal Court

This section examines how the intervention by the ICC in Kenya may have influenced the conduct and the results of the 2013 general elections, which were regarded as relatively peaceful (Mamdani 2013).

The 2013 general elections took place on 4 March 2013. The success of the elections has been attributed to many factors, such as the determination of Kenyans to avoid the mistakes of past elections, the large number of judicial and political reforms embarked upon by the government to strengthen governance institutions (directly and indirectly) responsible for conducting elections in Kenya, the improved security situation during the elections, as a result of adequate policing and the involvement of the ICC in prosecuting those that bore the greatest responsibility for the 2007/2008 PEV. The ICC has been identified as one of the important factors that influenced the elections (Mamdani 2013). Some of the influences attributed to the ICC are: raising the stake of the election (Lynch and Zgonec-Roze 2013), re-ethicising Kenya politics, shaping the political alliance that was formed to contest the elections, influencing the result of the elections and deterring election violence (Wamai 2013).

As mentioned above, the ICC involvement in Kenya helped to shape a political alliance, bringing together two hitherto political foes into a coalition. Kenyatta and Ruto then co-accused in the cases before the ICC became the presidential candidate and running mate of the Jubilee Coalition and in the process brought together their two ethnic groups—Kikuyu and Kalenjin—in a coalition that helped to ensure that there were limited outbreaks of violence between the two rival political groups (Lynch and Zgonec-Roze 2013). The involvement of the ICC contributed in shaping the way external actors' involvement in the internal affairs of Kenya is now viewed, leading to public debates on the acceptable roles of these actors, which include foreign diplomats, international election observers, international political analysts/media and the ICC (Lynch and Zgonec-Roze 2013).

The ICC is also perceived to have deterred people from resorting to violence during the election. Many politicians, citizens and members of the media allegedly acted more responsibly in both public and private spheres by avoiding "hate speech" and actions that could be construed as causing tension in a country that is deeply divided along ethnic lines, largely due to the fear of being investigated by the ICC (Wamai 2013, 2).

5.3.3 The ICC and the Peace Process in Kenya

This section examines the efforts by the GoK and the international community to build peace in Kenya after the 2007/2008 PEV. It focuses on the ways the ICC may be contributing to these efforts directly or indirectly by its various activities in Kenya and the tension between the ICC and the national institutions in Kenya. These impacts are examined through the prisms of the impact of the Court on accountability to the law, deterrence, promotion of victims' rights and reconciliation. The main mandate of the ICC in Kenya is to prosecute those who bear the gravest responsibility for the 2007/2008 PEV in Kenya. Using empirical data, this section explores the consequences of the execution of this mandate on the peace process in Kenya.

5.4 The International Criminal Court and Accountability to the Law in Kenya

Kenya has a long and sad history of impunity for those who had committed election violence (Jalloh 2009), and a legal system that has not lived up to the expectations of its citizens in ensuring accountability to the law, especially when politicians and important business leaders are involved (Jalloh 2009). Perpetrators of political crimes are rarely prosecuted, because of weak internal accountability mechanisms and institutional deficiencies (Human Rights Watch 2014). In fact, impunity still holds sway in Kenya, despite the various reforms initiated by the government since 2008 and despite the involvement of the ICC in the situation. For instance, most of the perpetrators of the 2007/2008 PEV are yet to be prosecuted (Human Rights Watch 2014). In 2012, a Committee appointed by the Director of Public Prosecution to review the cases of those detained during the PEV found that there was insufficient evidence in the 5000 files it reviewed to ensure proper prosecution (Human Rights Watch 2014).

This section examines how the intervention by the ICC influences accountability to the law in Kenya by examining: (a) the nexus between the involvement of the ICC and the enactment of accountability laws, (b) the link between the involvement of the ICC and the establishment of justice institutions, and (c) the nexus between the involvement of the ICC and the prosecution of offenders. These issues are examined by eliciting information from respondents and by analysis of relevant publications.

The involvement of the ICC in Kenya since the Court was mentioned in the Waki Commission's report as an alternative judiciary mechanism is said to have triggered and/or fast-tracked some judicial, legal and governance reforms. While some of these reforms are said to be genuine attempts by GoK to promote accountability to the law, others are deemed to have been designed to show that Kenya was capable of investigating and prosecuting the PEV so as to avoid accountability at the ICC (Dunaiski 2014; Wanyeki 2012). Some of these reforms are in law enforcement agencies, mainly police, prosecution, judiciary, probation and correctional services institutions. The involvement of the ICC in Kenya has also contributed towards influencing the establishment of good governance institutions, like the new Independent Electoral Commission and the National Cohesion and Integration Commission. There are also plans to establish an International Crimes Division of the High Court of Kenya.

There have been some new laws and regulations in Kenya after the involvement of the ICC. Some of these laws mimic international standards while others introduced some innovative reforms. This study does not conclude that the ICC directly facilitated the enactment of these laws and regulations, but affirms that since these laws and regulations came into place after the involvement of the ICC, and many of them mirror their international counterparts, it is likely that the involvement of the ICC influenced the decisions to enact them. The government enacted the Judicial Services Act (No. 1 of 2011), the Vetting of Judges and Magistrate Act (No. 2 of 2012), the Witness Protection Act, 2006 (as amended in 2012), the International Criminal Act, 2008, which domesticates the Rome Statute and the Supreme Court of Kenya Act (No. 7 of 2011).

Several respondents in Kenya argue that the intervention by the ICC influenced the enactment and or amendment of some of these laws for two main reasons. They state that the GoK enacted or amended the laws to prove that justice administration in Kenya is of international standard, and that judicial/law enforcement officials are capable of genuinely investigating and prosecuting those involved in the 2007/2008 PEV. Also, several respondents linked the intervention of the ICC to these reforms, arguing that the interventions sparked-off these changes, and that the government was propelled to make changes to impress the international community that the justice sector in Kenya is not in limbo and also to fight the admissibility challenge at the ICC. A lawyer from Kenya puts these points succinctly:

> Yes, the ICC may be contributing to accountability to the law in Kenya in the following ways: the ICC has brought some element of fear and respect for the law. Before the ICC, top politicians and business people did not respect the law, and these seem to be sustainable because the changes are not imposed but are coming from the people. Also, the ICC's involvement in Kenya may have contributed in facilitating the enactment of some accountability laws and the establishment of some good governance institutions. For instance, the national judicial system is currently trying to establish an International Crimes Division of the High Court.[8]

The head of an international non-government organisation working on justice reform in Kenya was one of the respondents who argue that the ICC may have had a positive impact on accountability to the law in Kenya. According to him, the ICC can promote accountability to

---

[8]Interview with a lawyer and researcher from Kenya, 2014.

the law in Kenya "through its activities, as such actions have prompted the government to embark on judicial reforms. However, promotion of accountability is not simply what one institution can do. Other agencies of government and other international institutions are contributing to the process, which has just begun".[9] A lecturer in Law at Kenyatta University, Nairobi, enumerated several areas that the ICC intervention in Kenya has impacted on accountability to law as:

> The initiatives by the judiciary to constitute an international crimes division; the amendment of various laws that are election-related to organise elections more effectively with respect to anticipating and/or dealing with violence; the general sensitisation of the public as they have followed the ICC cases about the types of crimes related to violence and the potential for consequences that stretch beyond the country; the sensitisation of the state about the potential for international bodies to take over the investigation and prosecution of certain crimes where the state fails to do so.[10]

Another respondent agrees that the ICC contributes to accountability to the law "through its involvement in Kenya since 2009, and by bringing charges against some prominent politicians in the country"; but he further argues that the ICC "can still do better by ensuring that more people are prosecuted".[11] A former staff member of the Human Rights Commission of Kenya also thinks that "the involvement of the ICC in Kenya will have a positive impact on accountability and the rule of law to the extent that Kenya seems to be doing more on accountability issues now than before the 2008 violence".[12] An international justice expert in Kenya agrees, arguing that the ICC's involvement in Kenya "has certainly generated a lot of interest in the judicial system of Kenya which has prompted those in government to take more action with respect to the rule of law and promotion of accountability".[13]

---

[9]Interview with an expert in security studies in Africa, 2014.

[10]Interview with a professor of law at Kenyatta University, Kenya, 2015.

[11]Interview with a director of a peace and conflict NGO in Kenya, 2013.

[12]Interview with a former staff of Kenya Human Rights Commission, 2014.

[13]Interview with a lawyer and researcher from Kenya, 2014.

These views were supported by a professor emeritus of Law in Kenya who states that:

> The ICC can help promote the rule of law and accountability, if the ICC persists in securing justice to serve the interests of at least three stakeholders: direct victims; indirect victims, including all Kenyans who have suffered assassinations, violence and electoral manipulation since Jomo Kenyatta invented electoral violence in 1969; and supporters of the rule of law, human rights and constitutional democracy.[14]

Another respondent in Kenya supports this view by arguing that: "in terms of the rule of law there is a linkage between judicial reform and the ICC. Reform was needed so that it may be argued that local courts are now a viable mechanism to prosecute rather than the ICC. Beyond that, it has made little contribution towards the rule of law". An international law consultant also argued that the ICC can promote the rule law in Kenya. He states:

> The Court can promote the culture of rule of law and accountability to the law by investigating situations and prosecuting those responsible for deadly conflicts. The international justice system could lead to accountability and checkmate the excesses of the leaders, including those in Kenya. But the international justice system may also lead to leaders being 'sit tights'.[15]

The ICC is also seen to have contributed to the promotion of accountability to the law by the fact that it prosecuted the country's top politicians. In the views of a researcher from Kenya, "the very act of prosecution could have already sent messages that nobody is above the law and nobody is untouchable. Thus, the ICC is contributing to the rule of law in Kenya by its proceedings which have clearly sent messages that nobody is above the law, and that nobody is untouchable".[16]

---

[14]Interview with a director of a peace and conflict NGO in Kenya, 2013.

[15]Interview with a consultant in international law in Nigeria, 2014.

[16]Interview with a research student from Kenya, 2014.

For respondents who think the ICC is not contributing to the promotion of the rule of law, the central argument is that the ICC is not showing a good example in the way it picks its cases and by its procedures. According to them, it cannot contribute to the development of the rule of law in Kenya, because it seems biased and political. According to a staff member of an NGO in Kenya, the "ICC has not been good in observing internationally accepted rules of procedures and established jurisprudence. It has, therefore, been seen as a body that is more political than legal".[17] Another interviewee thinks the ICC cannot fundamentally contribute to the rule of law in Kenya because the "Court is far removed from the people, and that only national institutions can contribute to the building of a culture of accountability, not an international Court".[18] Another reason the ICC cannot promote accountability is because "it does not have the power to arrest culprits and to enforce its judgments, which makes it a weak institution, with limited potential to genuinely impact on national judicial institutions, such as the ones in Kenya".[19] Thus, since the ICC cannot enforce its judgment by arresting culprits, its power and potential to promote the rule of law is limited.[20] A member of the defence team of Uhuru Kenyatta argues that the ICC has nothing to teach the people of Kenya on accountability to the law. According to him:

> The Kenyan state had an existing effective and independent legal system before the ICC's involvement in its affairs. The ICC has nothing to teach Kenya about accountability to law, given the failings of the OTP and ICC to present a credible case, and how they sought to support a case which was littered with false evidence.[21]

The impact of the intervention of the ICC on accountability to the law has not resulted in the prosecution of a good number of those who

[17]Interview with a project coordinator of an NGO in Kenya, 2013.

[18]Interview with, a researcher in peace and conflict studies from Kenya, 2014.

[19]Interview with a consultant in international law in Nigeria, 2014.

[20]Interview with a researcher in peace and conflict studies from Kenya, 2014.

[21]Interview with a lawyer and researcher from Kenya, 2014.

committed atrocities during the PEV in Kenya. Out of more than five thousand persons who were arrested after the violence, only fourteen have been convicted, while some cases are still pending. Many have been released for several reasons including, lack of sufficient evidence and want of diligent prosecution (Human Rights Watch 2013).

5.4.1 The International Criminal Court and Protection of Victims' Rights in Kenya

During the violence that lasted from December 2007 to February 2008, about 1100 persons were killed, 660,000 displaced (CIPEV 2008) and thousands injured through beatings, rapes, machete cuts and violent attacks that could be classed as crimes against humanity (Amnesty International 2014; Kenyans for Peace with Truth and Justice 2013).

Rule 85(a) of the Rules of Procedure and Evidence of the ICC defines victims as "natural persons who have suffered harm as a result of the commission of any crime within the jurisdiction of the Court".[22] Thus, all persons who have suffered harms or lost properties during the 2007/2008 PEV are deemed victims. This section explores how these victims have benefited (or otherwise) from the ICC's investigations and the prosecution of some of those who allegedly perpetrated the violence.

The Rome Statute provides for two distinct forms of victims' redress, which were discussed in Chapter 2 of this study. These are reparation by the Court, pursuant to article 75(2) of the Rome Statute, and support provided to victims by the TFV, independent of the Court's order. The TFV as at January 2018 does not have projects in Kenya for victims of the 2007/2008 PEV. The TFV, however, plans to extend its activities to Kenya, but has not done so. Thus far, in Kenya, 628 victims were permitted by the ICC to participate in The Prosecutor v. William Samoei Ruto and Joshua Arap Sang case,[23] and 725 victims were accepted in

[22]Rules of Procedure and Evidence of the ICC. https://www.icc-cpi.int/iccdocs/PIDS/legal-texts/RulesProcedureEvidenceEng.pdf.

[23]https://www.icc-cpi.int/CaseInformationSheets/RutoSangEng.pdf.

The Prosecutor v. Uhuru Muigai Kenyatta case.[24] However, this number represents less than six per cent of the estimated 352,000 direct victims of the PEV. Also, it is important to note that it is only victims of the crimes for which the accused are charged in the two main cases in Kenya that are eligible to participate in either cases in the ICC (Kenyans for Peace with Truth and Justice 2013).

Respondents were asked if these activities of the ICC are addressing the rights of victims of the violence, and if such activities could promote reconciliation, and also resettlement of victims in Kenya. Almost all answered that the ICC does not yet have projects in Kenya for the victims, which is evident from the facts on the ground and the records of the TFV. Most argue, however, that victims redress is one of the commendable aspects of the ICC since it will help victims overcome some of the troubles they went through. For instance, the legal representative of some of the victims at the ICC thinks that the ICC process is useful to victims as it has several impacts. He further argues that the Kenya cases are difficult because of high-profile persons involved, who are fighting back and making it hard to get reparation for victims. According to him, "the complication with the Kenyan situation is due to the fact that the cases have largely targeted people in power and so the opposition to the ICC process has been greater".[25]

Some of the respondents also argue that the ICC's intervention may have influenced the GoK to take some actions towards alleviating the sufferings of victims. For instance, the government established the Kenya Truth, Justice and Reconciliation Commission. The President of Kenya, in his 2015 State of the Nation's address, publicly apologised to the victims of mass atrocities in Kenya since independence and admitted that the government had failed them. The government also set up a fund of $110 million to help repair the harm caused by the government's actions (*New York Times* 2015). The majority view is that though these victim redress efforts have many shortcomings, such as being

[24]https://www.icc-cpi.int/CaseInformationSheets/KenyattaEng.pdf.

[25]Interview with a legal representative for victims from Kenya at the ICC, 2014.

selective and based on political affiliations, but these efforts may still be useful to victims. A transitional justice expert in Kenya states:

> The ICC cases have forced the government to begin addressing internally displaced persons (IDP) issues and providing minor and insufficient compensation to certain groups of victims. As mentioned earlier the ICC cases have forced the government to demonstrate some form of policy towards victims. One of these aspects is providing monetary reparations to IDPs from the PEV in a bid to do away with IDP camps for political reasons and to fit in line with government policies that the country has moved on.[26]

A researcher from Kenya argues that the ICC is only helpful to the extent that it has helped the government do something for the victims, like trying to resettle some of them, closing the IDP camps, attempting to pay compensation and developing new policies on victim protection.[27]

The impact of victims' redress on resettlement in Kenya was also explored. Many of those interviewed agreed that victim redress if properly addressed by the ICC through all its processes, and the GoK, through direct government intervention could assist in resettling the victims and in promoting the peace process in Kenya. A Kenya-based expert on African conflicts opines that victim redress could help "victims to resettle if the ICC can implement some projects, but they do not have projects to resettle people".[28] The opinion of another researcher from Kenya is instructive. He argues:

> It could be useful for resettlement and the peace process if well implemented by the ICC. Victims redress by the ICC through the TFV and the ICC proceedings in The Hague have the potential to promote resettlement and peace in Kenya. But since the TFV have not yet started its

[26]Interview with a legal representative for victims from Kenya at the ICC, 2014.

[27]Interview with a research student from Kenya, 2014.

[28]Interview with a lawyer and researcher from Kenya, 2014.

projects in Kenya, and the proceedings have not ended in The Hague, it is difficult to conclude.[29]

Another view is that the victim resettlement programme of the government has been politicised, with only those from certain parts of the country benefiting. For them, this might not facilitate resettlement and promotion of the peace process. A project coordinator of an NGO in Kenya argues that the "fact that reconciliation and resettlement have been driven by politicians has exposed the victims to political manipulation".[30] A lawyer from Kenya also argues that "the government is resettling some people, mostly from the ethnic group of the President, based on political imperatives, not facts on the ground".[31]

Another issue examined is whether the efforts of the ICC to address victims' problems could contribute to reconciliation in Kenya. The preponderance of opinion of respondents is that the efforts of the ICC in addressing victims' rights could contribute to reconciliation if the ICC could determine the cases quicker, and provided the ICC is not seen to be favouring one group more than others. A legal representative of some of the victims from Kenya at the ICC argues that victims redress is vital for the peace process in Kenya. According to him:

Many of the victims who suffered forcible displacement would ideally like to return to the locations they call home. Restitution of land therefore is important and reconciliation needs to take place within a milieu of ethnic integration, rather than having IDPs relocated to other locations which makes them feel that they have permanently lost the land and other property they previously owned. But, we need a bottom-up rather than a top-down approach.[32]

A lawyer from Kenya also argues that victim redress is good for reconciliation in Kenya, "but it depends on how it is implemented, and who is implementing it. The ICC should also make efforts to hold more sessions with the victims. The victims need assistance, and this

[29]Interview with a research student from Kenya, 2014.

[30]Interview with a project coordinator of an NGO in Kenya, 2013.

[31]Interview with a lawyer and researcher from Kenya, 2014.

[32]Interview with a legal representative for victims from Kenya at the ICC, 2014.

assistance could help them to resettle, reconcile and restart life again".[33] The mere presence of the cases, according to an international justice expert, "has shown victims that there is some hope for justice and reparations. This process has provided some measures of healings among victims simply by being able to talk about what happened to them".[34] Anything done to help victims will certainly help in reconciliation and the peace process. "Most of the victims are poor and helpless, and the ICC should try and put more life into the victims' projects, even more than it is doing in prosecuting the cases. Its efforts with victims could yield more results than prosecuting the cases".[35]

Some respondents doubt if there are links between the ICC and victims' redress in Kenya. For instance, the project coordinator of an NGO in Kenya argues that "the ICC is adding little to victims' redress, and that Kenyans have resolved on their own to reconcile or maybe they have done so as a result of fear or desperation, and not through any ICC victims' redress process".[36] The legal processes by the ICC will not do much for victims, because "prosecution of perpetrators of post-election violence requires cooperation from the state which has been untenable under Kenyetta's Jubilee government".[37] Also, "there appear to be no coherence in the identification of genuine victims or in the strategies to address their immediate and long-term problems by the ICC. There is little knowledge about the existing processes and systems from the ICC with regard to this issue".[38] In the view of another legal practitioner in Kenya:

> The victims are still stranded without a way forward on how they will be resettled or compensated. The Court is supposed to pay compensation

[33]Interview with a lawyer and researcher from Kenya, 2014.

[34]Interview with transitional justice expert in Kenya, 2014.

[35]Interview with a research student from Kenya, 2014.

[36]Interview with a project coordinator of an NGO in Kenya, 2013.

[37]Interview with a professor emeritus of Law in Kenya, 2015.

[38]Interview with a lecturer in Law at Kenyatta University, Kenya, 2014.

from the funds of the accused persons but it is apparent the cases are crumbling.[39]

The preponderance of opinion is that victims' redress by the ICC has the potential to contribute to the peace process in Kenya. But at this stage, the efforts of the ICC cannot be said to be having any meaningful impact on the peace process in Kenya because of the small number of victims permitted to participate in the cases, the failure of the ICC to convict any person from Kenya and the failure of the ICC through the TFV to embark on projects in Kenya.

5.4.2 The International Criminal Court and Deterrence in Kenya

The nexus between the ICC's intervention in Kenya and deterrence is examined in this section. Specifically, it examines the impact of the ICC's involvement in the relatively peaceful election in Kenya in 2013 and on deterrence of people from committing international crimes in Kenya in future. The central question examined is whether the investigation of the Kenya situation, the laying of charges against six persons by the ICC, and the trial of four prominent persons, including the President and the Vice-President of the Republic of Kenya has or will deter future atrocities.

There are claims and counter-claims about the impact of the ICC on deterrence in Kenya. The ICC, on one side, is seen to have contributed to the relatively peaceful elections in 2013 by deterring many people from committing electoral violence (Wamai 2013; Duinaiski 2014). On the other side, some respondents think it was the will of people to move forward after the PEV that led to the relatively peaceful 2013 elections. The ICC is also seen to have the potential to deter people, especially Kenyan political and business leaders from instigating people to commit electoral violence since it has established that it has the capacity to

[39]Interview with a legal practitioner in Kenya, 2014.

prosecute this class of people who hitherto had unofficial immunity from prosecution (Namiti 2014; Collevecchio 2011). The core issue in the argument is that the Court has the potential to lessen the risk of future conflict by raising the cost of instigating violence, by challenging the widespread conviction that Kenyan political and business leaders are above the law (Collevecchio 2011). However, the failure of the ICC to convict any of the persons indicted in Kenya makes the ICC appear weak and may reduce its impact on deterrence.

Respondents in this study were asked: "Do you think the ICC has the capacity to deter people from committing international crimes in Kenya in future?" The respondents have different views; however, most think the ICC has the potential to deter people from committing international crimes, and that the ICC alongside other institutions and factors contributed to the relatively peaceful 2013 general election in Kenya. Most respondents think that their leaders have got the message that the era of impunity is over, and that nobody is untouchable or above the law.

Those who argue against the deterrent impact of the ICC in Kenya submit that there is nothing to suggest that the ICC deterred people from committing electoral violence and also nothing to suggest that people will be deterred from committing international crimes in Kenya because of the ICC (Wanyeki 2012). Another argument is that for the ICC to deter it must not only deliver legal justice, but also social justice. Thus, issues that trigger political violence in Kenya, such as inequality, discrimination, and land conflicts, must be addressed too (Wanyeki 2012). The relative success of the 2013 elections was attributed to the reforms the country has undertaken since the 2007/2008 election violence, and the trust Kenyans have in the new institutions.

Some of those who accept that the ICC can contribute to deterrence in Kenya, however, caution that to realise this aim the ICC must be non-partisan and objective. In Kenya, ethnic politics is a big issue. People view national issues through ethnic lenses, which has coloured Kenyan politics. Thus, the performance of the ICC is also viewed from these perspectives. A peace advocate in Nairobi supports the view that the ICC can deter people, especially politicians, from committing electoral violence in Kenya in future. He argues, however, that to achieve this objective, the ICC needs to be "non-partisan", and "non-biased". His argument is:

> Yes. An unbiased, well-researched and properly investigated case can help to bring all the perpetrators to book and thus deter future violence driven by politicians. The ICC needs to stop being seen to be partisan, but get Kenyans to appreciate that the Court is a neutral body aimed at ensuring justice for victims of international crime.[40]

The ICC can deter people from committing international crimes, "however it must carry out its mandate properly and be more professional in its investigations and prosecution".[41] The ICC is good for deterrence since people, mostly politicians and business leaders are afraid of the Court, "but people are divided along ethnic and political lines which could make them not see the real values of the ICC".[42] The ICC "has demonstrated its capacity to call into accountability anyone who is suspected of such crime and so local warlords are forced to keep the peace. Also, and as a result of the cases, most people can relate to the situation and maintain peace".[43]

Most of those who think the ICC can deter, also agreed that the ICC played a significant, but not a sole role in ensuring the relatively successful election in 2013. They agree that this is a good example of the potential of the ICC to deter. An international justice expert in Nairobi states:

> The ICC is contributing to deterrence in Kenya. The ICC is one element that contributed to the deterrence in Kenya during the 2013 elections. Thus, there are links between the ICC's involvement in Kenya and the relatively peaceful elections in 2013. But there are other factors that contributed, such as the involvement of international organisations, the readiness of the security forces, and the willingness of the people to have a

[40]Interview with a director of a peace and conflict NGO in Kenya, 2013.

[41]Interview with an expert in security studies in Africa, 2014.

[42]Interview with a research student from Kenya, 2014.

[43]Interview with a legal practitioner in Kenya, 2014.

peaceful election and some legal, institutional and structural changes introduced by the government and people of Kenya.[44]

It is arguable that were it not for the ICC, Kenya "would have been on the brink of another episode of violence during the 2013 general and presidential elections. There has been more restraint by politicians when they speak, and judiciary as well as national institutions established to promote national cohesion and reconciliation have added to this".[45]

The ICC has the potential to deter. The ICC "has shown through its work that it cannot be pushed aside or manipulated. The fear of the ICC helped Kenya to have a peaceful election in 2013. People were afraid of the Court and behaved themselves during the election. Therefore, the ICC can deter, unlike a national judicial system".[46] This view was also supported by an international law expert in Nairobi, but he also cautions that domestic courts are in better positions to deter than the ICC:

> An argument can be made that the threat of the cases prevented violence during the 2013 general elections. However, there have been crimes committed between 2007 and 2013; for example, in Tana River and Mt. Elgon where it is unlikely the ICC was a cause for concern. The elevation of Kenyan actions to this level does alert the country to the fact that large-scale mass violations will prompt international actions. The prevention of international crimes remains largely a domestic function and the conduct of the cases makes it unlikely that the ICC will be able to influence this.[47]

There are also strong arguments that the ICC, because of its permanent nature, and demonstrated evidence of prosecution will deter potential criminals, including those who might want to commit electoral violence in Kenya in future. The central point is that the ICC,

[44]Interview with an expert in security studies in Africa, 2014.

[45]Interview with a legal representative for victims from Kenya at the ICC, 2014

[46]Interview with a lawyer and researcher from Kenya, 2014.

[47]Interview with transitional justice expert in Kenya, 2014.

despite its shortcomings, and the failure to convict any of the Kenyan leaders indicted, has already established itself as an international Court with the capacity to prosecute people who might commit international crimes. The ICC has the capacity to "deter in the sense that any person would know that if such were to happen then they cannot rely on a weak internal system to escape culpability".[48] Further, having raised the profile, a lot of the opinion shapers in the country are keen never again to have the tag of a banana republic hanging around the reputation of the country.[49]

The ICC can deter warlords in Africa from committing international crimes, including those who committed electoral violence in Kenya, because there is evidence of prosecution of people who committed international crimes; those who may be planning to commit international crimes may know that the ICC may catch up with them.[50] An international justice expert also adds that the ICC has the power to name and shame which is important for deterrence, where politicians are involved. According to her, the ICC can deter because the fear of the Court is everywhere. She cautions that the "ICC however needs to speed up cases to have some impact, and that there is need for reorganisation".[51] The power of the ICC to punish, which the Court has shown, is also cited as evidence that people are afraid of it. The "ICC can deter to some extent, and the fear of punishment may lead to deterrence by the ICC".[52]

Some respondents doubt the power and capacity of the ICC to deter people from committing international crimes, arguing that there is nothing to show that the ICC contributed to the peaceful election in Kenya, and that what was at play was the determination of the people to redeem themselves after the violence of 2007/2008. After the 2007 general elections, "Kenyans were determined not to have another bad election.

[48]Interview with a legal expert from Kenya, 2014.

[49]Interview with a legal expert from Kenya, 2014.

[50]Interview with a senior legal practitioner in Nigeria, 2014.

[51]Interview with an international accountability expert in Nigeria, 2014

[52]Interview with a legal practitioner in Nigeria, 2014.

The government and people of Kenya were prepared to make changes after the 2008 violence, and this led to reforms and improvement in the 2013 elections".[53] For a legal practitioner in Lagos, the ICC can only deter people if it has power to enforce and arrest[54] and, for a member of the defence team of Uhuru Kenyatta, the ICC's "involvement in Kenya is irrelevant to any future situation in Kenya or elsewhere because local violence may erupt anywhere".[55]

The conclusion drawn from the opinions of respondents is that the deterrent impact of the ICC is still controversial. On the one hand, the ICC's investigations and prosecutions have had a profound impact on what people think of the law and may have created some sort of fear or even respect for the law. On the other hand, the inability of the ICC to convict the accused persons may have diminished the respect most Kenyans had for the ICC in the early years of the ICC in Kenya. This diminishing position of the ICC may well have a negative impact on its deterrent impact in Kenya. However, a slight majority of respondents were convinced that the ICC contributed to the relatively peaceful 2013 elections by deterring people from funding, instigating and participating in violence. These respondents are also optimistic that this trend may continue, because it is now established that the ICC can indeed prosecute culprits, unlike national courts.

5.4.2.1 The International Criminal Court and Reconciliation

This section examines the process of reconciliation after the 2007/2008 PEV in Kenya. The first part deals with the various efforts at promoting reconciliation after the violence while the second part explores the nexus between the ICC and the reconciliation. The third and final part examines the contributions of the ICC to the process of reconciliation in Kenya. Reconciliation started immediately after the 2007/2008 PEV, with the African Union establishing a Panel of Eminent Personalities.

[53]Interview with a researcher in peace and conflict studies from Kenya, 2014.

[54]Interview with a legal expert in Nigeria, 2014.

[55]Interview with a member of the defence team of Uhuru Kenyatta at the ICC, 2015.

The mandate of the Panel was to resolve the crisis and mediate a political solution. The Panel, chaired by Kofi Annan, brought the PNU and the Orange Democratic Movement (ODM) into a process of reconciliation and political settlement called the Kenya National Dialogue and Reconciliation (KNDR). Another important step towards reconciliation was the establishment of the Truth, Justice and Reconciliation Commission of Kenya (TJRC) in 2008.[56] The TJRC was a part of the accountability component of Agenda Four of the KNDR aimed at addressing the root causes of the violence and the effects of injustices and gross violation of human rights in Kenya. It was hoped that by addressing these issues the TJRC could contribute towards the process of reconciliation, national unity and healing.

Respondents were asked if the ICC's intervention is contributing to reconciliation. There were divergent viewpoints from respondents. The majority of respondents argue that the ICC was not designed to facilitate reconciliation but to prosecute those who commit international crimes. Thus, the ICC is not a mechanism for reconciliation but for accountability and is not playing any role towards reconciliation in Kenya. Some respondents, however, think that the ICC has indirectly promoted reconciliation since the prosecution of Uhuru Kenyatta and Ruto may have contributed to the two candidates deciding to run as president and vice-president respectively during the 2013 and 2017 general elections. The joint ticket, according to them, brought together two top politicians from Kenya's main ethnic rival groups and may have contributed to the relative peace witnessed during the elections. Others also think that though the aim of the ICC is to prosecute and not to reconcile, accountability could over time, and if properly managed, promote stability and reconciliation in Kenya.

The first set of arguments is that the ICC was not designed to promote reconciliation, but to ensure accountability, by punishing those who committed crimes. Thus, according to some respondents the ICC

[56]The commission submitted its report on 3 May 2013. The 2220 page report has four volumes. Volume 1 deals with introductory matters, volume 2 is an account of human rights violations during the period covered by the report, volume 3 discusses national unity, peace and reconciliation, while volume 4 presents the findings and recommendations of the Commission.

is not expected to promote reconciliation in Kenya but to prosecute those who committed international crimes during the 2007/2008 PEV. In support of this view, a researcher on conflicts in Africa argues that:

> [the] ICC has not played many roles in reconciliation in Kenya. In fact there are no reconciliation efforts in Kenya. The big three ethnic groups are still fighting over political and economic largesse. Also, the ICC is more of a punitive institution and not designed to reconcile. In Kenya, reconciliation has political colouration and should be tackled from the political perspective.[57]

However, reconciliation is a "controversial and debatable issue in Kenya", and the ICC is "not working towards reconciliation in Kenya, but pursuing its primary function, which is to prosecute those who are involved in the post-election violence".[58] A peace and conflict expert from Kenya also argues that the ICC does not contribute to reconciliation in Kenya. According to him, "other factors are at play. In fact, the ICC has not promoted reconciliation in any country including Kenya. The countries that do not have the ICC have more reconciliation that those that have the ICC in their country".[59] It is also important to point out that the aim of law is justice not reconciliation, and that people should not confuse issues or put so many expectations on the ICC. The law is "focused on punishment not reconciliation. The ICC will not help in reconciliation in Kenya. We don't need to deceive ourselves or put so much expectation on the ICC, because it is designed only to sanction those who committed international offences and not to reconcile people in post-conflict societies".[60]

To the legal representative of some victims at the ICC, the impacts of the ICC on reconciliation have been "unfortunately, very little so far. Reconciliation appears to have happened only within the political class and with very little genuine reconciliation amongst the citizenry,

[57]Interview with a lawyer and researcher from Kenya, 2014.

[58]Interview with a research student from Kenya, 2014.

[59]Interview with a researcher in peace and conflict studies from Kenya, 2014.

[60]Interview with a legal practitioner in Nigeria, 2014.

particularly in locations where 'perpetrator communities' are living side by side with victim communities".[61]

Some respondents also think that the ICC's intervention has divided the country along political lines as those who support the government are against the ICC, while those who support the opposition are in support of the ICC. The "opposition is fighting the government through the ICC. In that sense, the people of Kenya are divided along political and ethnic divides. Those in support of the government are against the ICC, and those in support of the ODM are in favour of the ICC. Because of this reason the ICC cannot promote reconciliation and conflict transformation".[62] What the "Court succeeded in doing is to create divisions among the people".[63]

For respondents who think the ICC has contributed to reconciliation by indirectly facilitating a joint ticket between Uhuru Kenyatta and Ruto, the central argument is that without the ICC, it would have been unlikely for both candidates to run together. The ICC brought together two communities who had been in conflict with each other as the co-accused ran together thereby eliminating the possibility of conflict between them during the election period. However, "it is doubtful whether this constitutes reconciliation and Kenyan political history has shown that such political alliances are fluid – there has also not been any significant effort at reconciliation beyond the political rapprochement. Should the ICC cases that bind them together falter it is debatable whether the alliance will hold".[64]

A former staff member of the Kenyan Human Right Commission who supports this proposition argues that the ICC may have contributed in making Kenyatta and Ruto run under a joint ticket during the 2013 elections. This contributed to the peace Kenya had during the election and may have facilitated some sort of reconciliation between the two main ethnic groups in Kenya. But it is "arguable whether there

[61]Interview with a legal representative for victims from Kenya at the ICC, 2014.

[62]Interview with a legal expert from Kenya, 2014.

[63]Interview with a legal practitioner in Kenya, 2014.

[64]Interview with a lawyer and researcher from Kenya, 2014.

is real reconciliation between the two ethnic groups or just some sort of political agreement that is only temporary".[65]

Although the ICC has promoted reconciliation between the Kikuyu and the Kalenjin, "the ICC involvement has also pitted these two major groups against the rest of the country thereby escalating tensions. The ICC process should have been more tactfully and carefully handled. It lacked professionalism".[66] What the "Court succeeded in doing is to create a reason for the two most influential ethnic groups in the country to come together and dominate the other 40 tribes. These two were the most fractious groups and bringing them together has created a convenient reconciliation for political reasons".[67]

Some of those interviewed, however, were of the view that there are structural problems that make reconciliation in Kenya difficult, such as ethnic divides and bad governance. To them, unless these problems are addressed, no mechanism, including the ICC could promote reconciliation, since the foundation is weak. For instance, a researcher on African security states that there are structural problems that could not be helped by the ICC. For "reconciliation to take place in Kenya the people need to address these structural problems, such as, promoting an inclusive society, reducing ethnicity and ensuring openness and balance in governance".[68]

There were also those who think that the ICC, by promoting accountability, would also indirectly promote stability and reconciliation in the long-run. One argument here is that the ICC is not expected to promote reconciliation directly, but to contribute to the peace process by promoting accountability and stability. Another argument is that the ICC involvement in conflict could lead to reconciliation because it provides a platform for reconciliation in post-conflict societies as one cannot reconcile people that are aggrieved. To reconcile "we put our cards on the table on an equal basis. And the apparatus that can ensure

---

[65]Interview with a former staff of Kenya Human Rights Commission, 2014.

[66]Interview with transitional justice expert in Kenya, 2014.

[67]Interview with a legal practitioner in Kenya, 2014.

[68]Interview with an expert in security studies in Africa, 2014.

that there is accountability is the ICC. Thus, the ICC can promote reconciliation in Kenya by providing the platform for addressing wrongs done to some people".[69]

A related argument is that "It is important to have justice which could lead to peace and reconciliation. If people feel that they are getting justice it may pave the way to reconciliation".[70] The involvement of the ICC in post-conflict countries promotes stability and ensures justice. These are "the foundation for peace and reconciliation, which are also essential for development. The ICC cannot work against reconciliation in these countries. Rather, accountability will promote the rule of law and reconciliation".[71] For a lawyer for victims from Kenya, "reconciliation is a process that perhaps transcends generations, and it might be too early to assess the ICC's impact in this regard until well after the Kenya cases have been conclusively finalised".[72]

The impact of the ICC's involvement in Kenya on reconciliation, as can be discerned from the opinions of the respondents, is controversial and debatable. The opinion of the majority of respondents is that it is not the duty of the ICC to reconcile, and such issues should not be confused to create uncertainties about the mandate of the ICC in Kenya. This mandate is to prosecute those who committed atrocities during the PEV. For some respondents, the ICC intervention made Uhuru Kenyatta and William Ruto run on an "anti- ICC" ticket, which united the two main ethnic groups in Kenya, and thus "reconciled" them, at least during the 2013 elections. Yet, some of those interviewed were of the view that there are structural problems that make reconciliation in Kenya difficult, and unless these problems are addressed, no mechanism, including the ICC could promote reconciliation, since there is no foundation for reconciliation.

[69]Interview with an international law expert, 2014.

[70]Interview with an international accountability expert in Nigeria, 2014.

[71]Interview with a director of a community legal and justice organisation in Nigeria, 2014.

[72]Interview with a legal representative for victims from Kenya at the ICC, 2014.

5.4.3 Conclusion

The failure of the ICC to convict any of the six Kenyan leaders indicted represents an unmitigated disaster for the Court and for the fight against impunity in Kenya. These cases are good examples of why the ICC was established—to fight impunity in cases where political leaders are alleged to have committed crimes and to have used state powers to avoid prosecution. The collapse of the case against Ruto and Sang in April 2016 is arguably the last attempt in the struggle to investigate the PEV.

However, the importance of prosecuting a sitting president (Uhuru Kenyatta) and a sitting vice-president (William Ruto) should not, by any account, be underestimated. The prosecution of Uhuru Kenyatta was the first ever attempt to prosecute a sitting head of state from any African country. Thus, this action, seen from an international justice perspective, is a huge challenge against impunity in Kenya. It has sent a clear warning to all leaders in Kenya that the era of impunity is over. Despite its failure in Kenya, the ICC has challenged impunity for political leaders and has clearly increased the cost of committing crimes.

It is important to note that in criminal justice, what is central is not whether a person is found guilty or not, but whether the rule of law has prevailed. The rule of law has, to an extent, taken its course, so far in Kenya. Therefore, this chapter concludes that the ICC's involvement has sparked legal, judiciary and governance reforms in the country. While some of these reforms are genuinely meant to address some of the root causes of the 2007/2008 PEV, other reforms were simply responses designed to avoid accountability at the ICC by the country's top politicians, then on trial at the Court. The study concludes that the ICC has had and still is having a positive impact on the rule of law in general, and in the promotion of accountability to the law in particular. It also concludes that the ICC has had some deterrent impact on violence during the 2013 general elections in Kenya, to the extent that it is one of the institutions which helped ensure the relatively peaceful elections. It found that, because of the fear of being prosecuted by the ICC, many politicians, citizens and media practitioners conducted themselves responsibly and avoided conduct that could attract ICC's prosecution, such as "hate speech" and outright violence. The ICC was not seen to have contributed to the promotion of victims' rights as there were very limited ICC victim-related activities at the time of this study. The Court, so far, has had only a limited impact on promotion of reconciliation in Kenya. The study concludes that the ICC is contributing to the peace process in Kenya by its positive contributions to the promotion of accountability to the law and its deterrent capability which contributed to the relatively peaceful elections in 2013. The next chapter examines the 2010 PEV in Côte d'Ivoire, the process of building peace after the violence, and the impact of the ICC's involvement on the peace process in the country.

References

Amnesty International. 2014. "Crying for Justice: Victims' Perspectives on the Justice for the Post-election Violence in Kenya". Accessed September 30, 2018. http://www.amnesty.org.

Collevecchio, Edoardo. 2011. "Pointing Fingers for Peace: Can the ICC Deter Future Conflict in Kenya". Accessed January 20, 2015. http://www.inonafrica.com/.

Commission of Inquiry on Post-Election Violence. 2008. Accessed May 23, 2014. http://www.kenyalaw.org/Downloads/Reports/Commission_of_Inquiry_into_Post_Election_Violence.pdf.

Dunaiski, Maurice. 2014. "Accountability vs Stability? Assessing the ICC Intervention in Kenya". E-International Relations. Accessed August 20, 2015. http://www.e-ir.info/2014/01/09/accountability-vs-stability-assessing-the-iccs-intervention-in-kenya/.

Hoehn, Sabine. 2013. "Kenya: Is ICC Withdrawal Down to Court's 'Lack of Respect' for Kenyan Cooperation and Trail Relocation Request?" Accessed May 21, 2016. http://africanarguments.org/2013/09/09/kenya-is-icc-withdrawal-down-to-courtslack-of-respect-for-kenyan-cooperation-a.

Human Rights Watch. 2013. "High Stakes: Political Violence and the 2013 Elections in Kenya". Human Rights Watch Report. Accessed July 13, 2015. https://www.hrw.org/report/2013/02/07/high-stakes/political-violence-and-2013elections-kenya.

Human Rights Watch. 2014. "Country Summary: Kenya". Human Rights Watch Report. Accessed July 1, 2014. https://www.hrw.org/africa/kenya.

International Crises Group. 2012. "Kenya: Impact of the ICC Proceedings". International Crises Group: Policy Briefing, Africa Briefing No. 84, 2012. Accessed April 12, 2016. http://www.crisisgroup.org/en/regions/africa/horn-of-africa/kenya/b084-kenya-impact-of-the-icc-proceedings.aspx.

Jalloh, Charles Chernor. 2009. "Kenya's Dangerous Dance with Impunity". JURIST—Forum. Accessed August 13, 2014. http://jurist.law.pitt.edu/forumy/2009/08/kenyas, http://jurist.law.pitt.edu/forumy/2009/08/kenyas-dangerous-dance-with-impunity.php.

Jalloh, Charles Chernor. 2012. "Kenya vs the ICC Prosecutor". *Harvard International Law Journal* 53: 270–285.

Kenyans for Peace with Truth and Justice. 2013. "A Luxury Victims Cannot Afford". Kenyan for Peace, Truth and Justice Report, Issue 07/09 June 2013. Accessed May 24, 2015. http://kptj.africog.org

Kenya National Commission on Human Rights. 2008. "On the Brink of the Precipice: A Human Rights Account of Kenya's Post-2007 Election Violence". Accessed June 17, 2014. http://www.knchr.org/portals/0/reports/knchr_report_on_the_brink_of_the_precipe.pdf.

Lynch, Gabrielle and Misa Zgonec-Roze. 2013. "The ICC Intervention in Kenya". African/International Law. AFP/ILP 2013/01. Chatham House. Accessed October, 2014. https://www.chathamhouse.org/sites/files/chathamhouse/public/Research/Africa/0213pp_icc_kenya.pdf.

Mamdani, Mahmood. 2013. "Kenya: The ICC's Election". *Al Jazeera*. Accessed September 14, 2014. http://www.aljazeera.com/indepth/opinion/2013/03/20133982222657687.html.

Mueller, Sussane. 2014. "Kenya and the International Criminal Court: Politics, the Election and the Law". *Journal of East African Studies* 8: 25–42.

Namiti, Musaazi. 2014. "ICC Still a Deterrent Despite Major Setbacks". *Aljazeera*, September 10. Accessed June 12, 2015. http://www.aljazeera.com/indepth/opnion/2014.

New York Times. 2015. "Kenya: Official Apology for Past Wrongs". *New York Times*, March 27. Accessed January 20, 2016. http://www.nytimes.com/2015/03/27/world/africa/kenya-official-apology-for-past-wrongs.html.

Rigney, Sophie. 2014. "Unsettled Times at The Hague". Accessed November 19, 2014. http://insidestory.org.au/unsettled-times-at-thehague.

Wamai, Njoki. 2013. "The International Criminal Court and the Kenyan Election". Gates Cambridge. Accessed July 19, 2015. https://www.gatescambridge.org/multimedia/blog/international-criminal-court-and-kenyan-election.

Wanyeki, Muthoni. 2012. "The International Criminal Court Cases in Kenya: Origin and Impact". Institute for Security Studies, Paper 237. Accessed January 21, 2015. https://www.issafrica.org/uploads/Paper237.pf.

Wrong, Michela. 2014. "Has Kenya Destroyed the ICC? The Body Blow Dealt by Nairobi Have Human Rights Groups Questioning Whether the Court Can-or Should-Prosecute Atrocities in South Sudan and Other African States". Accessed April 9, 2015. http://foreignpolicy.com/2014/07/15/has-kenya-destroyed-the-icc/.

6

The International Criminal Court and the Peace Process in Côte d'Ivoire

6.1 Introduction

> I should also add that our investigations in the Côte d'Ivoire continue. We remain committed to our mandate under the Rome Statute and will continue to honour it. As we do, my Office is vigorously dedicated to doing its part, with the plight of the victims in Côte d'Ivoire foremost and always on our minds.[1]

Chapters 4 and 5 examined how the involvement of the ICC in the conflicts in Uganda and Kenya influenced the peace processes in these countries. This chapter examines the political situation in Côte d'Ivoire between 2002 and 2011 and the efforts to resolve the conflicts, particularly the impact of the ICC's prosecutions on the peace process in the country. Specifically, the chapter is concerned with the armed conflict of 2002/2003 that led to the partitioning of the country between government forces that controlled the South and *Forces Nouvelles (FN)* and

[1]Statement by the Prosecutor of the ICC on 15 January 2019 after Mr. Gbagbo and Mr. Blé Goudé was acquitted by Trial Chamber I. https://www.icc-cpi.int/Pages/item.aspx-?name=190115-otp-stat-gbagbo. Accessed 24 January 2019.

L. N. Malu, *The International Criminal Court and Peace Processes*,
Palgrave Studies in Compromise after Conflict,
https://doi.org/10.1007/978-3-030-19905-0_6

the rebel group that controlled the North. Also of special interest is the 2010/2011 post-election violence (PEV) between December 2010 and May 2011. The chapter relies on an analysis of data gathered from fieldwork in 2014 and 2015 on the situation in Côte d'Ivoire, examination of political developments in the country after the PEV, analysis of proceedings at the ICC and on a literature review. As in Chapters 4 and 5, this chapter will examine the impact of the ICC on the peace process in Côte d'Ivoire through the four analytical themes that were framed in Chapter 1 as core research questions of the study. These are the ICC and reconciliation, the ICC and deterrence, the ICC and promotion of victims' rights and the ICC and the promotion of accountability to the law in Côte d'Ivoire.

6.2 Côte d'Ivoire Since 1960

Côte d'Ivoire, a former colony of France, became independent in 1960. The country of twenty million people is located in West Africa (Cook 2011). Felix Houphouet-Boigny, who was its founding president, ruled the country under a one-party system (the official party was *Parti Democratique de la Côte d'Ivoire* [PDCI]) from 1960 to 1993. During his reign, Côte d'Ivoire was prosperous from its trade in coffee and cocoa. Indeed, it became a major economic power in West Africa and attracted many immigrants from other parts of the region, mainly from Burkina Faso, Mali and Liberia. These immigrants constituted an estimated 26% of the population, and citizenship became a major political issue that contributed to the crises that befell the country (Cook 2011; Dadson 2008).

Felix Houphouet-Boigny was succeeded by Henri Konan Bedie, who led the country till 1995 when a presidential election was held. Being the first truly competitive election held since independence under a multi-party system, the election was keenly contested. The main contestants were: Laurent Gbagbo of the Ivorian Popular Front (FPI), Henri Konan Bedie of the PDCI and Alassane Ouattara of the *Rassemblement des Republicains* (Rally of the Republicans [RDR]). Henri Konan Bedie won the presidential election, but was later overthrown in a coup on 24 December 1999 by soldiers who were disgruntled over low pay (Dadson 2008). The mutinous soldiers asked General Robert Guei, then the Chief-of-Staff to Bedie to lead the country (Human Rights Watch 2011).

In the 2000 election, as with the 1995 election, the contentious and divisive issue of citizenship was a major political problem. Under the 2000 constitution, to be eligible to contest for the office of president, both parents of a contestant must be Ivoirians. Ouattara and thirteen other presidential candidates were disqualified from contesting the 2000 election on various grounds, including the citizenship qualification condition. According to Owusu-Sekyere, "the political issue at the heart of the conflict is a constitutional one. In terms of the Constitution the president should be a 'pure' Ivorian, in that the parentage of the presidential candidate should be full-blood Ivorian without a mix from other countries, such as from its Burkina Faso or Mali neighbours" (2009). This constitutional provision was challenged by Ouattara, who argued that this constitutional requirement was "not an original provision but an insertion orchestrated to bar him from contesting the presidential election" (Owusu-Sekyere 2009).

The election was held on 22 October 2000, and early results showed Laurent Gbagbo winning, but General Guei dissolved the National Electoral Commission and declared himself the winner (Human Rights Watch 2011). After deadly protests by supporters of Gbagbo, General Guei was forced to leave, and Laurent Gbagbo declared himself the president. Laurent Gbagbo ruled Côte d'Ivoire from 2000 to 2010. He inherited an unstable country which eventually broke into two parts following the September 2002 rebel attacks.

6.3 The Armed Conflict in Côte d'Ivoire (2002–2003)

On 19 September 2002, a northern-based rebel group called the Patriotic Movement of Côte d'Ivoire (*Mouvement Patriotique de Côte d'Ivoire* [MPCI]) attacked important and strategic locations in Abidjan and the northern towns of Bouake and Korhogo. The rebellion was partially successful. Though it did not succeed in taking over the government and the main commercial city, Abidjan, the group, later joined by two other rebel groups, Movement for Justice and Peace (*Mouvement Pour la Justice et la Paix* [MJP]) and the Ivorian Movement for the Far West (*Mouvement Populaire Ivoirien du Grand Ouest* [MPIGO]) took control of the northern part of the country. The three rebel groups later merged into New Forces (*Forces Nouvelles* [FN]). Their main demands were an end to discriminations against the North and the removal of President Laurent Gbagbo (Dadson 2008).

The government responded swiftly, with attacks by government security forces on poor neighbourhoods in Abidjan, which were mostly populated by immigrants and northerners. In several raids, security forces destroyed houses and committed atrocities and human rights abuses, such as summary executions, arbitrary arrests, detention, rape, extortion and enforced disappearances. Also, in the North the rebels committed gross violations of human rights, such as summary execution, rape and illegal detentions and arrests (Human Rights Watch 2011). The armed conflict between the government and FN led to the splitting of the country into two parts. It dragged on until May 2003, when a ceasefire agreement was announced, and finally ended in 2005, when the ceasefire was fully observed. In 2007, the Ouagadougou Political Agreement was signed by the parties. The agreement was special because it was Ivoirians that initiated the idea and led the process. The agreement provided for the unification of the country, disarmament, identification of citizens, appointment of the leader of FN as prime minister and the holding of a presidential election in August 2008.

6.4 The 2010 Election and 2010–2011 Post-election Violence

After several delays, the presidential election was finally held in October 2010. The election was seen as a major democratic step to legitimise existing political institutions and promote the peace process

(Cook 2011). The main candidates for the election were: Alassane Ouattara of RDR, Laurent Gbagbo of the Presidential Majority (LMP) and Bedie of PDCI. The first round of the presidential election took place on 31 October 2010 with an impressive turnout of about 85% of registered voters. Gbagbo secured 38% of the total votes cast in the election; Ouattara got 32%, while Bedie got 25%. Since none of the candidates secured a majority, a run-off between Gbagbo and Ouattara took place on 28 November 2010. Ouattara won the run-off with 54.1% of the votes cast (Cook 2011).

Gbagbo did not accept the result which was announced by the Independent Electoral Commission (*Commission Electorale Independante*, CEI), certified by the United Nations Operation in Côte d'Ivoire (UNOCI), and considered free and fair by some monitoring groups, such as the European Union and the Carter Centre. Gbagbo approached the Constitutional Council for a review of the result. The Council held that Gbagbo won the election with 51% of the votes cast against Ouattara's 45%. Relying on the power granted to him by UNSC Resolution 1765,[2] and political agreements signed by the main political parties, the Special Representative of the Secretary General for Côte d'Ivoire, Choi Young-jin, on 3 December 2010 certified the result announced by the Independent Electoral Commission and further declared that the decision of the Constitutional Council was not based on facts. The European Union, ECOWAS, AU and the USA also certified the result of the election announced by the Independent Electoral Commission (Human Rights Watch 2011).

Nevertheless, Laurent Gbagbo was sworn in by the Constitutional Court on 4 December 2010, and Ouattara was also sworn in the same day (International Centre for Transitional Justice 2016). Both contenders formed governments and appointed prime ministers and ministers. The Economic Community of West African States (ECOWAS) and the African Union attempts to mediate the crisis failed, and Gbagbo refused to leave office. After months of impasse, the Republican Forces of Côte

[2]Resolution 1765 (2007), adopted by the Security Council at its 5716th meeting, on 16 July 2007. http://unscr.com/files/2007/01765.pdf. Accessed 17 January 2019.

d'Ivoire (Forces Républicaines de Côte d'Ivoire, FRCI), which was established by Ouattara in March, 2011(composed mainly of Soldiers from the *FN*), with the support of French forces launched a military offensive, leading to the arrest of Gbagbo on 11 April 2011. The crisis ended on 21 May 2011, with the swearing in of Ouattara. During the conflict, over 3000 civilians were reportedly killed, more than 150 women were raped (Cook 2011), and other grave violations of human rights committed by both sides. The new government led by Ouattara on 20 May 2011 established the Côte d'Ivoire's National Commission of Inquiry (Commission Nationale d'Enquête, CNE), which produced a report in July 2012 indicating the types of crimes committed during the PEV (International Centre for Transitional Justice 2016).

6.5 The International Criminal Court's Involvement in Côte d'Ivoire

In April 2003, Côte d'Ivoire submitted a declaration[3] accepting the jurisdiction of the ICC and later confirmed this declaration[4] in December 2010. In 2013, Côte d'Ivoire ratified the Rome Statute. Pursuant to article 15 of the Rome Statute, Pre-Trial Chamber III in October 2011 authorised[5] the commencement of an investigation in Côte d'Ivoire with respect to crimes within the jurisdiction of the Court committed since 28 November 2010 and with respect to crimes that may be committed in the future. Later in February 2012, Pre-Trial Chamber III expanded its authorisation for the investigation in Côte d'Ivoire to include crimes allegedly committed between 19 September 2002 and 28 November 2010.

[3]Copy declaration made by Côte d'Ivoire. https://www.icc-cpi.int/NR/rdonlyres/57B00915-8FDF-4532-9BDE-8AF338E3E364/279844/ICDEENG7.pdf. Accessed 23 January 2019.

[4]Copy of confirmation of declaration. https://www.icc-cpi.int/NR/rdonlyres/498E8FEB-7A72-4005-A209-C14BA374804F/0/ReconCPI.pdf. Accessed 23 January 2019.

[5]Decision Pursuant to article 15 of the Rome Statute on the Authorisation of an Investigation into the Situation in the Republic of Côte d'Ivoire, ICC-02/11-14, 3 October 2011.

Laurent Gbagbo and Simone Gbagbo were individually charged for allegedly bearing individual criminal responsibility, as indirect co-perpetrators for crimes against humanity: (a) murder, (b) rape and other sexual violence, (c) persecution, and (d) other inhuman acts, allegedly committed in the context of PEV in the territory of Côte d'Ivoire between 16 December 2010 and 12 April 2011. Also, in September 2013, Trial Chamber I unsealed an arrest warrant against Charles Blé Goudé, initially issued in December 2011. Charles Blé Goudé, a former minister, and youth leader who allegedly mobilised the youths against those who opposed the government, is alleged to bear individual criminal responsibility, as indirect co-perpetrator, for crimes against humanity, namely murder, rape and other forms of sexual violence, persecution and other inhuman acts, allegedly committed in Côte d'Ivoire between 16 December 2010 and 12 April 2011. The charges against Laurent Gbagbo and Charles Blé Goudé were later consolidated in one suit: *The Prosecutor v. Laurent Gbagbo and Charles Blé Goudé.* Their trial commenced in January 2016, but Côte d'Ivoire is yet to surrender Simone Gbagbo for trial at the ICC.[6]

On 15 January 2019, Trial Chamber I by majority, Judge Herrera Carbuccia dissenting, granted the Defence's motion for acquittal from all charges against Mr. Gbagbo and Mr. Blé Goudé. The Trial Chamber also ordered the immediate release of both Defendants pursuant to article 81(3)(c) of the Rome Statute and suspended the effects of the Decision to so that the Prosecution may file a request under article 81(3)(c)(i) of the Statute. The Prosecution later filed the "Urgent Prosecution's request pursuant to article 81(3)(c)(i) of the Statute" on continued detention. The majority of the Trial Chamber orally rejected the Prosecution's request and ordered the release of the Defendants. The Prosecution filed the "Prosecution's Appeal and urgent request for suspensive effect". On 18 January 2019, the Appeals Chamber, by majority, Judge Howard Morrison and Judge Piotr Hofmański dissenting,

[6]Decision on the Presiding Judge of the Appeals Chamber in the appeal of the Republic of Côte d'Ivoire against the decision of Pre-Trial Chamber I entitled "Decision on Côte d'Ivoire's challenge to the admissibility of the case against Simone Gbagbo", ICC-02/11-01/12-50, 18 December 2014.

held that "Mr Gbagbo and Mr Blé Goudé shall remain in ICC custody pending its decision on the Prosecution's Appeal.[7] The Appeals Chamber on 1 February 2019 ordered the release of both Defendants to a state willing to accept them in its territory and able to enforce the conditions set by the Court".[8]

6.6 Impact of the ICC's Intervention on the Peace Process in Côte d'Ivoire

Some of the likely consequences of the ICC's intervention on the peace process in Côte d'Ivoire are discussed here. This section examines if the ICC is facilitating or complicating or otherwise impacting on the peace process in the country. The peace process in Côte d'Ivoire includes, but is not limited to all efforts to end the 2002/2003 armed conflict, promote peace, and deal with the aftermaths of the 2010/2011 PEV. These include the numerous peace talks that took place between the rebels and the government, the establishment of the office of Prime Minister, the holding of the 2010 presidential election, the security sector reforms, the creation of the Truth and Reconciliation Commission and the National Commission for Victims' Reconciliation and Compensation. The affects of the ICC on the peace process are examined through the prisms of its impacts on reconciliation, deterrence, promotion of victims' rights and promotion of accountability to the law in Côte d'Ivoire.

6.6.1 Accountability to the Law in Côte d'Ivoire

Accountability to the law suffered during the years of conflicts in Côte d'Ivoire. In the North, where the FN ruled, there was almost a total collapse of justice institutions. Militants from the FN ruled without the

[7]Decision on the Prosecutor's request for suspensive effect of her appeal under article 81(3)(c)(ii) of the Statute and directions on the conduct of the appeal proceedings, ICC-02/11-01/15-1243, 18 January 2019.

[8]https://www.icc-cpi.int/CaseInformationSheets/gbagbo-goudeEng.pdf. Accessed 23 January 2019.

basic institutions of the rule of law. In the South, the rule of law also suffered significant neglect, but was not comparable to the situation in the North. Armed groups from both sides committed grave human rights abuses and international crimes against civilians along political, ethnic and religious lines after the 2000 election, during the 2002/2003 armed conflict, and after the 2010 election (Human Rights Watch 2011). The government of Alassane Ouattara has made restoration of the rule of law and accountability to the law one of the cardinal points of his administration.

The influence of the ICC involvement on accountability to the law in Côte d'Ivoire is assessed by examining: (a) the nexus between the ICC's intervention and enactment of accountability laws, (b) the link between the ICC's involvement and establishment of justice institutions, and (c) the link between the ICC's involvement and the prosecution of offenders. These issues are explored by eliciting information from respondents and by analysis of relevant publications.

Côte d'Ivoire is a civil law country that operates the monist system of application of international law in national environments. As a monist country, the Rome Statute became applicable to the country on the day it ratified the Rome Statute in 2013. Unlike the common law system where international treaties need to be domesticated before they become national law, the Rome Statute became operative in Côte d'Ivoire, without the requirement of domestication (Moffett 2014). The 2000 constitution of Côte d'Ivoire makes international treaties and agreements legal authority above domestic laws. Therefore, "once ratified, an international treaty is integrated into the domestic legal system without the need for any further action for its provisions to be enforceable in domestic law. Consequently, treaties may be invoked directly before Ivorian courts" (International Centre for Transitional Justice 2016). A direct implication of this development is that Ivorian prosecutors could rely on some of the provisions of the Rome Statute to prosecute persons who committed any international crime under the Rome Statute in Côte d'Ivoire where existing national laws do not have similar provisions (Moffett 2014). But, in spite of the country's ability under the monist system to apply the Rome Statute directly, Ivorian judges still prefer to rely "mainly on the provisions of the national

Criminal Code, the Code of Criminal Procedure, the Code of Military Operation, and the Code of Military Procedure to adjudicate serious crimes that occurred during the PEV" (International Centre for Transitional Justice 2016).

However, this norm-creation impact is one of the important contributions of the ICC to accountability to the law in Côte d'Ivoire. "The ratification of the Rome Statute makes it possible for the Statute to become applicable in Côte d'Ivoire. The onus is on the government to effectively use this window to promote accountability to the law, since offences not covered by national penal laws may be prosecuted using the Rome Statute".[9] Offences, such as torture and enforced disappearance which were allegedly committed by some accused persons during the conflicts are not laws covered by the penal code of Côte d'Ivoire, but could be prosecuted based on the provisions of the Rome Statute (Moffett 2014).

There are links between the ICC's involvement in Côte d'Ivoire and the creation of more justice institutions, or the introduction of reforms in some existing justice institutions. For instance, a transitional justice expert in Côte d'Ivoire thinks "the ICC involvement may have influenced the government to do more to promote accountability to the law, but further argues that the power of the influence may also be weak as the ICC is not on ground".[10] However, the efforts of the ICC are only supplementing what is happening at a national level. The primary responsibility for ensuring the rule of law is a matter for that country, but the involvement of the ICC will add impetus to what the national government is doing since there is a link between international accountability and promotion of the rule of law at the national level.[11]

Some justice institutions established after the ICC intervened in Côte d'Ivoire are the National Commission of Inquiry; the Dialogue, Truth and Reconciliation Commission; a Special Inquiry

---

[9]Interview with a professor of international criminal law at University of Ghana, Legon, 2014.

[10]Interview with an expert in Ivorian politics and development, 2015.

[11]Interviews with a professor of international law, 2014.

Unit/Special Inquiry and Investigation Unit; the National Commission for Victims' Reconciliation and Compensation; the National Commission for Reconciliation and Indemnification of Victims; and the National Programme for Social Cohesion. The Special Inquiry Unit (Cellule Spéciale d'Enquête, CSE) was established on 24 June 2011, by a ministerial order[12] to conduct judicial investigation into the events that occurred in Côte d'Ivoire since 4 December 2010. The CSE "carried the hopes of the international community and Ivorian civil society for a mechanism that could not only hold people accountable for violations and provide justice for victims but that could also foster national reconciliation" (International Centre for Transitional Justice 2016).

It was initially mandated to work for 12 months, but its mandate was renewed in 2012, and it was scrapped at the end of its second term in September 2013, by the Justice Minister before any trial began or even scheduled based on its investigations (International Centre for Transitional Justice 2016). Following protests from concerned organisations, the government replaced the CSE with the Special Inquiry and Investigation Unit (Cellule Spéciale d'Enquête et d'Instruction, CSEI). The 2013 presidential decree[13] that established the CSEI states that the CSE has been modified and transformed to CSEI with the responsibility of investigating "serious crimes and major offenses committed at the time of the crisis following the presidential election of 2010 and all offenses connected with or related to those serious crimes and major offenses" (International Centre for Transitional Justice 2016).

It is not clear whether the ICC influenced the establishment of these institutions or the introduction of these reforms. However, these developments certainly took place after the ICC intervened. Several respondents linked the ICC involvement in the country to the establishment of these institutions, stressing that the government would have probably done less, if the ICC had not intervened. They argue that the ICC's involvement brought the international searchlight on Côte d'Ivoire

[12]Order No. 020/MEMJ/DSJRH/MEF of 24 June 2011.

[13]Decree No. 2013-93 of 30 December 2013.

and may have contributed to influencing the government to take more action.[14] The "presence of the ICC in Côte d'Ivoire may be one of the factors that prompted the government to establish accountability to the law measures, but other factors such as the desire of the government to move the country forward on the accountability path should not be discountenanced".[15] The ICC has also helped in promoting accountability in Côte d'Ivoire, by its presence in the country, and its actions, such as "investigating the Côte d'Ivoire situation, prosecution of two former political leaders, public comments on the situation in Côte d'Ivoire, and meetings with government officials. All these actions have sent message to the government that accountability cannot be swept under the carpet".[16]

However, an expert in international criminal law argues that "the ICC cannot promote the rule of law and accountability unless the national government is involved. The people have to be involved in the entire rule of law process for the system to have impact. Therefore, there are doubts that the Court sitting in The Hague will have any impact on the rule of law".[17] The Court should be sitting in Côte d'Ivoire to have more impact. Finally, the ICC as a whole has the advantage of helping to promote accountability and in ending impunity, "but there should be a mechanism where the Court should work in the environment where the atrocities took place".[18]

Since the involvement of the ICC in Côte d'Ivoire, the GoC has enacted laws to establish the Truth and Reconciliation Commission (Ordinance No. 2011-167 of 13 July 2011, as extended by Order No. 2014-32 of 3 February 2014), the National Commission for Victims' Reconciliation and Compensation for Victims (Decree 24, March 2015), the National Commission for Reconciliation and Identification of Victims, the National Programme for Social

[14]Interviews with a professor of international law 2014, a senior research fellow on security and justice in West Africa, 2014, and an expert in Ivorian politics and development, 2015.

[15]Interview with an expert in Francophone West Africa, 2015.

[16]Interview with a lecturer in peace and conflict studies in Côte d'Ivoire, 2014.

[17]Interview with a professor of international criminal law at University of Ghana, Legon, 2014.

[18]Interview with a professor of international criminal law at University of Ghana, Legon, 2014.

Cohesion, and the Special Inquiry and Investigation Unit (CSEI), (Decree No. 2013-93 of 30 December 2013).

The government has prosecuted over 150 people who were involved in the 2010/2011 PEV, including Simone Gbagbo and Michel Gbagbo, the wife and the son of the former president. Michel was sentenced to five years in prison for his role in the violence, while Simone was sentenced to 20 years imprisonment for undermining state security. She was on trial with 82 other supporters of her husband, including two former military allies, General Bruno Dogbo Ble, former head of the Republican Guard, and the ex-Navy Chief Admiral Vagba Faussignaux. Both top security officers also received 20-year jail terms, while fifteen of those charged were acquitted (BBC News 2015). Simone Gbagbo's trial for war crimes during the 2010/2011 PEV began in 2016.

These prosecutions are commendable but not sufficient, in view of the high number of atrocities committed in the country. These prosecutions are just too small, too few and insignificant. The GOC must prosecute more persons from both sides and take care of the numerous victims of the atrocities committed in the country over a period of ten years.[19] According to David Tolbert, President of the International Centre for Transitional Justice, there is an urgent need for "serious, careful and effective efforts to acknowledge Côte d'Ivoire's past and account for grave abuses which can strengthen the country's economic and social progress" (Tolbert 2015). The GoC has been accused of lacking sufficient political will to prosecute those who committed massive human right violations during the PEV. According to the International Centre for Transitional Justice, at the national level although President Ouattara regularly promises to "end impunity and prosecute those responsible for human rights abuses committed during the PEV, those promises remain largely unfulfilled. The reality is that, to date, the judicial response has shown a lack of political will to prosecute all perpetrators of serious crimes committed by all political camps" (2016). One of the manifestations of this lack of political will is the struggle to fund the CSEI:

[19]Interviews with a research fellow on peace and conflict issues in West Africa, a professor of international law and an expert in international peace in West Africa, 2014.

"in 2014 the CSE was almost closed with no effort to advance the positive results of two years of work, before it was saved at the last minute by the CSEI's creation. Nevertheless, the two enforcement orders of the new CSEI took a long time to be adopted. Since then, the CSEI has continued to face financial uncertainty" (International Centre for Transitional Justice 2016).

It can be argued that the actions of Côte d'Ivoire represent an unbalanced attempt by a post-conflict country to ensure accountability, with a clear objective to develop domestic capacity to deal with the problem (Moffett 2014). The establishment of the ICC and the involvement of the Court in Côte d'Ivoire has contributed to promoting accountability to the law. However, the inability of the government to prosecute Ouattara loyalists who may have committed atrocities during the PEV remains a sore and dangerous point in the government efforts to promote accountability and the rule of law. Also, taking into due consideration the large-scale atrocities committed, the number of persons already prosecuted by Côte d'Ivoire for crimes committed during the 2010/2011 PEV, the number of persons prosecuted is still minimal and does not scratch the surface of accountability. The government needs to do more.

6.6.2 Victims' Rights in Côte d'Ivoire

One of the reasons for establishing the ICC was to provide justice for victims of international crimes under the Rome Statute. In line with these objectives, one of the central aims of the OTP, according to the 2012–2015 prosecutorial strategy, is to "impartially and independently strive *to bring justice to the victims* of the most serious crimes of concern to the international community".[20]

The main pro-victims' programmes of the government of Côte d'Ivoire are the Dialogue and Reconciliation Commission (*Commission Dialogue Vérité et Réconciliation*, CDVR), which submitted its report to the government in December 2014. Though the government has

[20]Office of the Prosecutor Strategic Plan, June 2012–2015. https://www.icc-cpi.int/iccdocs/otp/OTP-Strategic-Plan-2013.pdf. Accessed 20 January 2019.

regrettably, not yet made public the report, it has in March 2015 established the National Commission for Reconciliation and Compensation of Victims (*Commission Nationale pour la Reconciliation et l'Indemnisation des Victims*, CONARIV) to oversee a reparation programme for victims of violence from 1990 to 2012, and the National Programme for Social Cohesion (*Program National de Cohesion Sociale*, PNCS), to execute the reparation programme (Human Rights Watch 2015). The second notable programme is the accountability programmes of the government. The civil law system in use in Côte d'Ivoire permits victims to participate in proceedings in national courts, to present evidence through their lawyers and to claim damages and restitution (Moffett 2014).

The ICC, through its policy and practice, has brought more attention to the need to protect victims in international criminal justice. An expert in transitional justice in Côte d'Ivoire avers:

> [the] provisions of the Rome Statute has clearly shown that the ICC is desirous of providing an invaluable platform through which some of the victims of international crimes can at least tell their stories of the violent conflicts. The Rome Statute provided in many articles for methods of addressing abuses suffered by victims of conflicts. This is an important step towards victims' redress.[21]

The involvement of the ICC in Côte d'Ivoire is useful for the promotion and protection of the rights of the victims of the conflicts in the country since the ICC has numerous provisions for the protection and promotion of victims' rights.[22]

In practice too, the ICC has provided some of the victims of mass atrocities with opportunities to state the horrors they experienced,[23] and the ICC's victims' redress mechanisms have brought more attention to the need to respect victims, and provides an additional window for

[21]Interview with a transitional justice expert in Côte d'Ivoire, 2014.

[22]Interview with a lecturer in peace and conflict studies in Côte d'Ivoire, 2014.

[23]Interview with a lecturer in peace and conflict studies in Côte d'Ivoire, 2014.

victims to seek redress.[24] The ICC's intervention has also led to debates on the plight of victims which hitherto was not the case.[25] Nevertheless, only a few of the victims are directly involved in the proceeding at the ICC for the several reasons mentioned above, but particularly because of the narrowness of charges usually brought by the OTP which probably cover crimes the OTP has sufficient evidence to prove, and not all crimes committed. This leaves out the victims of the crimes not covered by the charges in the ICC proceedings and also excludes them from any possible reparation to be ordered by the Court. For instance, the OTP has only brought charges against three persons for crimes that relate to incidents within Abidjan, which excludes crimes that may have been committed by these persons in other parts of Côte d'Ivoire and by other persons from all sides of the violence (Human Rights Watch 2015). Laurence Gbagbo and Simone Gbagbo were accused of committing crimes against humanity in relation to four events, namely:

> [attacks] related to pro-Ouattara demonstrations at the headquarters of Radiodiffusion Television Ivoirienne (RTI), and in the aftermath, between December 16-19, 2010; the attack on a women's demonstration in Abobo on March 3, 2011; the shelling of Abobo market and the surrounding area on March 17, 2011; and the attack on Yopougon commune on or around April 12, 2011 (Situation in the Republic of Cote d'Ivoire, In the case of *The Prosecutor v. Laurent Gbagbo* of 12 June 2014). Blé Goudé is also accused of committing crimes against humanity in relation to these four events and an additional one in connection with an attack on Yopougon commune between February 25-28, 2011.[26]

The implication is that the ICC victims' redress mechanism does not reach many victims of the violent conflicts in the Côte d'Ivoire, who are entitled to legal protection under the Rome Statute.[27] Presently, only

[24]Interview with a transitional justice expert in Côte d'Ivoire, 2014.

[25]Interview with a professor of international criminal law at University of Ghana, Legon, 2014.

[26]The Prosecutor v. Charles Blé Goudé, ICC, Decision on the confirmation of charges against Charles Blé Goudé.

[27]Interview with an expert in Victims' rights, 2015.

727 victims[28] out of the estimated 74,000 direct victims are involved in the current proceedings at the ICC, prompting a respondent to argue that many victims in different communities who are the real victims of the conflicts may not have access to the ICC victims' redress programme, because the programme is not sufficiently focusing on them.[29] These developments were described by an expert in victims' rights as symbolic, since only few victims are involved in the proceedings, and these victims are represented by lawyers and do not attend court sessions.[30]

However, the ICC, through its victims' policies and practice, has brought attention to the need to protect victims in international criminal justice.[31] Also, the involvement of the ICC in Côte d'Ivoire may well have contributed to influencing the government to focus on the plights of victims.[32] There is evidence of a more robust victims-centred approach to justice, as the government is doing more in terms of establishing institutions that directly or indirectly deal with victims' rights, initiating victim friendly policies and enacting laws that focus on victims' rights or have provisions that protect victims' rights. As mentioned earlier, the government has established the National Commission for Reconciliation and Compensation for Victims and also the Dialogue and Reconciliation Commission, among others. In 2015, the government established a fund of 10bn CFA ($17 million) for the estimated 74,000 victims of the 2002/2003 armed conflict and the 2010/2011 PEV and commenced payment in August 2015 (BBC News 2015; Tolbert 2015).

The involvement of the ICC in Côte d'Ivoire has brought hope for thousands of victims who are crying out for justice for heinous crimes committed against them during the conflicts in the country. Yet, a perceived bias in prosecutions and a lack of access to the Court

---

[28]Please see https://www.icc-cpi.int/CaseInformationSheets/gbagbo-goudeEng.pdf. Accessed 23 January 2019.

[29]Interview with a research fellow on peace and conflict issues in West Africa, 2014.

[30]Interview with a lecturer in peace and conflict studies in Côte d'Ivoire, 2014.

[31]Interview with an expert in Victims' rights, respectively, 2015.

[32]Interview with a senior research fellow on security and justice in West Africa, 2014.

mechanisms by the numerous victims are some of the problems that make the Court's efforts to bring justice to victims of the violent conflicts in Côte d'Ivoire problematic. The inability of the ICC to establish projects and programmes for victims under its TFV mechanism because of paucity of funds is also lamentable.[33] The TFV's absence in Côte d'Ivoire limits the ICC's potential to act as a restorative justice mechanism.[34] Overall, the ICC's prosecution and the involvement of victims in the proceeding have helped some of the victims to have a sense of justice, generated more awareness and knowledge about the plight of victims and contributed to the establishment of more victims redress institutions.

6.6.3 Promoting Deterrence in Côte d'Ivoire

Advocates of international criminal justice insist that the involvement of international courts in conflict and post-conflict situations contributes to deterring future atrocities because "individual accountability is an important part of a preventive strategy, necessary for sustainable peace building" (Akhavan 2001). Thus, the involvement of the ICC in Côte d'Ivoire since 2011 could, on paper, serve as a deterrent to those who may be contemplating committing atrocities in the country. The Court's pursuit of accountability after the 2010/2011 PEV could serve as a warning to those who may be planning atrocities in the country that the era of impunity is about to end.[35] The failure of the ICC to prosecute those who perpetrated massive violations of human rights during the 2002/2003 revolt has been attributed to being partially responsible for the 2010/2011 PEV.[36] The thinking is that if the ICC had investigated and prosecuted those who committed international crimes during the 2002/2003 armed conflict, the Court would have been seen as a threat,

[33]Interviews with an expert in Ivorian politics and development, an expert in Francophone West Africa, and an expert in Victims' rights respectively, 2015.

[34]Interview with a professor of international criminal law at University of Ghana, Legon, 2014.

[35]Interview with a professor of international law, 2014.

[36]Interview with a lecturer in peace and conflict studies in Côte d'Ivoire, 2014.

and this could have contributed to deterring people from committing international crimes during the 2010/2011 PEV (Chepsoi 2011).

The attempts by the ICC to prosecute key personalities involved in the 2010/2011 PEV were described as capable of sending a strong message that the era of impunity is over. For instance, a transitional justice expert argues that:

> [the] prosecution of some of those who allegedly bear the greatest responsibility for the 2010/2011 post-election violence is a clear departure from the past when impunity for such offences was common, and a strong indication that those who masterminded or participated in violence could be made to face trial at The Hague.[37]

Against the backdrop that those who planned the 2000 election violence and the 2002/2003 armed conflict were not prosecuted, the current ICC's prosecutions are perceived as invaluable for the country's quest to promote accountability, and to end impunity. These prosecutions are significant and clear indications that if the national judicial system is reluctant to prosecute, the international community will step in. The main aim of establishing the ICC is "to ensure that there is no impunity, particularly when the national government is shielding some persons or is reluctant to prosecute, or is incapable of prosecuting those who committed international crimes".[38] The central argument is that the ICC is investigating the crimes committed in Côte d'Ivoire and "that accountability for these crimes is important".[39] Punishment deters. Therefore, it is likely that political leaders in Côte d'Ivoire have taken note of the plight of those in The Hague and may not like to walk the same road. The prospect that "a person can be charged and convicted by a national or international court can be a deterrent to such a person and to other persons. If there is concrete evidence of prosecution by the national government and the ICC, people will be deterred".[40]

[37]Interview with a transitional justice expert in Côte d'Ivoire, 2014.

[38]Interview with a professor of international criminal law at University of Ghana, Legon, 2014.

[39]Interview with a professor of international criminal law at University of Ghana, Legon, 2014.

[40]Interview with a professor of international law, 2014.

Prosecution of some leaders in the country is good for deterrence since there is the likelihood that prosecution could help in deterrence. Though, "this is difficult to prove, but, it is certain that politicians in the country are watching the ordeals of those in the custody of the ICC and may be more careful".[41]

However, the prosecutions of only members of the Gbagbo camp may be negatively impacting on the ability of the ICC to contribute to deterrence (Moffett 2014) since it reduces the credibility and acceptability of the Court. The ICC needs to prosecute individuals from both camps that committed grave crimes in order to have respect. The prosecution of only Gbagbo supporters has made the opposition to view the ICC as partial, against the opposition, and on the side of the government.[42] It is only high-quality justice, not partial justice that will lead to deterrence in Côte d'Ivoire. Thus, for the ICC to deter, it must not sow seeds of injustice and discontent among the people by prosecuting only those from certain parts of the country or camp.[43]

Trust and confidence in the ICC is important if the Court will have any significant deterrent influence in Côte d'Ivoire. Trust and confidence depends on perception. According to a lecturer in peace and conflict studies, the perception that ICC will deter people from committing international crimes in Côte d'Ivoire depends on the confidence and trust people have in this institution as a mechanism for justice. So, "if they trust the ICC, it will contribute to deterrence, but if not it will not serve any purpose, whatsoever".[44] An expert in Ivorian conflicts and development also thinks that:

> If the ICC trials are fair, and result in legal sanctions and justice only if and where warranted; and the potential for ICC legal sanctions—even short of a conviction—will make people think twice. What might militate against such an outcome is the fact that the ICC and other international legal forums typically only indict those for whom evidence

[41]Interview with a lecturer in peace and conflict studies in Côte d'Ivoire, 2014.

[42]Interview with a research fellow on peace and conflict issues in West Africa, 2014.

[43]Interview with a senior research fellow on security and justice in West Africa, 2014.

[44]Interview with a lecturer in peace and conflict studies in Côte d'Ivoire, 2014.

> (which is of course open to legal contestation about its validity) appears to indicate are the "most responsible"—i.e., top leaders. Such sanctions may well not motivate foot soldiers and low-level commanders not to take up arms or to act lawfully.[45]

This raises another limitation to the power of the ICC to deter in that it is focusing only on those who bear the greatest responsibility for the atrocities committed during the conflicts in Côte d'Ivoire. This limitation creates a vacuum that cannot be filled easily by the national institutions in view of the large number of persons who may have committed international crimes. During the conflicts, thousands of foot soldiers fought on both sides of the divide and committed atrocities of different types. In view of the weak capacity of the justice institutions in Côte d'Ivoire, most of these foot soldiers and followers will escape prosecution. Therefore, the fact that the ICC is only focusing on the big fish reduces its deterrent impact on the middle-cadre officers, foot soldiers and followers that also played significant roles in the conflicts.[46] This, therefore, makes a good case for more robust involvement of national institutions in the prosecution of international crimes to complement the work of the ICC.

Evidence shows that violent conflict in Côte d'Ivoire has been de-escalating (Mindaoudou 2016). Côte d'Ivoire, a country that was embroiled in violent conflicts for over ten years, is witnessing a gradual return to peace. For instance, the 2015 election was relatively peaceful—unlike the 2010 elections that culminated in the death of over 3000 persons, the 2015 elections witnessed minimal violence (Mindaoudou 2016). This is not to suggest that the ICC's intervention was the major cause of the de-escalation of the conflict, but that, the ICC's intervention is a contributory factor. The ICC's involvement in Côte d'Ivoire alongside other factors, such as the improved security situation,[47] the governance reform of the government and the

[45]Interview with a legal researcher, 2015.

[46]Interview with an expert in Ivorian politics and development, 2015.

[47]UNSG Resolution 2162 of 25 June 2014, renewing the mandate of United Nations Operation in Côte d'Ivoire.

post-conflict peacebuilding efforts of the government played major roles in reducing election violence during the 2015 presidential election.[48] Therefore, it is reasonable to argue that the ICC is contributing to conflict prevention through deterrence, by its various activities. Such actions include but are not limited to the prosecution of some persons, the ICC numerous public comments on the situation, its investigations of the violent conflicts and the issue of arrest warrants. Also, as a permanent international Court, the ICC is a constant reminder to all would-be violators of international norms that their conduct can be punished.

In Côte d'Ivoire, the ICC's investigations of the 2002/2003 armed conflict and the 2010/2011 PEV and the prosecution of key political leaders have clearly demonstrated that punishment is likely for those who commit international crimes.[49] Given the high level of impunity for crimes committed by political leaders in Côte d'Ivoire during the years of violent conflicts and before the ICC's intervention, it is reasonable to conclude that the ICC has increased the likelihood of sanction despite not convicting any of the persons indicted so far. This increased likelihood of sanction, evidenced by the existence of the ICC as an institution of international crime justice, the ratification of the Rome Statute by Côte d'Ivoire, the investigation of some of the crimes committed by the ICC, the indictment of some leaders in the country and the prosecution of some high-profile persons, *contributes* to deterrence.

6.6.4 Reconciliation in Côte d'Ivoire

After over a decade of bitter struggle for political power culminating in the defeat of Laurent Gbagbo at the polls in 2010, the 2010/2011 PEV, the indictment of the former president, Laurent Gbagbo, his wife and a major supporter by the ICC, and the crackdown on and detention of

[48]Interview with a lecturer in peace and conflict studies in Côte d'Ivoire, 2015.

[49]Interview with a legal researcher, 2015.

several other supporters of Gbagbo, Ivoirians are still struggling to find ways to live together. The country continues to be deeply divided along ethnic and political lines (Kofi 2014). "Hate speech" is still common in the media (IRIN 2012). The main political parties are yet to agree to work together to promote national reconciliation (Kofi 2014). Years after the violence, a solution to building long-term, sustainable peace has yet to be found (Oussou 2015). The FPI boycotted the 2012 parliamentary election and the 2015 presidential election and refused to fully participate in the political process. Political leaders from both the Gbagbo and Ouattara camps still trade blame as to which of the groups was responsible for the 2010/2011 PEV (Wells 2013). The national reconciliation process may have "come to a standstill, with rampant corruption and widespread injustice---such as arrests and discrimination --directed almost exclusively towards the allies of former president Gbagbo---and Gbagbo himself has been sent to The Hague to face allegations of mass murder, even though both sides in the conflict committed awful crimes" (Oussou 2015, 1).

The government is aware that reconciliation is one of its main challenges. The president has repeatedly emphasised the need for reconciliation if the country is to move forward. In September 2011, the government established the CDVR to lead the process of reconciliation in the country. Headed by former Prime Minister Charles Konan Banny, the CDVR was mandated to investigate human rights violations during the violent conflicts in the country. The CDVR was also tasked with creating the conditions for lasting peace by providing tools for conflict prevention and monitoring political developments. In November 2013, the CDVR released its first conclusions, "but many concerns were raised, including about the fundamental lack of initiatives established to mitigate divisions and heal wounds" (Oussou 2015).

The government also places emphasis on accountability for those who committed crimes during 2010/2011 PEV, with the expectation that these efforts will lay the foundation for reconciliation. Thus, it has prosecuted several persons at the national courts. After the initial crackdown on opposition leaders, the government later released some political leaders, unfroze several bank accounts and returned many seized houses (Al Jazeera 2014). In January 2016, the president announced state pardons for over 3100 persons imprisoned for various offences, including involvement in the 2010/2011 PEV. In August 2018, the government granted amnesty to about 800 persons, including the former First Lady, Simone Gbagbo, convicted for offences committed during the 2010/2011 PEV (BBC News 2018). The ruling party had also invited the opposition to dialogue and to participate in the political process.

Despite these efforts, the country is still divided along political and ethnic lines and seems to be limping towards the future with trepidation, despite the gains in the economic and development fronts as massive development projects are going on in the energy, communications, education and transportation sectors (Al Jazeera 2014). The current efforts at promoting reconciliation in Côte d'Ivoire revolves around institutions like: CDVR, CONARIV and the PNCS. The government is continuously consulting with stakeholders, such as the executive committee of the National Chamber of Traditional Kings and Chiefs, religious leaders and representatives of CONARIV (Mindaoudou 2016).

One vexatious issue is whether the involvement of the ICC in Côte d'Ivoire is contributing to the process of reconciliation in Côte d'Ivoire, or complicating it or having no impact on it. The actions of the ICC can complement the efforts of other transitional justice mechanisms such as the CDVR and national courts, and grass-roots efforts at reconciliation, such as religious, local and traditional institutions already at work. However, a majority of respondents think that what is needed in Côte d'Ivoire is amnesty and other forms of conflict resolution, not prosecution. One such respondent is a professor of philosophy, who states that "Côte d'Ivoire has seen so much division, instability and violent conflicts". What is needed to promote reconciliation in the country is "amnesty, mediation, and consultations, not prosecution. Prosecution will exacerbate the conflict in Côte d'Ivoire instead of promoting peace, stability, national cohesion and reconciliation".[50] A former US Assistant

[50]Interview with an expert in international peace in West Africa, 2014.

Secretary of State for African Affairs, Herman Cohen, also suggests that amnesty will be good for conflict transformation in Côte d'Ivoire, arguing that:

> President Alassane Ouattara needs to break through the tension and suspicion with a grand gesture. He should issue an amnesty to the former first lady Simone Gbagbo who is about to go on trial for war crimes in an Ivoirian Court. At the same time, he should begin a major economic development program in Western Côte d'Ivoire where the ethnic groups tends to be pro-Gbagbo, and where the fighting caused tremendous hardship. (Cohen 2015)

A researcher in peace studies interviewed in Accra argues that "peace will not return to Côte d'Ivoire through prosecutions, but through national dialogue and inclusions in the politics of the country, because prosecution by the ICC and the government divides the country more".[51] The president in August 2018 responded to these arguments as he granted amnesty to 800 persons. In an address to the nation on 6 August 2018, the president said that through the amnesty he wanted to bring about "peace and real reconciliation" (BBC News 2018).

On the other hand, the ICC's intervention in Côte d'Ivoire may assist in promoting reconciliation.[52] Accountability by the ICC and national courts is important for reconciliation.[53] Accountability through the ICC could "indeed assist in creating the conditions that will make reconciliation possible, such as providing justice for victims and punishing those who committed crimes".[54] An expert in Ivorian conflicts argues that the present prosecution could make leaders think twice and embrace peace, mediation and reconciliation. In his words:

[51]Interview with an expert in international peace in West Africa, 2014.

[52]Interview with a professor of international law, 2014.

[53]Interview with a transitional justice expert in Côte d'Ivoire, 2014.

[54]Interview with a professor of international criminal law at University of Ghana, Legon, 2014.

> The ICC actions also might make leaders who bother to contemplate lessons learned from them to think twice about using political violence as a tool; to the extent that this is true, these leaders would presumably seek non-violent means; i.e., politics, political deliberative forums (parliament, the media, etc.) potentially other forums, such as formal mediation meetings/processes, as a means of accomplishing their goals and exerting pressure on their opponents, and so on.[55]

One of the main problems negating the process of reconciliation is that only leaders of the opposition groups, particularly the members and supporters of the FPI, are being prosecuted. There "appear to be a reluctance to prosecute all perpetrators: only cases targeting members of the so-called pro-Gbagbo clans and forces have reached an advanced phase. Similarly-- waves of conditional releases, or political releases, requested by the Ministry of Justice demonstrate a partisan intent to control the administration of justice" (International Centre for Transitional Justice 2016). One-sided justice in Côte d'Ivoire is not good for reconciliation.[56] Since it is only the members of the opposition groups that are being prosecuted nationally and by the ICC, there is the impression that the government is hunting the opposition. It is "somewhat ironic that a government that has made accountability one of its cardinal points, is also not providing justice for all, but for a few".[57] Côte d'Ivoire is making a gradual return to peace, development and stability, but the problem of reconciliation remains a sour and difficult issue hindering the process. The government has made commendable efforts to promote reconciliation in this deeply divided country. The government needs to do much more than it is currently doing. It should take concrete steps to promote inclusive governance, even development, national cohesion and stability in the country.

[55] Interview with a legal researcher, 2015.

[56] Interview with an expert in Ivorian politics and development, 2015.

[57] Interview with a senior research fellow on security and justice in West Africa, 2014.

6.7 Conclusion

This chapter examined the political situation in Côte d'Ivoire between 2002 and 2011, the efforts to resolve the violent conflicts, and how the involvement of the ICC influences the peace process in the country. It found that the ICC has positive influence on accountability to the law and general deterrence, and to that extent has positive impacts on the peace process. However, the ICC is at this staging not having significant influence on the promotion of rights of victims of violent conflicts in the country. Only very few victims are involved in the proceeding at The Hague, and these few are yet to be paid reparation since the case against Laurent Gbagbo and Charles Blé Goudé is not concluded but is facing serious problems. Also, the TFV has not commenced any project in the country. Thus, to a large extent, the ICC is not contributing to the peace process through the promotion of the rights of victims. The impact of the ICC on reconciliation is found to be divisive, mainly because the ICC is at present prosecuting only those from the Gbagbo camp, and the opposition deems the ICC to be against it.

Nevertheless, after several years of conflict, the prosecution of some political leaders in Côte d'Ivoire by the ICC has brought international justice closer to the country. It signifies that to an extent the era of impunity and lawlessness may be over. Through the prosecution of leaders who were hitherto seen as beyond the reach of the country's criminal justice system, the ICC has stamped its imprint of international accountability on the country. This will contribute to national efforts towards accountability and deterrence. National and international accountability, however, face the problem of acceptance by the Gbagbo camp that accuses the ICC and the government of executing partial justice. In view of the power and influence of this group, this perception has the potential to erode the capacity of the ICC and national agencies to facilitate post-conflict peacebuilding. Thousands of victims of the conflicts are yet to see justice done. However, the ICC provides one of many possible windows to redress some of the harms done to them, although the road to peace in Côte d'Ivoire remains complex.

References

Akhavan, Payam. 2001. "Beyond Impunity: Can International Criminal Justice Prevent Future Atrocities?" *The American Journal of International Law* 95.7: 7–31.

Al Jazeera. 2014. "Ivory Coast Struggles with Reconciliation". Al Jazeera, August 10. Accessed February 20, 2015. http://www.aljazeera.com/news/africa.

BBC News. 2015. "Ivory Coast's Former First Lady Simone Gbagbo Jailed". British Broadcasting Corporation, March 10. Accessed February 1, 2016. http://www.bbc.com/news/world-africa-31809073.

BBC News. 2018. "Ivory Coast Ex-first Lady Simone Gbagbo Granted Amnesty". British Broadcasting Corporation, August 7. Accessed January 2, 2019. http://www.bbc.com/news/world-africa-45095830.

Chepsoi, Timothy. 2011. "Can the ICC Prosecutions Stem Election Violence". Accessed February 2, 2015. http://www.iwpr.net/global-voices/can-icc-prosecutions-stem-electoral-violence.

Cohen, Herman. 2015. "It Is Time for Côte d'Ivoire and the ICC to End the Nation's Cycle of Revenge and Retribution, Amnesty Simone Gbagbo and Indict Blaise Compaoré". Accessed February 3, 2015. http://africanarguments.org/.

Cook, Nicholas. 2011. "Côte d'Ivoire's Post-election Crisis". Congressional Research Service. Accessed February 28, 2015. http://www.fpc.state.gov/documents/organization/156548.pdf.

Dadson, Eunice. 2008. "Examining the Role of Third-Party Mediation in Côte d'Ivoire's Conflict: Peacemakers or Spoilers?" Kofi Annan International Peacekeeping Training Centre Paper No. 24, 2008. Accessed February 23, 2015. http://www.kaiptc.org/Publications/Occasional.

Human Rights Watch. 2011. "They Killed Like It Was Nothing: The Need for Justice for Côte d'Ivoire Post-election Crimes". Human Rights Watch Report. Accessed October 5, 2011. https://www.hrw.org/report/2011/10/05/they-killed-them-it-was-nothing/need-justice-cote-divoires-post-election-crimes.

Human Rights Watch. 2015. "Making Justice Count: Lessons from the ICC Work in Côte d'Ivoire". Human Rights Watch Report. Accessed September 21, 2015. https://www.hrw.org/report/2015/08/04/making-justice-count/lessons-iccs-workcote-divoire.

International Centre for Transitional Justice. 2016. "War Crimes Trial for Gbagbo's Wife Slated for May 31 in Abidjan". International Centre for Transitional Justice Briefing. Accessed March 13, 2016. https://www.ictj.org/news/war-crimes-trialgbagbos-wife-slated-may-31-abidjan.

IRIN. 2012. "Analysis: Côte d'Ivoire Needs Top Down Reconciliation". IRIN, December 20. Accessed February 28, 2015. http://www.irinnews.org/analysis/2012/12/20/côte-divoire-needs-top-down-reconciliation.

Kofi, Christopher. 2014. "Côte d'Ivoire Reconciliation at Dead End". Accessed February 26, 2015. http://mg.co.za/article.

Mindaoudou, Aïchatou. 2016. "Press Briefing on the Situation in Côte d'Ivoire". Office of the Special Representative of the Secretary-General for Côte d'Ivoire, January 13. Accessed February 20, 2016. http://ww.onuci.org/spip.php?article133426.

Moffett, Luke. 2014. *Victims Before the International Criminal Court.* New York: Routledge.

Oussou, Kouame Remi. 2015. "Reconciliation in Côte d'Ivoire: Mission Impossible?" Accessed February 28, 2015. https://reliefweb.int/report/c-te-divoire/reconciliation-cote-d-ivoire-mission-impossible.

Owusu-Sekyere, Benard. 2009. "Towards a Sustainable Reconciliation in Côte d'Ivoire". Accessed February 22, 2019. http://www.operationspaix.net/DATA/DOCUMENT/5131-v-Towards_a_Sustainable_Peace_and_Reconciliation_in_Cote_d__8217Ivoire.pdf.

Tolbert, David. 2015. "Doing Right by Victims in Côte d'Ivoire: Qattara's Second Term". The Huffington Post, November 11. Accessed November 24, 2015. http://www.huffingtonpost.com/david-tolbert/doing-right-by-victims.

Wells, Matt. 2013. "Political Leaders Stall Needed Reconciliation in Côte d'Ivoire". Accessed February 26, 2015. https://www.huffingtonpost.com/matt-wells/political-leaders-stall-n_b_3677143.html.

7

Comparative Analysis of the Consequences of the Involvement of the ICC in Côte d'Ivoire, Kenya and Uganda

7.1 Introduction

> I reiterate that the purpose of the trial is to uncover the truth, for the sake of doing justice for the victims; and to prevent mass atrocities recurring in the future.[1]

In Chapters 4, 5 and 6 of this book, qualitative data from the field were used to analyse the impact of the involvement of the ICC on the peace processes in Uganda, Kenya and Côte d'Ivoire. In this chapter, arguments that were made in the three chapters are further explored, analysed and distilled to show the patterns of the consequences of the interventions of the ICC. The assessment juxtaposes the qualitative findings from the field with the published literature on international justice and conflict transformation, and the ICC's practice from the field. This approach also involves a comparative analysis of how the ICC

[1]ICC chief prosecutor in a press statement on 27 January 2016, before the commencement of the trial of Laurent Gbagbo and Charles Blé Goudé on 28 January 2016, https://www.icc-cpi.int/Pages/item.aspx?name=otp-stat-27-01-2016. Accessed 21 January 2019.

L. N. Malu, *The International Criminal Court and Peace Processes*,
Palgrave Studies in Compromise after Conflict,
https://doi.org/10.1007/978-3-030-19905-0_7

involvement affects the peace processes in the three countries. The analysis in this chapter is premised on the research questions discussed in Chapter 1. Therefore, the following issues are comparatively discussed: the ICC and accountability to the law, the ICC and promotion of victims' rights, the ICC and reconciliation, and the ICC and deterrence.

7.2 Will the Involvement of the ICC in Côte d'Ivoire, Kenya and Uganda Promote Accountability to the Law?

This section addresses the first research question. Promotion of the rule of law is one of the expected roles of the ICC. Paragraph 3 of the Preamble to the Rome Statute states, among other things, that "the most serious crimes of concern to the international community as a whole must not go unpunished and their effective prosecution must be ensured by taking measures at national level and by enhancing international cooperation". Paragraph 4 of the Preamble also states that the international community will work to put an end to impunity for the perpetrators of international crimes and to contribute to the prevention of such crimes.

In Chapter 2, it was that because of the vastness of the concept of the rule of law and the difficulty of empirically studying it, this book focuses on accountability to the law which is one aspect of the concept of rule of law. Moreover, the wordings of Paragraph 4 of the Preamble incorporate the concept of accountability to the law. Also, as noted in this chapter, the socio-legal environment in the three countries before the involvement of the ICC was that of impunity and the withering of the rule of law. Against this background, the need for the promotion of accountability to the law becomes imperative if the ICC is to contribute to sustainable peace. The findings of this study with respect to the impact of the ICC on accountability to the law are: (a) the ICC influenced the enactment of accountability laws, to the extent that in the three countries, some laws that promote accountability to the law were enacted/amended after the ICC became involved, (b) the ICC influenced the establishment of justice institutions in the three countries, to the extent that in the three cases, some justice institutions were established/reformed after the ICC intervened, (c) the ICC attracted international attention and debate to accountability and the dangers of impunity in the countries, and (d) the ICC involvement has not generally influenced the prosecution of more persons who committed atrocities during the violent conflicts by national courts.

There are some links between the ICC's involvements in these countries and the creation of more justice institutions, or the introduction of reforms in some existing institutions. It is not clear whether the ICC directly influenced the establishment of these institutions or the introduction of these reforms. However, what is clear is that firstly, these developments took place after the ICC intervened, and secondly, these reforms and institutions that were established attempt to mirror international standards or models. In Uganda, the GoU established the International Crimes Division of the High Court of Uganda in 2011 to try those who committed international crimes. The International Crimes Division is modelled after international tribunals, comprising a Bench of at least three Judges, a Registry, an Office of the Prosecutor (OTP) and that of the Defence Counsel (Nouwen 2012). Another important development is the establishment of the Justice, Law and Order Sector which works on justice reforms, law and order. These developments were linked to the involvement of the ICC in Uganda by several respondents in Uganda.

Côte d'Ivoire has also established new justice institutions after the ICC intervened in the country, such as the National Commission of Inquiry, a Special Inquiry Unit/Special Inquiry and Investigation Unit, the Dialogue, Truth and Reconciliation Commission, the National Commission for Victims' Reconciliation and Compensation, the National Commission for Reconciliation and Identification of Victims, and the National Programme for Social Cohesion. Several respondents in Côte d'Ivoire linked the ICC's intervention in the country to the establishment of these institutions, stressing that the government would have probably done less if the ICC had not intervened.

In Kenya, there have been some reforms in the justice sector after the PEV and since the ICC intervention. The main institutions include law enforcement agencies: police, prosecution, judiciary, probation and correctional services institutions. The involvement of the ICC in Kenya has also contributed to influencing the establishment of good governance institutions, like the new Independent Electoral Commission and the National Cohesion and Integration Commission. There are also plans to establish an International Crimes Division of the High Court of Kenya.[2] Respondents in Kenya also linked the ICC's intervention to these reforms, arguing that the ICC's interventions sparked off these changes, and that the government was propelled to make changes to impress the international community, to show that the justice sector in Kenya is not in limbo, and to fight the admissibility challenge at the ICC.

Nouwen (2013) agrees that the ICC's intervention has led to the establishment of justice institutions in Uganda, but also states that the establishment of these institutions does not, without further support, lead to accountability to the law. Jurdi (2011) also states that the ICC's involvement in Sudan had some impact on the judicial system of the country, leading to the establishment of the Special Court for Darfur, the Judicial Investigations Committee, the setting-up of other committees to investigate violations of human rights and the restarting of the investigation of Ahmad Harun by the Attorney-General of Sudan. He further argues that the existence of the ICC and its practice "has created some contributions at the national level, but it has not reached a systematic level". Thus, it is argued that, in these countries, the ICC is influencing the establishment of justice institutions and the introduction of reforms.

There have been some new laws and regulations in the three countries after the ICC's involvement. Some of these laws mimic international standards while others introduced some innovative reforms. This book does not conclude that the ICC directly facilitated the enactment of these laws and regulations but affirms that since these laws and regulations came into place after the involvement of the ICC, and many of them mirror their international counterparts, it

[2]Interview with a professor emeritus of law from Kenya, 2015.

is likely that the involvement of the ICC influenced the decisions to enact some of these laws and regulations.

In Kenya, the government enacted/amended the Judicial Services Act (No. 1 of 2011), the Vetting of Judges and Magistrate Act (No. 2 of 2012), the Witness Protection Act, 2006 (as amended in 2012), the International Criminal Act, 2008, which domesticates the Rome Statute and the Supreme Court of Kenya Act (No. 7 of 2011). Several respondents in Kenya argue that the ICC's intervention has influenced the enactment of some of these laws. Firstly, the respondents state that the GoK amended some of the laws to prove that justice administration in Kenya was of an international standard, and capable of genuinely investigating and prosecuting those involved in the 2007/2008 PEV. This was to position the government to fight the admissibility case then pending at the ICC. The second reason is to avoid a recurrence of election violence. A respondent in Kenya argues that the ICC's involvement in Kenya "has generated a lot of interests in the judicial system which has prompted the GoK to take more actions with respect to the rule of law and the promotion of accountability".[3]

In Uganda, the GoU enacted the International Criminal Act, 2010, signed the Accountability and Reconciliation Agreement with the LRA and published a comprehensive Transitional Justice Policy. Also, the Prevention of Genocide Commission Bill was introduced in the Ugandan Parliament in 2015. Many respondents in Uganda, as in Kenya, argued that the ICC's involvement in Uganda influenced the decision of the government to take these steps, and that the reforms will facilitate accountability to the law.

Since the involvement of the ICC in Côte d'Ivoire after the 2010/2011 PEV, the government has enacted laws to establish the Truth and Reconciliation Commission of Côte d'Ivoire (Ordinance No. 2011-167 of 13 July 2011, as extended by Order No. 2014-32 of 3 February 2014), the National Commission for Victims' Reconciliation and Compensation for Victims (Decree 24 of March 2015), the National Commission for Reconciliation and Identification of Victims and the

[3]Interview with a professor emeritus of law from Kenya, 2015.

National Programme for Social Cohesion. Côte d'Ivoire has not enacted any law to reform the justice sector. This could be because Côte d'Ivoire is a monist country and could directly incorporate the Rome Statute without the need to domesticate it through local laws. Some of those interviewed in Côte d'Ivoire also think there is ICC influence in the enactment of some of these laws.

The views of scholars like Wanyeki (2012) and Dunaiski (2014) tally with some aspects of these conclusions. They argue that the ICC's involvement in Kenya influenced the enactment of laws mimicking international standards on the rule of law, while Nouwen (2013) linked the ICC's involvement in Uganda to the enactment of the 2012 International Crimes Act of Uganda.

The major criticism against these developments is that they were meant to ward off international intrusion and protect sovereignty, and not genuine attempts by the national governments to promote accountability (de Vos 2015). Dunaiski (2014) argues that the Kenyan government's admissibility challenge against the jurisdiction of the ICC "prompted important judicial reforms aimed at bringing the cases home".

The second criticism is that some of these developments were allegedly designed as a public relations stunt, to show that something is being done, to earn the respect of the international community and to win the support of donors. For instance, de Vos (2015) argues that the main motivation for enacting the Uganda 2010 ICC Act was because Uganda wanted to appear good in the eyes of the international community before hosting the 2010 Review Conference. According to him, "by 2010, an increasingly Hague-centric framework for punishment has taken hold; hastened by a perceived need to pass the legislation prior to the start of the ICC Review Conference". Also, there was thinking in Uganda that "echoing international standards could provide the state with a shield against international criticisms" (Nouwen 2013).

The third criticism is that some national institutions were created as an alternative to the ICC and not to complement the ICC or because of the ICC's involvement (de Vos 2015). For instance, with respect to the situation in Uganda, Nouwen (2013) avers that the Government of Uganda began to explore alternatives to the ICC when it fell out with the Court, and that most of the ideas for alternatives to the ICC were developed during the Juba Peace Talks, when the interests of the government seemed to have diverged from that of the ICC.

Thus, because of these reasons, the sustainability of the accountability to the law influenced by the ICC may be doubtful, purely because governments were driven by short-term opportunistic strategies, not genuine desire to promote accountability to the law (Nouwen 2013).

Also, the enactment of these laws and the establishment of justice institutions have not led to the prosecution of more people for crimes committed during the armed conflict in Northern Uganda, and the 2008/2009 PEV in Kenya. In the two countries, the number of persons prosecuted for crimes committed during the violent conflicts is worryingly low. However, in Côte d'Ivoire, the government prosecuted over 150 people who were involved in the 2010/2011 PEV, including Simone Gbagbo and Michel Gbagbo. In Uganda, so far, only Thomas Kwoyelo[4] is being prosecuted in the International War Crime Division of the High Court of Uganda. Kwoyelo was charged in August 2010 with 12 counts of violating Uganda's Geneva Conventions Act. The charge was amended by the DPP to add 53 additional violations under the Penal Code Act (International Centre for Transitional Justice 2015).

In Kenya, there are few statistics on the prosecution of those who committed international crimes during the PEV. While the government claims that several persons who committed crimes during the PEV have been prosecuted, Human Right Watch reports that only fourteen persons were convicted:

> As of February 2013, Human Rights Watch was aware of only seven serious crimes related to the violence, which had resulted in convictions. This conclusion was based in part on extensive research conducted for a 2011 report on accountability for offences related to the post-election violence. In one of these cases, the two accused had their convictions overturned on appeal. In total, by that time, only 14 people appeared to have been convicted for serious election-related crimes. (Human Rights Watch 2016, 36)

[4]The case is still pending because the Supreme Court of Uganda in April 2015 ruled that Thomas Kwoyelo's trial before the International Crimes Division of the High Court of Uganda must resume (Uganda v. Thomas Kwoyelo, Constitutional Appeal No. 01 of 2012).

The 2016 Report also states that:

> A multi-agency taskforce established by Kenya's Director of Public Prosecutions in February 2012 to undertake a comprehensive review of the status of investigation and prosecution of cases of post-election violence, transmitted its final report to President Kenyatta in March 2015. The taskforce found that of 6,081 cases were reported for investigation, 366 cases were taken to Court for prosecution. Of these, 10 were murder cases, but only 4 resulted in convictions. In 4,575 files returned from the taskforce to the police, the police reported that they were unable to proceed in the vast majority of cases on grounds that complainants could not be reached or were unable to identify suspects. (Human Rights Watch 2016)

What is evident is that the DPP has prosecuted very few persons involved in the PEV, and none is a high-ranking officer or leading politician in Kenya.

The conclusion drawn from these analyses is that the establishment of rule of law institutions and the enactment of laws and regulations that mirror international standards do not automatically result in the promotion of accountability to the law at the national level. Rather, these developments are important first steps in the long and tedious process of promoting accountability to the law. These laws and institutions should be put into action, by investigating and prosecuting persons who committed crimes and by ensuring that cases in court are expeditiously disposed of. As the cases in Uganda, Kenya and Côte d'Ivoire indicate, the willingness of national governments to genuinely embark on judicial reforms and take concrete actions to ensure that those who committed atrocities during violent conflicts are as important as the influence of international justice on accountability to the law in these countries. Thus, where there is a will to embark on judicial reforms, and the zeal to investigate and prosecute international crimes (as in Côte d'Ivoire), there is a likelihood that the presence of the ICC will add impetus to these efforts and lead, over time, to the promotion of accountability to the law. In this way, if the current momentum is maintained in Côte d'Ivoire, the efforts of the government are not derailed, and the GoC and the ICC prosecute persons from both sides

Table 7.1 No of persons prosecuted for crimes committed during the conflicts by national courts in Côte d'Ivoire, Kenya and Uganda

S/No	Country	No of persons prosecuted by national court	Type of national court	Date prosecution commenced	State of the national judicial proceeding
1	Côte d'Ivoire	150	National Courts	2010–2015	Completed
2	Kenya	14	National Courts	2010–2013	Completed
3	Uganda	1	War Crimes Division of the High Court of Uganda	2010	Pending

of the political divide, there is optimism that the ICC could have more impact on accountability to the law in Côte d'Ivoire than in Kenya and Uganda. Nouwen (2012) with respect to Uganda corroborates this view, arguing that the primary cause of impunity in Uganda has been the lack of investigation and prosecution, not the absence of courts and jurisdiction. However, as Freeland (2010) opines, the "incorporation of these international crimes into domestic laws will mean that greater pressure will exist for accountability at national levels". Prosecution is more likely to contribute to norm creation at the national level by reinforcing applicable international norms (Rosenberg 2012) (Table 7.1).

7.3 Will the Intervention of the ICC in Côte d'Ivoire, Kenya and Uganda Promote Reconciliation?

> The trouble with peace and reconciliation is that, unlike warfare and torture, they tend to require time and patience. (Thomas Buergenthal 2015)[5]

[5]Thomas Buergenthal, interviewed by *Newsweek*, 6 July 2015. https://www.newsweek.com/british-judiciarylord-jannericc-judgeauschwitzjewsholocaustprofessor-law-602725. Accessed 21 January 2019.

The task of this section is to answer the second research question of this study. Reconciliation in this book is described as the process of transiting from revenge, resentment and bitterness to dialogue, a shared future and friendly situations. The task is relevant because one of the justifications for the involvement of international justice mechanisms in post-conflict situations is that such interventions could lead to reconciliation (Fletcher and Weinstein 2002). However, promotion of reconciliation is not mentioned in any provision of the Rome Statute as one of the aims of the ICC.

Field data on how the ICC influences reconciliation which were discussed in Chapters 4, 5 and 6 are juxtaposed with published literature on the nexus between international justice and reconciliation, to comparatively discuss *how* the ICC influence reconciliation in the three countries. In Chapter 2, the nexus between the ICC and reconciliation was discussed, and it was noted that there are divergent views on the nature, scope and specific impact of criminal prosecutions on reconciliation. The main argument of the proponents of the ICC is that the Court creates conditions which are conducive for reconciliation, which is important for peacebuilding (Bensouda 2008; Fisher 2010). There is another view that there is insufficient evidence to conclude that international justice contributes to national reconciliation (Drumbl 2007; Fletcher and Weinstein 2002; Tolbert 2013). Clark (2014) also submits that reconciliation is an unrealistic and inappropriate goal for the court because individuals, communities and societies should be left alone to chart the course of reconciliation at their own time, and that the court should not set any agenda and decide for the people involved.

The findings of this study corroborate some of these views. However, a preliminary but important issue that emerged from the interviews is that in the three countries, people were already divided along ethnic and political lines before the ICC intervened. These divisions, some deep and long-standing, were because of many factors, such as political alienation, years of acrimonious relationships and the scramble for power and resources among the main ethnic/political groups. In Uganda, economic and political divisions and disparities between the North and South, partly created by the colonial government and exacerbated by the post-independent governments, created animosity between the

North and South. In Kenya, political differences, bickering and struggles for power among the major ethnic groups characterised the development of the country since independence. In Côte d'Ivoire, after the death of Felix Houphouet-Boigny in 1993, the country commenced a drift towards a division between the North and South, culminating in the 2002/2003 armed conflict and the partitioning of the country along this line.

These divisions, obviously, make the process of promoting reconciliation complex, because the actions of the ICC are usually seen through group or ethnic perspectives and not national or objective lenses. Thus, the ICC's investigations, indictments and prosecutions were interpreted from these narrow perspectives. The apparent result is that, no matter the quality of the decision of the ICC in each stage of its work, such decisions are criticised and opposed by the group that felt that the decision was against it. Such decisions also alienate the group that felt "cheated" from the ICC and from the "favoured" group, thereby creating more obstacles to the already complex road to reconciliation in these countries. In Uganda, several of those interviewed agreed that the North feels that the ICC is against it since the Court has not indicted any person from the Ugandan Army but has focused on the LRA. Thus, these respondents argue that the ICC does not promote reconciliation in Uganda, and that the ICC negatively influenced the North/South relations, as it further portrayed the North as fighters and rebels. In Côte d'Ivoire, Gbagbo supporters and many people from the South openly accuse the ICC of supporting the North and the government, and of conducting partial justice. Several respondents argue that the sequential prosecution policy of the ICC, which means that the ICC is only focusing on persons that have the greatest responsibility for atrocities, many of whom are from the Gbagbo camp, certainly gives this impression. In Kenya, the long-standing acrimonious relationship among the major ethnic groups and political parties is playing out and eroding the efforts of the ICC in the country. While the opposition party and ethnic groups that support the opposition are in support of the ICC, the party in government and the ethnic groups that support the government think otherwise—that the ICC is witch-hunting the president and the vice-president.

Table 7.2 Agencies and groups that work on reconciliation and reconciliation-related matters in Côte d'Ivoire, Kenya and Uganda

Country	Truth and reconciliation commission	Governmental agencies	ICC	TFV	Religious groups	NGOs
Uganda	Nil	• Justice, Law and Order Sector • Amnesty Commission of Uganda	ICC	TFV	Yes	Yes
Kenya	Truth, Justice and Reconciliation Commission of Kenya (TJRC)	National Cohesion and Integration Commission	ICC	Nil	Yes	Yes
Côte d'Ivoire	The Dialogue, Truth and Reconciliation Commission (CDVR)	National Commission for Reconciliation and Compensations for Victims	ICC	Nil	Yes	Yes

Another germane point made by most of the respondents in the three cases is that the ICC should not be the sole or only mechanism entrusted with the task of promoting reconciliation, but should work with community, national and international agencies or groups in this regard. This view corroborates those of scholars like Fletcher and Weinstein (2002) who argue that for international criminal justice to achieve reconciliation goals in transitional societies, it must be part of a larger process of peacebuilding, not the sole or central transitional justice mechanism; and that of Mendez (2010), who submits that the right approach should be to devise how to apply different transitional justice mechanisms to ensure complementarity and compatibility with the construction of democracy, international law and the search for reconciliation. The appropriate mix, according to him, will depend on the contexts, the circumstances, and the free and rational choices made by local actors, not the international community.

In practice, this suggestion is being implemented, as there are different agencies, groups and individuals working on reconciliation and reconciliation-related issues, which gives the hope that with the appropriate mix, contexts and circumstances they may be contributing to the process of reconciliation. Some agencies that work on reconciliation and reconciliation-related matters in these countries as shown in Table 7.2 are: Truth and Reconciliation Commissions, governmental agencies/ institutions, non-governmental organisations, religious groups, community groups, the ICC and the Trust Fund for Victims (TFV). This study did not investigate how to achieve the appropriate mix but proceeds on the assumption that such agencies need to be compatible and complementary.

One of the findings of the study is that the ICC does not contribute to reconciliations in the short term in these countries. This finding corroborates the views of scholars like Drumbl (2007), who argues that international courts do not care much about how their sentences could assist in reconciling the victims and the offenders, and Fletcher and Weinstein (2002) who contend that reconciliation is based on the ability of the individual to forgive or forget, and not an action the Court or the community can mandate. Clark (2014) also argues that individuals, communities and societies should be left alone to chart the course of reconciliation at their own time.

Many respondents agree that the role of the ICC is to prosecute those who commit mass atrocities and not to reconcile them. They also argue that the ICC is not competent and well positioned to promote reconciliation since the issues involved in reconciliation are complex, deep-rooted and beyond any court's competence. In Uganda, many respondents argue that reconciliation in the country is complex, broad and political, and goes back to colonial rule and the so-called un-answered questions of Uganda, which requires a holistic approach, not criminal prosecution by the ICC.[6] They also argue that people do not appreciate prosecution as a means of ending the conflict, since the ICC has not "touched" many people deeply in Uganda to promote reconciliation, but that people prefer the local methods of conflict resolution.

[6]Interviews with a lecturer in peace and conflict studies in Uganda, and a community leader in Uganda, respectively, 2013.

Some respondents also think that the ICC cannot contribute to resolving structural injustice in Uganda which, according to them, is the foundation of the South/North divide.

In Kenya, reconciliation is seen by some respondents to be beyond the ICC, since divisions in Kenya go back to early independent years and beyond, and because of the exclusion policy of past administrations. They also argue that the ICC, as with any legal institution, was not designed to promote reconciliation, but to ensure accountability by punishing those who committed crimes. Thus, the ICC is not expected to promote reconciliation in Kenya but to prosecute those who commit international crimes during the 2007/2008 PEV.

The second finding is that the ICC seems to be exacerbating the tension in Côte d'Ivoire through its sequential prosecution policy, which has so far resulted in the prosecution of only persons from the Gbagbo camp. As discussed in Chapter 6, supporters of Laurent Gbagbo who lost out in the power game are angry that the ICC is prosecuting only their leaders, while there is ample evidence that atrocities were committed by people from both camps. Several respondents solidly faulted the decision of the ICC to prosecute only persons from the Gbagbo camp, describing it as counterproductive and capable of derailing the government's efforts to reconcile different groups in the country.

Therefore, it is argued that the ICC has not contributed to reconciliation in the three countries in the short term, nor have the parties to the violent conflicts in these countries been reconciled. At best, many of those affected by these conflicts are simply living together, in peaceful coexistence, because as neighbours they must live together and not because they have been reconciled. With specific reference to the impacts of the ICTY on reconciliation, Clark (2014) argues "that reconciliation does not exist in BiH, Croatia or Kosovo and that at best there is peaceful coexistence; but these have resulted less from the ICTY's work than from simple pragmatism and the practical demands of everyday life". At the national level, in Côte d'Ivoire, Kenya and Uganda, the extreme ethnic politics, uneven development among the major groups and bitter competition among the elites that characterised the political space and contributed to the violent conflicts in these countries still exist. It is obvious that reconciliation in the immediate aftermath of a violent conflict is unrealistic, and it is an over-expectation to expect a court to contribute to reconciliation immediately after conflict (Clark 2014).

Bloomfield et al. (2003) describe reconciliation as a process of enabling victims and perpetrators of crimes in a post-conflict community to move from a divided past to a shared future. That process could start with peaceful coexistence without overt violence and could blossom to reconciliation over time. The contributions of the ICC to the process will be better assessed over the long term and not in the short term, and as the legal representative of some of the victims at the ICC in one of the cases from Kenya opines, "reconciliation is a process that perhaps transcends generations".[7]

7.4 Will the Involvement of the ICC in Côte d'Ivoire, Kenya and Uganda Promote Respect for Victims' Rights?

The third research question of this study, which is whether the ICC involvements in the three countries promote victims' rights, is explored here. This question is germane because one of the main reasons for establishing the ICC, according to the Preamble to the Rome Statute, is to end impunity for perpetrators of international crimes. Thus, one of the central aims of the OTP, according to the 2012–2015 prosecutorial strategy, is to "impartially and independently strive *to bring justice to the victims* of the most serious crimes of concern to the international community".[8]

In Chapter 2 of this book, it was noted that the ICC Statute has new and creative provisions for the protection of victims' rights, and that the ICC mechanisms also suffer from some inherent weaknesses which may negate the full implementation of these victim-protection

[7]Interview with a legal representative for victims from Kenya at the ICC, 2014.

[8]Office of the Prosecutor, Strategic Plan June 2012–2015. https://www.icc-cpi.int/iccdocs/otp/OTP-Strategic-Plan-2013.pdf. Accessed 23 January 2019.

provisions. Protection of victims' rights or involving victims in criminal trials is relatively new to international criminal justice. Protection of victims' rights is therefore in its infancy in international criminal law as international criminal justice has for a long time focused entirely on punishment of perpetrators of international crimes with little attention devoted to the roles and rights of victims and survivors of international crimes (Garkawe 2003; Goetz 2008; McCarthy 2012). Thus, the various innovative provisions of the Rome Statute that focused on victims' rights discussed in Chapter 2 highlight the level of importance the ICC mechanism attaches to the protection of victims' rights. For instance, the right to participate in the proceedings of the ICC with legal reputation was described as providing both moral and legal recognitions which could even be more satisfying than financial compensation (Goetz 2008). On the other hand, the involvement of courts in post-conflict situations could have negative consequences on victims in the following ways: it tends to ignore or sideline the feelings of victims of violent conflicts, political obstacles may make it impossible for criminal trials to connect to victims (Bloomfield et al. 2003), and as discussed earlier, it may lead to re-victimisation.

The views of several respondents in the three countries corroborate these arguments. Most of the respondents think that the ICC through its policy and practice has brought more attention to the need to protect victims in international criminal justice. They argue that the provisions of the Rome Statute have clearly shown that the ICC is desirous of providing an invaluable platform through which some of the victims of international crimes can at least tell their stories of the violent conflicts. In practice too, the ICC has provided some of the victims of mass atrocities in the three countries with opportunities to state the horrors they experienced. In Kenya, many respondents argue that the ICC has opened doors, no matter how inadequate, for victims to be heard and has brought international attention to the plights of the victims of the 2007/2008 PEV. In Côte d'Ivoire, several respondents argue that the ICC's victims' redress mechanisms have brought more attention to the need to respect victims and provide an additional window for victims to seek redress. In Uganda, several respondents argue that the ICC's intervention has led to debates and conferences on the plight of victims of the war in the North which hitherto was not the case.

However, only a few of the victims of the crimes committed in these countries are directly involved in proceedings at the ICC for several reasons already mentioned in this book. One major drawback is the narrowness of charges usually brought by the OTP, which probably cover those crimes the OTP has sufficient evidence to prove, but not all crimes committed. This leaves out the victims of the crimes not covered by the charges in the ICC proceedings, and out of any possible reparation that may be ordered by the Court.

Several respondents interviewed in the three countries argue that the ICC's victims' redress mechanisms, particularly those provided in article 75 of the Rome Statute, protect only a very few of the victims of the conflicts and are insufficient and incapable of providing redress to many victims. This deficiency is inherent in the ICC mechanism which is complementary to national courts and focuses only on those who bear the greatest responsibility for the crimes committed in the conflict. The implication is that the ICC victims' redress mechanism does not reach many of the victims of the violent conflicts in the three countries, who are entitled to legal protection under the Rome Statute. In Côte d'Ivoire, Pre-Trial Chamber I granted only 727[9] persons the status of victims authorised to participate in the proceedings, out of the estimated 74,000 direct victims of the conflicts in the country. In Kenya, only 628[10] victims participated in the William Samoei Ruto and Joshua Arap Sang case, and 725[11] in the Uhuru Muigai Kenyatta case, out of an estimated 350,000 displaced and 3561 injured during the PEV. Several respondents in Kenya argue that the ICC can only accommodate a few of the victims and that national authorities should also get involved in protecting victims who have been suffering since the 2007/2008 PEV.

[9]Please see https://www.icc-cpi.int/CaseInformationSheets/gbagbo-goudeEng.pdf. Accessed 23 January 2019.

[10]Please see https://www.icc-cpi.int/CaseInformationSheets/RutoSangEng.pdf. Accessed 23 January 2019.

[11]Please see https://www.icc-cpi.int/CaseInformationSheets/KenyattaEng.pdf. Accessed 23 January 2019.

In Uganda, only one out of five persons indicted by the ICC is currently on trial at The Hague. Thus, only 4107 victims[12] of the crimes covered by the charges against Dominic Ongwen at the ICC are participating in the proceeding. This number does not in any way represent the thousands of persons who are direct and indirect victims of the conflict that lasted for over twenty years.

This finding from the field is supported by the literature. For instance, McCarthy (2012) notes that the overwhelming number of perpetrators and victims the Court has to deal with makes it difficult for the ICC to cater for the majority of victims of the crimes in conflict countries, while Goetz (2008) argues that the problems inherent in the ICC victims' redress mechanism make it impossible for the Court to reach the majority of victims.

The Trial Chamber of the ICC in the *Lubanga Dyilo Case Reparation Decision*[13] of 7 August 2012 held, *inter alia*, that only victims within the meaning of rule 85 (a) of the Rules of Procedure and Evidence and regulation 46 of the Regulations of the Trust Fund, who suffered harm as a result of the crimes (i.e. enlisting and conscripting children under the ages of fifteen and using them to participate in the hostilities) for which Mr. Lubanga Dyilo was found guilty, are eligible to claim reparations against him. The Appeals Chamber in the *Reparation Appeal Decision*[14] in the same case of 3 March 2015 also held that, where an award for reparations is made to the benefit of a community, only members of the community meeting the relevant criteria are eligible. However, it does not matter whether the persons who qualified as victims participated in the proceeding at the ICC or not. The implications of these decisions are that only direct and indirect victims of the crimes that the convicted person was charged with could benefit from

[12]Please see https://www.icc-cpi.int/CaseInformationSheets/OngwenEng.pdf. Accessed 23 January 2019.

[13]"Decision establishing the principles and procedures to be applied to reparations" of 7 August 2012, ICC-01/04-01/06-2904.

[14]Judgement on the appeals against the "Decision establishing the principles and procedures to be applied to reparations" of 7 August 2012 with AMENDED order for reparations, ICC-01/04-01/06-3129,03 March 2015.

Table 7.3 Number of victims in ICC cases and the total number of victims

S/No	Country	Estimated no of victims	No of victims in the ICC proceeding	Gap
1	Côte d'Ivoire	74,000	Laurent Gbagbo Blé Goudé Case: 726	73,274
2	Kenya	1333 deaths 350,000 displaced 3561 injured	Ruto and Sang case: 628 Kenyatta case: 725	352,208
3	Uganda	66,000 abducted 1.5 m displaced, 120,000 deaths	Ongwen case: 4107	1,563,974

any reparations ordered by the Court. This leaves out those victims of the crimes committed where nobody was charged, but happily includes victims of the crimes charged whether they participated in the proceedings, and the communities where the offences charged took place.

Following from the above discussion, it is further canvassed that the victims' redress mechanisms of the ICC, particularly those provided by article 75, could at best be described as symbolic in the sense that only a few of the victims are likely to be involved. This conclusion is fully supported by evidence of ICC practice in the cases as indicated in Table 7.3, data from interviews conducted in the three cases and published literature. Moffett's (2014) conclusion that the ICC victims' redress is symbolic since only a few persons are covered by the mechanism, and that such persons are only represented by Counsel, is supported by many respondents who argue that in the main, these measures are symbolic because victims are not real participants but are merely represented, and that there are some disconnects between actualities and what is being represented. The involvement of the ICC in Côte d'Ivoire, and specifically the Court's victims' redress mechanisms, is also described by respondents as symbolic in the sense that they are not far-reaching, and because they are limited to the cases the ICC is prosecuting; but, also significant because they open more windows of opportunities for the victims to seek redress. In Kenya, about half of those interviewed agree that the ICC cannot and should not pretend to have the primary responsibility of resettling the victims, since it is the main duty of the government. In Uganda, a summary of the arguments of respondents on this point is that the ICC and the GoU have abandoned the victims, as there are few victims involved in the proceeding at The Hague and very little progress at home.

Related to the arguments made above, that the ICC, through its victims' policies and practice, has brought attention to the need to protect victims in international criminal justice is another argument that the involvement of the ICC in the three countries seems to have influenced the respective governments, to pay more attention to the plight of victims of the crimes committed in their countries. There is a noticeable trend in all the countries towards a victim-centred approach to justice. Each of the governments seems to be doing more in terms of establishing institutions that directly or indirectly deal with victims' rights, initiating victims' friendly policies and enacting laws that focus on victims' rights or have provisions that protect victims' rights. To different degrees, these governments have developed a victim-oriented agenda since the ICC's interventions.

In Côte d'Ivoire, the GoC has established the Dialogue and Reconciliation Commission, the National Commission for Reconciliation and Compensations for Victims, the National Commission for Reconciliation and Identification of Victims, and the National Programme for Social Cohesion. In 2015, the GoC established a fund of 10bn CFA francs (US$17million) for the estimated 74,000 victims of the 2002/2003 armed conflict and the 2010/2011 PEV and promised to commence payment in July 2015 (BBC News 2015). The National Programme for Social Cohesion began the payment of financial compensations from this fund to victims in August 2015 (Tolbert 2015).

In Kenya, apart from establishing the Kenya Truth, Justice and Reconciliation Commission, the President of Kenya, in his 2015 State of the Nation Address, publicly apologised to the victims of mass atrocities in Kenya since independence and admitted that the government has failed them. He asked the Finance Ministry to set up a $110 million fund to help repair the harm of government actions (*New York Times* 2015).

In Uganda, the GoU has established the Justice, Law and Order Sector, published a National Transitional Justice Policy which provides that victims be identified, and reparation paid, and established the

International Crime Division of the High Court which has victims' protection as part of its mandate. In all three countries, victims-oriented programmes are already on course, but there are differences in the scope, reach and relevance of these projects to the needs of victims. This book does not argue that the ICC directly influenced these developments but affirms that they took place *after the ICC become involved.*

In Kenya, many of those interviewed state that the presence of the ICC may well have prodded the government to be more interested in the plight of the victims. One respondent states that the ICC's intervention propelled the government to "begin addressing IDP issues and providing minor and insufficient compensation to certain groups of victims".[15] Another argues that "the ICC is only helpful to the extent that it has helped the government of Kenya do something for the victims, like trying to resettle some of them, close the IDP camps, attempting to pay compensations, and developing new policies on victims' protection".[16] In Côte d'Ivoire, most respondents think the ICC's involvement may have prompted the GoC to be more victim sensitive, while in Uganda many respondents do not see any tangible efforts by the GoU to address victims' rights besides the projects of the TFV.

The differences in the impacts of the ICC's interventions on the protection of victims' rights in these countries are attributable to the environment at the national level, particularly how national governments react to the involvement of the ICC, and the seriousness of the government in implementing victims' redress. For instance, the GoC seems to have devoted more attention to the plight of victims than the GoU and the GoK, which has resulted in more victim-oriented programmes in Côte d'Ivoire than in Kenya and Uganda, to the extent that the GoC has established more agencies for the protection of rights of victims and has set out a timetable for payment of compensation. To overcome this justice gap observable in all the countries, and to ensure better protection of victims, there is need for more victim-protection initiatives by state parties (Table 7.4).

---

[15]Interview with a transitional justice expert in Kenya, 2014.

[16]Interview with an expert in security studies in Africa, 2014.

Table 7.4 National victims protection projects in Côte d'Ivoire, Kenya and Uganda

S/No	Country	Victim project established by the government	Type of project/ agency	Year of establishment
I	Côte d'Ivoire	1. Dialogue and Reconciliation Commission	TRC/Governmental	2012
		2. National Commission for Reconciliation and Compensations for Victims	Victims/ Governmental	2015
		3. National Commission for Reconciliation and Indemnification of Victims	Victims/ Governmental	2015
		4. National Programme for Social Cohesion	Victims/ Governmental	2015
2	Kenya	Truth, Justice and Reconciliation Commission of Kenya	TRC/Governmental	2008
3	Uganda	1. Justice, Law and Order Sector	Transitional Justice/ Governmental	2001
		2. National Transitional Justice Policy	Transitional Justice/ Governmental	2001
		3. International Crimes Division of the High Court of Uganda	National Court	2011

Article 79 of the Rome Statute established the TFV for the benefit of victims of crimes within the jurisdiction of the Court and the families of victims. The TFV supports and implements "programmes that address harms resulting from genocide, crimes against humanity and war crimes". McCarthy's argument that the TFV mechanism has the potential to provide justice to a wider range of victims, beyond those covered by the retributive justice mechanism of the Court (because, unlike prosecution, reparation or victim support provides a "potentially more tangible and concrete form of justice" [2012]), was corroborated by most respondents in the three countries. These respondents argue that the TFV's projects will have a long-lasting impact on victims by contributing to reconciliation and rehabilitation which could indeed assist victims in rebuilding their lives and their communities. The TFV projects were also described as capable of promoting sustainable peace in these communities because they will assist victims to return to a normal community life.

In Uganda, where the ICC has some projects, 15 out of 22 respondents interviewed argue that the TFV projects are very useful to individuals and communities that suffered from the brutality of the LRA and government forces during the armed conflict in the North. In Kenya, where the TFV had not established any project at the time of the study, a majority of those interviewed argue that TFV projects will help victims and communities return to normal lives and promote the peace process in the country. They also lamented the absence of the TFV, despite the strong presence of the ICC in the country. In Côte d'Ivoire, where the TFV has not established any project, many respondents think such projects are needed as they will facilitate sustainable peace by promoting restorative justice and reconciliation.

The conclusion to draw from the analysis is that the impact of the ICC on victims' rights are still not significant, because of the minimal number of victims participating in the proceedings, and because the ICC has not convicted any of those charged with crimes from these countries. Further, the TFV is only working in Uganda and does not have projects in Côte d'Ivoire and Kenya, because it has very limited resources and can only execute few projects in some countries. Also, when the Trial Chamber makes reparation orders, the orders will only be for the benefit of the victims of the offences in which people were charged.

The ICC's reparation provisions are novelty in international criminal law because they provide victims of conflicts with actual rights to reparation; thus, it is becoming an expectation in international law that victims of international crimes are entitled to reparation as a right (Clamp 2014). However, the involvement of some victims in the trial at The Hague could lead to re-victimisation, in the sense that most court trials involve many litigious and hostile processes that may expose the victims to another round of humiliation (Bloomfield et al. 2003) (Table 7.5).

Table 7.5 TFV projects in Côte d'Ivoire, Kenya and Uganda

S/No	Country	Number TFV projects	Number of persons impacted	Types of projects
1	Côte d'Ivoire	Nil	Nil	Nil
2	Kenya	Nil	Nil	Nil
3	Uganda	18	39,750	Counselling, material support, vocational training, prosthetic limbs and orthopaedics support, reconstructive surgery

7.5 Can the ICC Contribute to Deterrence in Côte d'Ivoire, Kenya and Uganda?

> The second goal of my visit is related to my Office's preventive mandate. It is absolutely crucial to prevent further crimes from being committed, no matter the situation or circumstance.[17]

This section provides answers to the fourth research question of this study. In Chapter 2, deterrence theory and the application of deterrence to conflict and post-conflict situations as a theory of punishment for those who committed mass atrocities during conflicts were discussed. The Preamble to the Rome Statute provides, inter alia, that the Court is established to end impunity for the perpetrators of international crimes and to contribute to the prevention of international crimes. This has been interpreted to mean that deterrence as a fundamental principle of international criminal justice is one of the aims of the ICC (Mendes 2010). The chief prosecutor of the ICC amplified this on 4 July 2015, during a visit to Guinea when she stated that one of the goals of her visit was related to her office's preventive mandate because "it is absolutely crucial to prevent further crimes from being committed, no

[17]Press Statement of the Prosecutor of the ICC, 6 July 2015. https://www.icc-cpi.int/Pages/item.aspx?name=otp-stat-150704. Accessed 22 January 2019.

matter the situation or circumstance".[18] However, people can also obey the law because they think that the law is just, or because those enforcing the law are legitimate and have the right to dictate behaviour, not just because they were deterred (Tyler 2006, 4). The focus on deterrence in this book is because of the reference to deterrence, as one of the aims of the ICC in the Preamble to the Rome Statute.

Deterrence theory is based on the belief that punishment can deter offenders from reoffending, and others from offending, because people fear punishment. As noted in Chapter 2, deterrence can be specific or general. Both specific deterrence and general deterrence are based on the cost-benefit analysis and on the principles of severity, swiftness and certainty. Opinions of scholars on the application of deterrence theory to punishing international crimes are somewhat divided. Pro-deterrence scholars like Akhavan (2001), Grono (2012), Kim and Sikkink (2009), Scheffer (1999) and Whiting (2012) argue that the international justice system could have a long-time deterrent impact. On the other hand, Drumbl (2007) argues that there is no systematised and conclusive evidence that potential extraordinary international criminals are deterred by the punishment of others following a criminal trial. Ku and Nzeribe (2006) also state that international criminal justice does not deter people from committing crimes but might even exacerbate conflicts in weak states. There are also "middle-of-the-road" scholars like Rosenberg (2012) and Wippman (1999) who state that the argument that international criminal law deters should be treated with caution.

Justice Richard Goldstone states that deterrence should not even be a goal of the international criminal justice system because it is an impossible task (Mendes 2010) and notoriously difficult in the international context (May and Hoskins 2010). The linkages between international prosecutions and actual deterrence of future atrocities are at best a "plausible assumption" (Rosenberg 2012). In the expanding field of conflict prevention and international criminal justice, the interrelationship of varying preventive mechanisms together with greater certainty

[18]Press Statement of the Prosecutor of the ICC, 6 July 2015. https://www.icc-cpi.int/Pages/item.aspx?name=otp-stat-150704. Accessed 22 January 2019.

of prosecution, reinforced by the establishment of the ICC, gives hope that international criminal justice could play a more deterrent function (Rosenberg 2012).

Wippman (1999) believes that the link between international criminal prosecution and deterrence of future atrocities is "at best a plausible but largely untested assumption". On the other hand, Akhavan (2001) and Castillo (2007) aver that the international criminal justice system can indeed have a deterrent effect on leaders and even subordinates. According to them, resort to international criminal prosecution alongside other policy instruments could play substantial roles in discrediting and containing destabilising political leaders and their subordinates, and thereby weakening their influence. Also, in support of the deterrence capability of the international legal system, Aloyo et al. (2013) argue that no legal theory posits that everyone will be deterred, because not everyone is fully and equally rational, and because some people are high risk takers and may be willing to take the risk. Rather, what legal sanctions do, and what the international justice system is doing, is to *increase the disincentives for committing international crimes so that the crime is no longer worth the costs.*

The "increased use of human rights prosecutions and truth commissions around the world can be a valuable policy tool to contribute to lessening repression" (Kim and Sikkink 2009). The court may not be able to deter atrocities, but it can at least constrain a person's action by creating norms that will provide fewer tools to commit atrocities (Whiting 2012). This view is supported by Grono (2012), who argues that the ICC will have a long-term impact on deterrence.

The findings of this study corroborate the work of pro-deterrence scholars with some caveats. The results of the field study show that the ICC contributes to general deterrence in the three countries with varying results. It shows that the ICC contributes to general deterrence by challenging the culture of impunity, through its investigations and prosecutions, and by contributing to the promotion of accountability to the law.

The first pertinent issue in discussing the nexus between the ICC and deterrence is to understand the socio-legal environment in the three countries before the ICC's interventions, to properly situate them.

This context is the high level of impunity (particularly about prosecuting political leaders) that encased the legal systems of these countries before the ICC's interventions. In Kenya, no recognisable efforts were made by the government to try those who financed, masterminded and participated in election violence since independence, leading to a culture of impunity, which facilitated the recurrence of violence in subsequent elections (International Crisis Group 2012; Kenya National Commission on Human Rights 2008). There was a manifest lack of political will at high levels to genuinely address election violence as well as fears of prosecuting powerful people that perpetrated or financed election violence, which resulted in a "culture of impunity" and the withering of the rule of law (Jalloh 2009). This "culture of impunity" therefore encouraged some politicians to use ethnic violence as a political weapon against opponents, being certain that their crimes would go unpunished (Dunaiski 2014). In Côte d'Ivoire, after more than a decade of conflict and impunity between 2002 and 2010 that led to a collapsed judicial system in the North, and a limping one in the South, the country is just at the beginning stages of the process of rebuilding its justice institutions. In Uganda, accountability to the law suffered during the years of conflict. In the North, where the LRA held power, there was almost a total collapse of justice institutions. In the South, the rule of law also suffered as neither the LRA nor government forces that committed grave human rights abuses during the years of conflict in the North were prosecuted (Human Rights Watch 2005).

Against the background of years of unbridled impunity which has led to partial withering of the rule of law, in some cases caused by years of conflicts, as in Côte d'Ivoire and Uganda, and by weakness, corruption and incapacitation of the institutions responsible for administration of justice, in Kenya, the attempts by the ICC to prosecute key personalities involved in the violent conflicts were described by several respondents in these countries as capable of sending strong messages that the era of impunity is over.

Thus, the ICC has shown through its investigations and prosecutions that it has the capacity to impose sanctions, and that people can no longer rely on a weak internal system to escape culpability. The prosecution of some of those who allegedly bear the greatest responsibility for humanitarian atrocities is therefore *a clear departure from the past, and a strong indication that those who mastermind or participate in violence can be made to face trial at The Hague.*

The central point made by many respondents is that the ICC, despite its shortcomings and vulnerabilities, and the failure to convict any of the Kenyan leaders, has already established itself as an international court which could prosecute people who commit international crimes by investigating the atrocities committed and by attempting to sanction them. The argument that can be distilled in support of the deterrent impact of the ICC is that the ICC has made a clear statement through its investigations and prosecutions that the era of impunity is over. The fear of investigation and possible prosecution by the ICC influenced some people to act responsibly by avoiding acts that could attract the attention of the ICC, thus leading to general deterrence.

In Kenya, the ICC commenced investigations in 2009 and in 2010 issued summonses to six leaders in Kenya who were accused of masterminding, facilitating and funding the 2007/2008 PEV. This action made people to refrain from actions that could cause tension and from outright violence before, during and after the 2013 elections (Dunaiski 2014; Wamai 2013). A Solicitor and Advocate in Kenya clearly describe the impact of the ICC's intervention on the "culture of impunity" in Kenya thus:

> The persons taken to the ICC belonged to the high-class society in Kenya and traditionally those have always been above the law in this country. This had led to a culture of impunity to the extent that when the political class was given the opportunity to set up local mechanisms no one had the confidence that it could be done and would be above board. Secondly, the perpetrators did not imagine that the ICC would be able to investigate and act as they were in charge of virtually every organ of government.[19]

[19]Interview with a legal practitioner in Kenya 2014.

In his view "the fact that some people were charged was therefore a shock to the culture of impunity. The act of indicting persons previously perceived to be above the law gave a minor boost to the rule of law".[20] Nonetheless, the inability of the ICC to speedily conclude the cases from Kenya and the failure of the OTP to prove any of the charges against any of the top politicians charged erodes its capacity to contribute to deterrence.

In Côte d'Ivoire, the investigation of the 2010/211 PEV, the incapacitation and the prosecution of some top politicians were described as a strong statement by the ICC that those who commit atrocities could be punished, no matter the individual's position. Some respondents argue that these developments have contributed to a reduction in the level of violence in the country since 2011 and the relative peace in the country before the 2015 general elections. However, the failure of the OTP to charge individuals from both the Gbagbo and the FN was seen by some respondents as capable of reducing the deterrence capability of the ICC, because many Gbagbo supporters see the Court as "partial" and lacking legitimacy. The failure of the ICC to convict those charged may also have negative impact on the deterrence capability of the Court. Also, in Uganda, by "being there" the ICC has clearly stated that the era of impunity and "living above the law" for politicians that stretches back to the first Obote regime in 1962, and continued with subsequent regimes, including that of Yoweri Museveni may be over.[21] Breaking the cycle of impunity is important to peacemaking because a climate of impunity emboldens perpetrators to commit new crimes even at larger scales (Mendez and Kelley 2015).

These findings are in line with the major argument of deterrence theorists that threatening punishment deters crimes by increasing their costs. According to the cost-benefit argument of deterrence, the ICC increases the costs of committing crime by increasing the certainty and severity of prompt punishment (Dan Terzian 2011; Akhavan 2001; Castillo 2007; Aloyo et al. 2013). This finding does not suggest that

[20] Interview with a legal practitioner in Kenya 2014.

[21] Interview with a former head of the Uganda Human Rights Commission, 2013.

no further violations will take place after the ICC's interventions in these countries, or that international crimes have disappeared in these countries because of the deterrent impact of the Court. Rather, as a permanent international Court, the ICC is a constant reminder to all would-be violators of international norms that their conduct can be punished (Aloyo et al. 2013). Thus, because of the presence of the ICC and its permanent nature, the possibility of ICC's intervention is one factor future human rights abusers in Côte d'Ivoire, Kenya and Uganda may now take into consideration when making decisions.

In Chapter 2, the main principles of deterrence theory: severity, certainty and swiftness were discussed, and it was argued that against the old belief that severity of punishment will more likely lead to deterrence, there seem to be consensus in recent literature on deterrence that the likelihood and swiftness of punishment will more likely deter crimes than the severity of punishment (Sikkink 2011). Thus, measures such as increased policing, increased efficiency of law enforcement agencies and increased risk of apprehension are thought to have reduced crimes (Jo and Simmons 2014). In Africa, higher conviction rates have also been found to have the tendency to reduce crimes. Thus, the best measure to reduce crimes in Africa is *to increase the likelihood of punishment rather than the severity of punishment* (Jo and Simmons 2014).

In line with this argument, the ICC's investigations of the situations and prosecutions of key political leaders have clearly demonstrated that punishment is likely for those who commit international crimes. Given the high level of impunity for crimes committed by political leaders before the ICC's interventions, it is plausible to assume that the ICC has increased the likelihood of sanctions despite not convicting any of the persons indicted. The "increased likelihood of sanction", evidenced by the existence of the ICC, as an institution of international criminal justice, the ratification of the Rome Statute by governments of the three countries, the investigation of some of the crimes committed during the conflicts by the ICC and the prosecutions of some high-profile persons, *contributes* to deterring people from committing international crimes. This conclusion is in consonance with general deterrence theory which implies that investigations, indictments and prosecution should trigger a likelihood of punishment and increase deterrence (Jo and Simmons 2014; Dan Terzian 2011).

It was also argued in Chapter 2 that international criminal justice institutions may in the long term contribute to deterrence through the promotion of accountability to the law at the national level which may encourage states to prosecute and norm proliferation, which is the creation of a normative situation where extraordinary crimes are no longer accepted (Rosenberg 2012; Burke-White 2001). The enactment of laws and amendment of some existing ones to reflect international standards on accountability will mean that greater pressure will exist for accountability for those who may commit atrocities in future (Freeland 2010). The involvement of the ICC in the three countries has influenced the establishment of rule of law institutions, which is *contributing* to the creation of normative situations where extraordinary crimes are no longer accepted. Also, the ICC's involvement in the countries has contributed to influencing the creation of favourable conditions for good governance, internal monitoring and law enforcement which have improved prosecutorial deterrence (Jo and Simmons 2014). All these changes in the legal, judiciary, policing and law enforcement fields have come to the knowledge of leaders and became part of their calculations.

The results of the qualitative evidence presented and discussed in Chapters 4, 5 and 6 support the conclusion that the ICC contributes to general deterrence. The findings are in line with deterrence theories discussed in Chapter 2, that an increase in the likelihood of an imposition of sanctions and the actual imposition of sanctions will contribute to a decrease in violations. The assumption is based on the cost-benefit analysis that the ICC increases the costs of committing crime by increasing the certainty and severity of prompt punishment (Dan Terzian 2011). Before the intervention of the ICC, impunity for leaders almost enveloped the criminal justice system of the three countries. Political and business leaders were very rarely prosecuted for political crimes. Since the ICC's intervention, prosecution of leaders who commit international crime became more likely. The cost of committing international crimes increased, and the benefits have remained relatively constant.

Owing to the difficulties of measuring deterrence, the claim of deterrence can best be substantiated through specific examples (Mendez and Kelly 2015). A practical result of deterrence is conflict prevention. Evidence shows that violent conflicts in the three countries have been de-escalating. This is not to suggest that the ICC interventions directly led to the gradual de-escalation of these conflicts, but that the intervention of the ICC is a *contributory factor*. For instance, the Northern Uganda conflict has not been escalating, but rather has been de-escalating since the intervention of the ICC. The LRA has since 2005 virtually left Uganda, and life is gradually returning to normal in Northern Uganda. The ICC's intervention in Kenya is one factor that contributed to the relatively peaceful general elections in 2013 (Mamdani 2013; Lynch and Zgonec-Roze 2013; Wamai 2013). Côte d'Ivoire, a country that was enmeshed in violent conflicts for over ten years, is witnessing a gradual return to peace. Unlike the 2010 elections that directly culminated in the death of over 3000 persons, the 2015 elections witnessed minimal violence.

Therefore, it is reasonable to argue, based on the opinions of most of the respondents and the situations on the ground, that by its various activities, the ICC is contributing to conflict prevention through deterrence. Such actions include but are not limited to, prosecution of some persons, the ICC's numerous public comments on the situations, its investigations of the violent conflicts and the issue of arrest warrants.

7.6 The ICC and the Peace Processes in Côte d'Ivoire, Kenya and Uganda

A peace process in this study is seen as the process of ending conflicts and building peace after conflicts. Thus, in Uganda, the peace process includes but is not limited to all efforts to end the conflict between the LRA and the GoU, and build peace in the country, such as the Juba Peace Talks, the establishment of the Amnesty Commission, the creation of the International War Crime Division of the High Court of Uganda and the creation of Justice, Order and Law Sector. In Côte d'Ivoire, it includes all efforts to end the 2002/2003 armed conflict, promote peace and deal with the aftermaths of the 2010/2011 PEV. These include but are not limited to the numerous peace talks that took place between the rebels and the government, the establishment of the office of prime minister, the holding of the 2010 election, the security sector reforms, the creation of the Truth and Reconciliation Commission and the National Commission for Victims' Reconciliation and Compensation. In Kenya, the peace process commenced after the PEV with the appointment of the African Eminent Persons Group, the formation of the National Coalition Government, the promulgation of the 2010 Constitution and the numerous justice and governance reforms introduced by the GoK.

Although there is no direct mention in the Rome Statute that the ICC should promote peace (Nouwen 2012), it has been argued by several scholars that the ICC's intervention in a conflict or post-conflict situation can directly or indirectly impact on a peace process (International Centre for Transitional Justice 2013; Roht-Arriaza 2006; Turano 2011; Schabas 2001; Teitel 2000; Minow 1998). However, there is no consensus on *how* the ICC influences a peace process (Clark 2011). Article 16 on "deferral of investigation or prosecution" made an indirect reference to international peace and security. It provides that "no investigation or prosecution may be commenced or proceeded with under this Statute for a period of 12 months after the Security Council and in a resolution adopted under Chapter VII of the Charter of the United Nations, has requested the Court to that effect". Chapter VII refers to "actions with respect to threats to the peace, breaches of the peace, and acts of aggression".

This section uses two methods to comparatively assess the impact of the ICC's involvement on the peace processes in the three countries. First, it draws from the conclusions of this study in this chapter on the influence of the ICC on the four variables used to verify the nexus between the ICC and peace processes. Second, this study relies on the responses of respondents on the impact of the ICC on peace processes. Respondents were asked whether the ICC complicates/stalls, or facilitates, or has other impacts on the peace process in each country. The majority of those interviewed in the three cases contend that the ICC contributes positively to peace processes in the respective countries. Of the 22 persons interviewed in Uganda, 14 think the ICC has contributed positively to the peace process in Uganda by promoting accountability, by fighting impunity, by bringing international attention to the conflict which made the "GoU to sit up" and by contributing to the

Juba Peace Talks. Most of the respondents, however, think that the most important contribution of the ICC to the process is that it has created a sense of accountability, which was not there before the ICC intervention. A staff member of an international organisation in Uganda states: "the ICC contributes to the peace process by creating a sense of accountability that those who commit international crimes will be punished. The ICC has also influenced the promotion of awareness of the use of law in conflict resolution".[22] This point that the ICC influences the peace process through the promotion of accountability to the law was also amplified by a human rights advocate and law teacher in Uganda when she states:

> Another positive impact is that the dynamics changed on the part of the government because it introduced a new wave of accountability, and the government became more responsible in prosecuting the war since it is bound by the ICC Statute. The conflict became an arena of international watchers, and this promoted transparency, accountability and even fear of repercussions by the international community acting through the ICC. Another positive impact was that it promotes victims' rights, because of the internationalisation of the conflict.[23]

The ICC is also perceived to have contributed to the peace process in Uganda by drawing the attention of the international community to the humanitarian crises in Northern Uganda. The main argument, which was supported by many respondents, was that the intervention of the ICC brought a wave of international attention to Uganda which was unprecedented, and which forced the GoU to sit up and to act according to international standards on accountability. Speaking on how the ICC "internationalised" the conflict, which also assisted the peace process, she further states that:

---

[22]Interview with a human rights advocate and lecturer in law at Makerere University, Uganda, 2013.

[23]Interview with a human rights advocate and lecturer in law at Makerere University, Uganda, 2013.

> One of the positive impacts of the ICC is that it introduced a situation where the fighters knew that it was not a Northern Uganda issue, and they cannot hide from the gaze of the international community. In the ICC we see the international community. The ICC "internationalised" the conflict and brought international gaze on the conflict. The implication was that the world was watching, and this introduced an impetus to try peace.[24]

Also elaborating on how the ICC's intervention "internationalised" the conflict and propelled all local actors to worker harder, which helped the peace process, a lecturer in peace studies in Uganda argues that "the positive impact it had was that when the ICC intervened, there were activities and knowledge that apart from the government of Uganda, there was a bigger brother ready to take action".[25]

The ICC helped the peace process by propelling LRA to join the Juba Peace Process. This view was canvased by some of the respondents who think that it was doubtful if the LRA would have joined the Juba Peace Talks and if the ICC had not indicted its leaders. They argue that the LRA leadership calculated that they could neutralise the ICC intervention and arrest warrants by seeking peace. However, other respondents submit that the intervention of the ICC stalled the Juba Peace Talks and frustrated the peace process. For instance, the project coordinator of an NGO that works on peace and reconciliation argues that the intervention of the ICC "negatively interfered with the local mechanism. This development may have usurped the local mechanisms, and distorted the conflict resolution mechanisms known to the people".[26]

The preponderance of opinion of respondents in Kenya is that the ICC has positive effects on the peace process in the country by creating a sense of fear, panic and restraint on the political leadership,[27] which

---

[24]Interview with a human rights advocate and lecturer in law at Makerere University, Uganda, 2013.

[25]Interview with a lecturer in peace and conflict studies in Uganda, 2013.

[26]Interviews with a lecturer in peace and conflict studies in Uganda, 2013.

[27]Interview with a research student from Kenya, 2014.

forced them to play according to the rules enacted by the ICC, and for those in power to introduce justice and good governance reforms in Kenya. This sense of restraint and fear, according to a researcher from an international peace and justice organisation based in Kenya, "contributed to the peaceful elections in 2013, and still contributes to Kenya's march towards good governance".[28] This line of argument was amplified by a Kenyan lawyer who states that "the ICC is facilitating the peace process in Kenya through its contributions to deterrence. The Court may have contributed to deterring people from committing election violence during the 2013 election. It is also likely to contribute to deterrence in the long run".[29] The ICC played a role in the "prevention of major violence following the 2013 general elections as it was clear that there would be consequences for anyone involved in incitement for the same".[30] The ICC also made the 2013 elections one in which Kenya needed to demonstrate that it "was peaceful, and therefore stable enough to conduct local tribunals".[31] In a lesser sense, the "ICC process gave judicial reform some momentum so that local processes could be used as an alternative to the ICC processes under the principle of complementarity".[32]

A lecturer in law interviewed from Kenya, while supporting the argument that the ICC promotes the Kenyan peace process by creating awareness about international crimes which in turn promotes accountability to the law and deterrence, argues that a "large percentage of Kenyans are now aware that there can be consequences extending beyond the national machinery for the punishment of crimes, which then acts as a deterrence for persons who may wish to engage in wanton acts that breach the peace".[33] She further states that:

[28]Interview with an expert in security studies in Africa, 2014.

[29]Interview with a lawyer and researcher from Kenya, 2014.

[30]Interview with a transitional justice expert in Kenya, 2014.

[31]Interview with a transitional justice expert in Kenya, 2014.

[32]Interview with a transitional justice expert in Kenya, 2014.

[33]Interview with a professor of law at Kenyatta University, Kenya, 2014.

> Kenyans are now aware of the sub-categorisations of violence-related crimes beyond the individuals who may be arrested for physical execution of the crime. They are now aware that there are crimes pertaining to funders, planners, holders of offices that ought to act to prevent and/or stop violence, media broadcasters etc. This means that Kenyans are now aware they cannot sponsor violence remotely and escape the consequences, and they cannot hold offices which are responsible for maintaining the peace and escape sanction where they do not act accordingly.[34]

The central point is that the ICC promotes the peace process by challenging the culture of impunity. The ICC process has an impact on the culture of impunity in the country by investigating the crimes committed during the violence and prosecuting some leaders for the violence that took place during the 2007 elections. All of "Kenya's elections since the introduction of multi-party elections have been characterised by some element of ethnic tension and violence though not to the scale of the 2007 elections".[35] There have been feeble attempts to address the violence. At the local level, politics is defined and determined by inter-clan rivalry while at the national level it is the tribe. By "demonstrating that leaders can be held to account for their actions and puncturing the shield of impunity, the ICC helped to tone down ethnic tensions".[36]

The realisation that "one can be held to account may in time inform the political culture and over time lead to real peace processes in Kenya".[37] Another respondent summarised these opinions by averring that the ICC's main contributions to the peace process in Kenya are in the areas of accountability and deterrence. "The arrest of the initial six suspects demonstrated a higher power and many people with violent tendencies realised they could be sent to the Court if they were involved in such crimes and these people preach peace incessantly".[38] However, the failure by the ICC to sanction any of the leaders indicted gives the

---

[34]Interview with a professor of law at Kenyatta University, Kenya, 2014.

[35]Interview with a legal practitioner in Kenya, 2014.

[36]Interview with a legal practitioner in Kenya, 2014.

[37]Interview with a legal practitioner in Kenya, 2014.

[38]Interview with a legal representative for victims from Kenya at the ICC, 2014.

impression that the leaders can get away with atrocities even with the ICC, as they do with national courts.[39]

The majority of respondents' interviewed in Côte d'Ivoire think the ICC involvement is good for the peace process because it promotes accountability to the law, by serving as a useful mechanism to tackle impunity. The incarceration of Laurent Gbagbo was perceived by most of those interviewed as one prime factor that promotes peace. They argue that Gbagbo was a prominent actor in the conflict in the country for several years and his indictment and incarceration opened the road to the peaceful resolution of the conflict. According to an expert in international criminal law, "the ICC has done well to put Gbagbo out, which is good for diffusing of tension and which could facilitate the peace process".[40] The removal of Gbagbo by the ICC is good for the peace process in Côte d'Ivoire. It is true that keeping Gbagbo in prison prevents the escalation of the conflict, but for how long? The existence of a very strong part (camp Ouattara) and the existence of a crushed one create a relative state of peace which Alassane Ouattara benefits from today.[41]

Nevertheless, the failure of the ICC to indict people from all sides of the conflict does not promote the peace process but rather sows seeds of discord. A lecturer in peace and conflict studies in Côte d'Ivoire states that the way the peace process has been conducted from the start has been awkward, because it seems a justice of victors. There were "two sides to the conflict, but it seems now that only the side of Laurent has been paying the price. Therefore, the peace process is flawed in the first place, and this can have a very negative impact on the reconciliation process too".[42] Gbagbo is not the only person that committed atrocities in Côte d'Ivoire and "the ICC should do well to prosecute all those that are involved in committing international crimes in Côte d' Ivoire. This way the Court will be contributing more substantially to the peace

[39]Interview with professor emeritus of Law in Kenya, 2015.

[40]Interview with an expert in international criminal law, 2014.

[41]Interview with an expert in Francophone West Africa, 2014.

[42]Interview with a lecturer in peace and conflict studies in Côte d'Ivoire, 2015.

processes in the country".[43] A respondent in Ghana also does not think that the ICC promotes the peace process in Côte d'Ivoire. He recommends mediation and reconciliation instead of prosecution as the way to peace in Côte d'Ivoire. According to him, "prosecution of leaders in Côte d' Ivoire may exacerbate the conflict in the country. But, alternative mechanisms of conflict transformation promote a deep sense of remorse. Amnesty and other mechanisms of conflict resolution are more likely to lead to reconciliation and peace than prosecution".[44]

The preponderance of view is that the ICC contributes positively to the peace processes, by contributing to the promotion of accountability to the law, fighting impunity and through general deterrence. However, the ICC is seen by some respondents to be weak in the promotion of reconciliation, in its methodology which has led to failure to convict, in its influence on victims' rights, and in Uganda, and for having negative impacts on the Juba Peace Process.

7.7 The Nexus Between the Four Variables and Peace Processes in Côte d'Ivoire, Kenya and Uganda

This section analyses the impact of the four variables on peace processes. In Chapter 1, it was conceptualised that the ICC will be contributing positively to the peace process in the three countries if it promotes accountability to the law, deterrence, victims' rights and reconciliation. It was also argued that in each case, the degree and scope of impact will depend on the nature and scope of the impacts of the ICC on all or some of the variables. In Chapters 4, 5 and 6, data from the field were used to examine the impact of the ICC on the four variables. In Chapter 4, it was argued that the ICC has positive impacts on the peace process in Uganda by contributing positively to accountability to the

[43]Interview with a professor of international law, 2014.

[44]Interview with a peace activist in West Africa, and also a professor of philosophy at University of Ghana, Legon, 2014.

law and general deterrence. In Chapter 5, it was argued that the ICC contributes positively to the peace process in Kenya to the extent that it promotes accountability to the law by influencing the enactment of new laws and by contributing to deterrence through the promotion of accountability to the law. In Chapter 6, it was found that the ICC's involvement in Côte d'Ivoire has contributed positively to the peace process by promoting accountability to the law, by creating awareness of the plight of victims and by contributing to general deterrence. In this chapter, it was argued that the ICC does not contribute to reconciliation, and that in Côte d' Ivoire, the ICC is indeed having a negative impact on the process of reconciliation through its sequential prosecution policy, which has alienated the opposition. It was submitted that the ICC has positive influence on accountability to the law, deterrence and victims' rights in the three countries.

These conclusions are in line with the views of scholars such as Darehshori and Evenson (2010) who argue that the ICC's interventions in post-conflict situations promote the peace process and accountability to the law. They state that the existence of arrest warrants for leaders suspected of international crimes does not necessarily undermine the peace process. Freeland (2010), while discussing the effectiveness of international criminal justice, argues that it would be naïve to measure the effectiveness of an international justice system solely on the cessation of an armed conflict, and has called for a more nuanced approach to ending wars in which international accountability will be part of more holistic measures. Nouwen (2012) submits that the ICC by operationalising international law and by deterring crimes is inevitably contributing to peacebuilding in Africa. Lanz (2007) similarly argues that the peace and justice controversy in Northern Uganda should be understood as a manifestation of the tensions between different actors with different agendas and priorities, and that the ICC, despite its limitations, promotes the peace process in Uganda.

Clark (2011), in "Peace, Justice and the International Criminal Court", concludes that while "tensions can and do arise between peace and justice, this does not necessarily mean that the ICC represents a threat to peace". The way forward, according to her, is "to explore whether and how the ICC can contribute to peace as part of a comprehensive and holistic justice strategy". Goldstone (1996) argues that though "one must not expect too much from justice, for justice is merely one aspect of a multifaceted approach needed to secure enduring peace in a transitional society", justice can be a useful tool for "peace-keeping or peace-building. With it, countries emerging from periods of serious human rights violations can hope for an enduring peace. Without it, the terrible rate of war crimes will not abate". Zyberi (2015) also concludes that international courts by emphasising individual criminal accountability for mass atrocities "play a retributive as well as a preventive and deterrent role, which is potentially important for purposes of maintaining or restoring peace". Garcia-Godos (2015) thinks accountability "plays an important role in the pursuit of long-term peace because it contributes to rebuilding trust in post-conflict societies". Wegner (2015, 11) states that the nexus between the ICC and conflict resolution depends on some factors. He argues that the "procedural decisions taken by the Office of the Prosecutor and other organs of the Court, as well as local and regional perception of justice have an important impact on whether the ICC hampers or furthers conflict resolution", while Kersten (2016) argues that the effect of the ICC intervention is ultimately and inevitably mixed. In the views of Gissel (2017), the level and timing of the ICC involvement are key to the ICC impact on peace processes.

On the other hand, Drumbl (2007) argues that it has not been established that international justice contributes to peace. Similarly, with respect to the impacts of the ICTY on social peace in the former Yugoslavia, Meernik (2005) argues that there is little evidence to support the notion that "the ICTY had a positive impact on social peace in Bosnia" and that the effect "was the opposite of what was intended". He submits that "more often than not, ethnic tension responded with increased hostility towards one another after an arrest or judgement". Clark (2014) states that the negative impacts of the ICC on peace are normally mentioned with respect to Northern Uganda, to the extent that the issuance of arrest warrants to five leaders of the LRA and the refusal of the OTP to withdraw the arrest warrants contributed to the refusal of LRA to sign the peace agreement and therefore impacted negatively on peace.

Further to the points made above, it is argued that accountability to the law promotes the peace process by contributing to the promotion of the rule of law, by strengthening the capacity of the state to tackle impunity and by providing more access to justice. International courts, according to Zyberi (2015), contribute to "strengthening of the rule of law and human rights protection, which are important for a peaceful society". Accordingly, without accountability to the law, "human rights will be denied, crime will flourish, impunity for past conflict-related crimes will persist, undermining legitimacy and prospects for reconciliation" (United States Institute for Peace 2015) and peace. In this chapter, the high level of impunity in the three countries was analysed. Promotion of accountability to the law will put more pressure on the conditions that promote and sustain impunity, which could lead to the prosecution of more persons, since the aim of accountability to the law is to "mitigate against capture of justice institutions by political and economic spoilers that enables impunity, favouritism and unequal application of the law" (United States Institute for Peace 2015). In the three countries, unlike before, attempts are being made to punish those that committed grave crimes during the violent conflicts. Apart from the ICC's prosecutions, at least 150 persons have been prosecuted for crimes committed during the 2010/2011 PEV in Côte d'Ivoire, fourteen persons have been prosecuted in Kenya, and one person is being prosecuted in Uganda. These prosecutions are significant because they represent a departure from the past when people who committed atrocities were rarely prosecuted. Curbing impunity will contribute to the peace process since impunity has been identified as one of the causes of the recurring violence (CIPEV 2008).

Therefore, promotion of accountability to the law will contribute to reducing impunity, and reduction in the level of impunity will contribute to peace through the promotion of the rule of law. The rule of law is based on justice and security, two of the most essential prerequisites for sustainable peace and development (UNDP 2011). Also, incorporation of new laws, amendment of existing ones and judicial reforms will mean that greater pressure will exist for judicial accountability for perpetrators of gross violation of human rights to be initiated at local levels (Freeland 2010).

It is argued in this study that the ICC contributes to general deterrence. The practical impact of deterrence is conflict prevention. Some of the aims of conflict prevention is to strengthen likely *preventors*, such as the ICC, and reduce likely causes of war or mass violence (Miall et al. 1999). Bosco (2011) states that the ICC contributes to conflict prevention by deterrence through preliminary examination, the conduct of investigations, choice of charges, sentencing policy and public outreach. Zyberi (2015) opines that international Courts, by emphasising individual criminal accountability for mass atrocities, "play a retributive as well as a preventive and deterrent role, which is potentially important for purposes of maintaining or restoring peace". According to Corradetti, the ICC contributed to conflict prevention through deterrence during the 2013 elections in Kenya, and "the significant decrease of violence in the aftermath of the contested electoral turn-outs of 2013 has been accompanied by a general popular trust in the actions of the ICC (social deterrence)" (2015).

There are two main aspects of conflict prevention. One is establishing measures for the prevention of violent conflicts. This involves developing short-, medium- and long-term measures for conflict prevention. The second aspect of conflict prevention involves preventing relapses into wars or violent conflicts after peace agreements have been fully executed by the parties. The ICC contributes to conflict prevention in these countries, in the second sense, through deterrence. The practical impact has been an avoidance of relapses to conflicts which has contributed to de-escalation of conflicts in Kenya, Côte d' Ivoire and Uganda, since the ICC intervention. Evidence of de-escalation of conflicts was discussed in this chapter and shown from the facts on the ground as large-scale violent conflicts have not occurred since the ICC intervened. In this way, the ICC contributes to the peace processes in these countries.

It was argued in this chapter that the ICC contributes to the promotion of victims' rights in two ways. The first is by influencing some national governments to establish pro-victim rights institutions, to the extent that some of these pro-victims' rights agencies were established after the ICC intervened. Also, the ICC's reparation provisions are a novelty in international criminal law because they provide victims of conflicts with actual rights to reparation. However, the ICC victims' redress is also symbolic since only a few persons are covered by the mechanism and such persons are only represented by Counsel (Moffett 2014). The ICC, therefore, does not impact on the peace process through its impacts on victims' rights, since these contributions are very minimal and have not concretised to have any significant impact on peace processes. This conclusion is further buttressed by facts. As of January 2019, only 6187 victims were approved to be represented by lawyers in cases from the three countries at the ICC. This is a negligible number, taking into account the estimated numbers of victims of the violent conflicts in these countries. Also, since none of the persons from these countries has been convicted, the ICC has not ordered any kind of reparation for victims. As of March 2018, the TFV has only executed some projects in Uganda and has not commenced any project in Côte d'Ivoire and Kenya. Further, the involvement of some victims in the trial as witnesses at The Hague could lead to re-victimisation.

The discussions in this book indicate that the ICC does not promote reconciliation in the three countries. In Côte d'Ivoire, the intervention of the ICC was shown to be divisive and contributes negatively to the process of reconciliation in the country. This is a fundamental drawback. Shinoda (2005) argues that the contributions of international justice to reconciliation are limited, and that the link between international prosecution and reconciliation is loose. Clark (2014) also submits that international justice does not contribute to reconciliation, and argues that the ICTY has not contributed to ethnic reconciliation in BiH, Croatia or Kosovo. Also, none of the six persons from the three countries that have appeared before the ICC pleaded guilty to any or all charges. A guilty plea is in many ways similar to some non-judicial mechanisms of dealing with perpetrators of mass violence and could have positive influence on reconciliation (Vincente 2003). The Trial Chamber of the ICTY in its sentencing decision in *The Prosecutor v. Biljana Plavšić (Sentencing Judgement*, of 27 February, 2003, 25) held among other things, "that acknowledgement and full disclosure of serious crimes are very important when establishing the truth in relation to such crimes. This, together with acceptance of responsibility for the committed wrongs, will promote reconciliation".[45] Though, Mrs. Plavšić's guilty plea later became controversial Subotic (2012), however, the main issue still remains as states by Combs (2007, 224) that generally, defendants who "acknowledged their atrocities rather than deny the obvious, who accept responsibility rather than blame their enemies, and who apologise to victims rather than continue to demonise them stand a better chance of reintegrating and advancing peace efforts".

Therefore, it is argued that in Côte d'Ivoire, Kenya and Uganda, the ICC does not contribute to reconciliation in the short term and to that extent does not contribute to the peace processes in the three countries.

7.8 Conclusion

This chapter comparatively examined how the ICC influences accountability to the law, victims' rights, reconciliation and deterrence in Côte d'Ivoire, Kenya and Uganda. The chapter argues that the ICC promotes accountability to the law in the three countries to the extent that it influences the enactment of accountability laws, the establishment of justice institutions, attracts international attention and debate to accountability and the dangers of impunity in the countries, and generally influenced the prosecution of more persons who committed atrocities during the violent conflicts by national courts.

It was also submitted that the ICC does not contribute to reconciliations in the short term in these countries but is rather exacerbating the tension in Côte d'Ivoire through its sequential prosecution policy which has so far resulted in the prosecution of only persons from the Gbagbo camp. The impacts of the ICC on victims' rights are insignificant to promote peace, because of the minimal number of victims participating in the proceedings, and because the ICC has not convicted many of those charged with crimes from these countries. Finally, it was argued

[45]The Prosecutor v. Biljana Plavšić, Sentencing Judgement of 27 February, 2003, Case No: IT-00-39&40/1-S 24.

that the ICC contributes to conflict prevention, through general deterrence, by challenging impunity in the three countries, through actions like prosecution of some persons, numerous public comments on the situations, investigations of the violent conflicts, and by issuing arrest warrants.

This chapter concludes that the ICC contributes to peace processes through its positive impact on general deterrence and accountability to the law. On the other hand, the ICC's influence on victims' rights and reconciliation does not result in positive result on peace processes. The effect of the ICC on victims' rights, at this stage, is seen to be too minimal to make any positive contribution to peace processes. Also, the ICC is found to be having no impact on reconciliation, and so this aspect does not contribute to peace processes. In Côte d'Ivoire, the intervention of the ICC was found to be having a negative influence on reconciliation and to that extent affects peace process negatively in that country. Generally, the weaknesses of the ICC are the slow pace of justice by the Court, the inability of the Court to ensure that most of those that committed atrocities are arrested and prosecuted, the inability of the Court to ensure proper investigations of crime situations and prosecution of suspected persons (a major issue in Kenya and Côte d'Ivoire) and the failure of the Court to prosecute suspects from all sides of the divide, which is causing uncertainties in Côte d'Ivoire and Uganda.

References

Akhavan, Payam. 2001. "Beyond Impunity: Can International Criminal Justice Prevent Future Atrocities?" *The American Journal of International Law* 95.7: 7–31.

Aloyo, Eamon, Yvonne Dutton, and Lindsay Heger. 2013. "Does the International Criminal Court Deter Torture?" One Earth Future Foundation. Accessed May 30, 2013. http://oneearthfuture.org/research/publications/does-international-criminalcourt-deter-torture.

BBC News. 2015. "Ivory Coast's Former First Lady Simone Gbagbo Jailed". British Broadcasting Corporation, March 10. Accessed February 1, 2016. http://www.bbc.com/news/world-africa-31809073.

Bensouda, Fatou. 2008. "Justice, Reconciliation and the Role of the ICC". Accessed April 15, 2013. http://www.idea.net/resources/analysis/www.idea.net/resources/analysis/.

Bloomfield, David, Teresa Barnes, and Luc Huyse, eds. 2003. "Reconciliation After Violent Conflict". International Institute of Electoral Assistance and Democracy. Accessed February 11, 2016. http://www.un.org/en/peacebuilding.

Bosco, David. 2011. "The International Criminal Court and Crime Prevention: By-Product or Conscious Goal?" *Michigan Journal of International Law* 19: 163–197.

Burke-White, William. 2001. "Reframing Impunity: Applying the Liberal International Law Theory to an Analysis of Amnesty Legislation". *Harvard International Law Journal* 42: 467–535.

Castillo, Pablo. 2007. "Rethinking Deterrence: The International Criminal Court in Sudan". UNISCI Discussion Paper, No. 13. Accessed June 11, 2013. http://www.pendientemigracion.usm.es/info.

Clamp, Kerry. 2014. *Restorative Justice in Transition*. London: Routledge.

Clark, Janine. 2011. "Peace, Justice and the International Criminal Court". Journal *of International Criminal Justice* 9: 521–545.

Clark, Janine Natalya. 2014. *International Trials and Reconciliation*. New York: Routledge.

Combs, Nancy Armoury. 2007. *Guilty Pleas in International Criminal Law: Constructing a Restorative Justice Approach*. Stanford: Stanford University Press.

Commission of Inquiry on Post-Election Violence. 2008. Accessed May 23, 2014. http://www.kenyalaw.org/Downloads/Reports/Commission_of_Inquiry_into_Post_Election_Violence.pdf.

Corradetti, Claudio. 2015. "The Priority of Conflict Deterrence and the Role of the International Criminal Court in Kenya's Post-Electoral Violence 2007–2008 and 2013". *Human Rights Review* 16: 257–272.

Dan Terzian. 2011. "What Measures Should Be Taken to Maximize the Crime Prevention Impact of the International Criminal Court?" Accessed August 5, 2015. http://iccforum.com/forum/prevention.

Darehshori, Sara, and Elizabeth Everson. 2010. "Peace, Justice and the International Criminal Court". Oxford Transitional Justice Research Working Papers Series. Accessed May 1, 2013. http://www.otjr.csls.ox.ac.uk.

de Vos, Christian. 2015. "All Roads Leads to Rome: Implementation and Domestic Politics in Kenya and Uganda". In *Contested Justice: The Politics and Practice of International Criminal Law Intervention*, edited by Christian de Vos, Sara Kendall, and Carsten Stahn, 377–378. Cambridge: Cambridge University Press.

Drumbl, Mark. 2007. *Atrocity, Punishment and International Law*. Cambridge: Cambridge University Press.

Dunaiski, Maurice. 2014. "Accountability vs Stability? Assessing the ICC Intervention in Kenya". E-International Relations. Accessed August 20, 2015. http://www.e-ir.info/2014/01/09/accountability-vs-stability-assessing-the-iccs-intervention-in-kenya.

Fisher, Martina. 2010. "Transitional Justice and Reconciliation: Theory and Practice". Accessed April 12, 2013. http://www.berghofhandbook.net/documents/publications/fisher_tj_and_rec_%20handbook.

Fletcher Laurel, and Harvey Weinstein. 2002. "Violence and Social Repair: Rethinking the Contributions of Justice to Reconciliation". *Human Rights Quarterly* 24: 573–639.

Freeland, Steven. 2010. "Effectiveness of International Criminal Justice". Accessed September 20, 2015. http://www.austlii.edu.au/au/journals/ALRS/2008/16.html.

Garcia-Godos, Jemima. 2015. "It Is About Trust: Transitional Justice and Accountability in the Search for Peace". In *Promoting Peace Through International Law*, edited by Cecilia Marrcela Bailliet and Kjetil Mujezinovic Larsen, 321–343. Oxford: Oxford University Press.

Garkawe, Sam. 2003. "Victims and the International Criminal Court: Three Major Issues". *International Criminal Law Review* 3: 345–367.

Gissel, Line Engbo. 2017. *The International Criminal Court and Peace Processes in Africa*. London: Routledge.

Goetz, Mariana. 2008. "The International Criminal Court and Its Relevance to Affected Communities". In *Courting Conflict? Peace and the ICC*, edited by Nicholas Waddel and Phil Clark, Royal African Society. Accessed May 20, 2013. http://www.royalafricansociety.org.

Goldstone, Richard. 1996. "Justice as a Tool for Peacemaking: Truth Commissions and International Criminal Tribunals". *N.Y.U. International Law and Politics* 28: 485503.

Grono, Nick. 2012. "The Deterrent Effect of the ICC on the Commission of International Crimes by Government Leaders". Accessed April 23, 2014. http://www.crisesgroup.org/en/publication.

Human Rights Watch. 2005. "Uprooted and Forgotten: Impunity and Human Rights Abuses in Northern Uganda". Human Rights Watch Report. Accessed October 16, 2014. https://www.hrw.org/reports/2005/uganda0905/uganda0905.pdf.

Human Rights Watch. 2016. "To Consolidate This Peace of Ours". Human Rights Watch Report. Accessed February 28, 2016. http://www.hrw.org/report/2015/12/08/consolidate-peace-ours/human-rights-agenda-cote-divoire.

International Centre for Transitional Justice. 2013 "Criminal Justice". International Centre for Transitional Justice Briefing. Accessed May 10, 2013. http://www.ictj.org.

International Centre for Transitional Justice. 2015. "Pursuing Accountability for Serious Crimes in Uganda's Courts". International Centre for Transitional Justice Briefing. Accessed August 13, 2015. https://www.ictj.org/sites/default/files/ICTJ-Briefing-Uganda-Kwoyelo-2015.

International Crises Group. 2012. "Kenya: Impact of the ICC Proceedings". International Crises Group: Policy Briefing, Africa Briefing No. 84. Accessed April 12, 2016. http://www.crisisgroup.org/en/regions/africa/horn-of-africa/kenya/b084-kenya-impact-of-the-icc-proceedings.aspx.

Jalloh, Charles Chernor. 2009. "Kenya's Dangerous Dance with Impunity". JURIST—Forum. Accessed August 13, 2014. http://jurist.law.pitt.edu/forumy/2009/08/kenyas-dangerous-dance-with-impunity.php.

Jo, Hyeran, and Beth Simmons. 2014. "Can the International Criminal Court Deter Atrocity?" Accessed April 13, 2015. http://papers.ssrn.com/sol3/papers.cfm?abstract_id=2552820.

Jurdi, Nidal Nabil. 2011. *The International Criminal Court and National Courts: A Contentious Relationship*. Surrey: Ashgate.

Kenya National Commission on Human Rights. 2008. "On the Brink of the Precipice: A Human Rights Account of Kenya's Post-2007 Election Violence". Accessed June 17, 2014. http://www.knchr.org/portals/0/reports/knchr_report_on_the_brink_of_the_precipe.pdf.

Kersten, Mark. 2016. *Justice in Conflict*. Oxford: Oxford University Press.

Kim, Hunjoon, and Kathryn Sikkink. 2009. "Explaining the Deterrence Effect of Human Rights Prosecutions for Transitional Countries". *International Studies Quarterly* 54: 1–46.

Ku, Julian, and Jide Nzeribe. 2006. "Do International Criminal Tribunals Deter or Exacerbate Humanitarian Atrocities?" *Washington University Law Review* 84: 777833.

Lanz, David. 2007. "The ICC's Intervention in Northern Uganda: Beyond the Simplicity of Peace vs. Justice". Accessed September 4, 2014. http://www.reliefweb.int/sites/reliefweb.int/files/resources/EC66215A0071F156C12573910051D06D-Full_Report.pdf.htm.

Lynch, Gabrielle, and Misa Zgonec-Roze. 2013. "The ICC Intervention in Kenya". African/International Law. AFP/ILP 2013/01. Chatham House. Accessed October, 2014. https://www.chathamhouse.org/sites/files/chathamhouse/public/Research/Africa/0213pp_icc_kenya.pdf.

Mamdani, Mahmood. 2013. "Kenya: The ICC's Election". Al Jazeera. Accessed September 14, 2014. http://www.aljazeera.com/indepth/opinion/2013/03/20133982222657687.html.

May, Larry, and Zachary Hoskins. 2010. *International Criminal Law and Philosophy*. Cambridge: Cambridge University Press.

McCarthy, Conor. 2012. "Victims' Redress and International Criminal Justice". *Journal of International Criminal Justice* 10: 352–372.

Meernik, James. 2005. "Justice and Peace? How the International Criminal Tribunal Affects Societal Peace in Bosnia". *Journal of Peace Research* 42: 271–289.

Mendes, Errol. 2010. *Peace and Justice at the International Criminal Court: A Court of Last Resort*. Cheltenham: Edward Elgar.

Mendez, Juan. 2010. "National Reconciliation, Transitional Justice, and the International Criminal Court". *Ethics and International Affairs* 15: 25–44.

Mendez, Juan, and Jeremy Kelly. 2015. "Peace Making, Justice and the ICC". In *Contested Justice: The Politics and Practice of International Criminal Court Interventions*, edited by Christian de Vos, Sara Kendall, and Carsten Stahn, 479–496. Cambridge: Cambridge University Press.

Miall, Huge, Oliver Ramsbotham, and Tom Woodhouse. 1999. *Contemporary Conflict Resolution*. Cambridge: Polity.

Minow, Martha. 1998. *Between Vengeance and Forgiveness: Facing History After Genocide and Mass Violence*. Boston, MA: Beacon Press, 1998.

Moffett, Luke. 2014. *Victims Before the International Criminal Court*. New York: Routledge.

New York Times. 2015. "Kenya: Official Apology for Past Wrongs". *New York Times*, March 27. Accessed January 20, 2016. http://www.nytimes.com/2015/03/27/world/africa/kenya.

Newsweek. 2015. "Former International Court of Justice Judge: Dick Cheney Should Face Prosecution". *Newsweek*, July 6. Accessed 21 January, 2019. https://www.newsweek.com/british-judiciarylord-jannericc-judgeauschwitz-jewsholocaustprofessor-law-602725.

Nouwen, Sarah. 2012. "The International Criminal Court: A Peacebuilder in Africa?" In *Peacebuilding, Power, and Politics in Africa*, edited by Curtis Devon and Dzinesa Gwinyayi, 171–192. Athens: Ohio University Press, 2012.

Nouwen, Sarah. 2013. *Complementarity in the Line of Fire: The Catalysing Effect of the International Criminal Court in Uganda and Sudan*. Cambridge: Cambridge University Press.
Roht-Arriaza, Naomi. 2006. "The New Landscape of Transitional Justice". In *Transitional Justice in the Twenty-First Century: Beyond Truth Versus Justice*, edited by Naomi Roht-Arriaza and Javier Mariezcurrena, 1–16. Cambridge: Cambridge University Press.
Rosenberg, Sheri. 2012. "The Relationship Between the International Criminal Court and the Prevention of Mass Atrocities". Accessed April 24, 2014. http://www.genocidepreventionnow.org/Portals/0/docs/Relationship_ICC_Prevention_HU.pdf.
Schabas, William. 2001. "International Law Responses to Conflict". In *Turbulent Peace: The Challenges of Managing International Conflict*, edited by Chester Croaker, Fen Hampson, and Pamela Aall, 603–618. Washington, DC: United States Institute for Peace.
Scheffer, David. 1999. "War Crimes and Crimes Against Humanity". *Pace International Law Review* 112: 319–340.
Shinoda, Hideaki. 2005. "Peace-Building by the Rule of Law: An Examination of Intervention in the Form of International Tribunals". *International Journal of Peace Studies* 17: 1–20. Accessed March 26, 2016. http://www.gmu.edu/programs/icar/ijps/vol7_1/Shinoda.htm.
Sikkink, Kathryn. 2011. *The Justice Cascade: How Human Rights Prosecutions Are Changing World Politics*. New York: W.W. Norton.
Subotic, Jelena. 2012. "The Cruelty of False Remorse: Biljana Plavsic at The Hague". *Southeastern Europe* 36.1: 39–59.
Teitel, Ruti. 2000. *Transitional Justice*. Oxford: Oxford University Press.
Tolbert, David. 2013. "Can International Justice Foster Reconciliation?" Accessed April 16, 2013. http://www.aljazeera.com/indepth/opinion/2013/04/201341074354441 90.htm.
Tolbert, David. 2015. "Doing Right by Victims in Côte d' Ivoire: Qattara's Second Term". *The Huffington Post*, November 11. Accessed November 24, 2015. http://www.huffingtonpost.com/david-tolbert/doing-right-by-victims.
Turano, Laura. 2011. "The Gender Dimension of Transitional Justice Mechanisms". *New York University International Law and Politics* 43: 1045–1085.
Tyler, Tom. 2006. *Why People Obey the Law*. Princeton: Princeton University Press.

United Nations Development Program. 2011. "Strengthening the Rule of Law in Crisis-Affected and Fragile Situations". Accessed June 2, 2015. http://www.undp.org/content/dam/undp/library/crisis%20prevention/Global%20Programme%20Phase%20II%20-%20FINAL.pdf.

United States Institute for Peace. 2015. "Accountability to Law". Accessed March 23, 2016. http://www.usip.org/guiding-principles.

Vicente, Alejandra. 2003. "Justice Against Perpetrators: The Role of Prosecutor in Peacemaking and Reconciliation". Working Paper No. 2, April, 2003. Accessed April 2, 2016. http://www.badil.org/phocadownloadpap/Badil_docs/Working_Papers/WP-E-02.pdf.

Wamai, Njoki. 2013. "The International Criminal Court and the Kenyan Election". Gates Cambridge. Accessed July 19, 2015. https://www.gates-cambridge.org/multimedia/blog/international-criminal-court-and-kenyan-election.

Wanyeki, Muthoni. 2012. "The International Criminal Court Cases in Kenya: Origin and Impact". Institute for Security Studies, Paper 237. Accessed January 21, 2015. https://www.issafrica.org/uploads/Paper237.pdf.

Wegner, Patrick. 2015. *The International Criminal Court in Ongoing Intrastate Conflicts*. Cambridge: Cambridge University Press.

Whiting, Alex. 2012. "The International Criminal Court Impact". Accessed April 22, 2013. http://today.law.harvard.edu/whiting-offers-views-on-the-international-criminal-courts-impact/.

Wippman, David. 1999. "Atrocities, Deterrence, and the Limits of International Justice". *Fordman International Law Journal* 23: 473–488.

Zyberi, Gentian. 2015. "The Role and Contribution of International Courts in Furthering Peace as an Essential Community Interest". In *Promoting Peace Through International Law*, edited by Cecilia Marrcela Bailliet and Kjetil Mujezinovic Larsen, 345–367. Oxford: Oxford University Press.

8

Conclusions and Recommendations

It is necessary to prevent the repetition of violence and to dismantle the structures that enable violence in the first place...we may not have empirical proof that prosecution of international crimes prevents their recurrence in future; we do know that a climate of impunity is an invitation to perpetrators to commit new abuses and perhaps even to escalate existing conflicts. (Mendez Juan and Kelly Jeremy)[1]

8.1 Introduction

This book examined the impact of the ICC on peace processes in three countries. It examined how the new institution (ICC) has struggled to prosecute people who allegedly committed gross human rights violations during violent conflicts and has revealed some of the weaknesses in the conception of the ICC, which, among other things, did not take

[1]Mendez, Juan, and Kelly Jeremy. 2015. "Peace Making, Justice and the ICC". In *Contested Justice: The Politics and Practice of International Criminal Court Interventions*, edited by Christian de Vos, Sara Kendall, and Caesten Stahn, 479–496. Cambridge: Cambridge University Press.

L. N. Malu, *The International Criminal Court and Peace Processes*,
Palgrave Studies in Compromise after Conflict,
https://doi.org/10.1007/978-3-030-19905-0_8

full consideration of the difficulties and complexities of prosecuting international crimes. The quest by the international community to punish those who commit atrocities is based on the belief that promoting international accountability promotes respect for human rights, peace and security.

International accountability for crimes has grown rapidly since the Second World War. Three types of international mechanisms have been developed and deployed. These are international tribunals, internationalised or hybrid courts and the ICC (Williams 2012). But there are uncertainties and controversies about how international justice mechanisms influence peace processes. In this book, the impact of the involvement of the ICC on selected post-conflict situations was analysed. Also, by examining the interactions between the ICC and national institutions, this book showed the tensions and challenges of the involvement of the ICC in these countries, and how the collision of international accountability and national sovereignty influences peace processes. This chapter presents the important issues from the discussions of the involvement of the ICC in the three countries, as well as the causes and nature of the violent conflicts, the review of literature, and the analysis of the major findings of the study to provide a synthesis of the main arguments of this book. It summarises the research findings, outlines the major recommendations, acknowledges the limitations of the study and closes with a final observation.

8.2 Summary of the Main Issues Discussed in This Book

This book has examined how the ICC influences the peace processes in Côte d'Ivoire, Kenya and Uganda. Relying on qualitative studies, this study comparatively analysed the long and the short-term impact of the interventions of the ICC in Uganda (in 2004), in Kenya (after the 2007/2008 post-election violence) and in Côte d'Ivoire (after the 2010/2011 post-election violence). The aim of this study is to provide an evidence-based account of how the involvement of the ICC in these countries influences the processes of promoting peace. The study developed and relied on an analytical framework that is based on four variables: deterrence, victims' rights, reconciliation and accountability to the law (which were transformed into the research issues of the study), to gauge how the ICC contributes to peace processes. It was argued that the ICC will be contributing positively to peace processes in Côte d'Ivoire, Kenya and Uganda if the Court promotes reconciliation, accountability to the law, the rights of victims of atrocities and deters future atrocities or gross human rights violations. Also, the ICC may not be contributing to the peace process in a country by not contributing to, or by complicating efforts to promote accountability to the law or protection of victims' rights or deterrence or reconciliation. It was also submitted that the level of influence will depend on the nature, degree and scope of impact on all or some of the variables.

Drawing upon interviews with national experts in these three countries, and relying on its analytical framework, it argues that the ICC's intervention has had multiple impacts on the situations across these countries, and that, despite some arguments to the contrary, the ICC contributes positively to peace processes through deterrence and the promotion of accountability to the law. However, there is minimal evidence that the ICC contributes to peace processes in these countries through the promotion of reconciliation and victims' rights.

The essence of international accountability is to punish the perpetrators of atrocities, and according to paragraph 5 of the Preamble to the Rome Statute "put an end to impunity for the perpetrators of these crimes, and contribute to the prevention of such crimes". This, in the words of paragraph 3, is because such "grave crimes threaten the peace, security and well-being of the world". This study contributes to knowledge of international accountability by explaining just how the ICC contributes to peace processes and to the existing body of knowledge of international accountability in four ways. First, it contributes to the research methodology in international justice by formulating a framework for assessing how international accountability contributes to the peace process. Second, the study provides an evidence-based account of how the ICC influences peace processes. It shows *how* the ICC influences the peace processes in the three countries and provides evidence of *what* the ICC brings to the table in a peace process. These contributions are useful to the peace and justice debate, transitional justice discourse and understanding of conflict transformation. Third, this study provides valuable insights into how international accountability is confronting impunity. These contributions, put together, provide useful guides on which aspect of the ICC's work contributes to peace processes.

8.3 Summary of Main Findings

The major findings of this study, which were discussed in Chapter 7, are summarised in this section. Each finding answers a research question of this book, and an aggregation of all the findings satisfies the objective of the study.

8.3.1 The Impact of the Intervention of the ICC on Promotion of Accountability to the Law

The study found that the impact of the ICC on accountability to the law in the three countries is positive. This, as demonstrated in Chapters 4, 5, 6 and 7, is to the extent that the ICC has challenged the culture of impunity in these countries. The ICC also contributed to influencing the establishment of new institutions, and the enactment of new laws that promote accountability. However, the nature and scope of the impact varied in different countries. Each country has its own peculiarities, the nature of the conflict, type of conflict ending, government system, political structure, dynamics and legal system, which influence how the ICC's involvement in its internal affairs impact on accountability to the law.

The influence of the ICC could be divided into three types: norm creation, establishment of new or modified institutions for justice administration and challenging impunity. Norm creation is perhaps where the ICC created the most impact. Since the interventions of the ICC, new laws, acts, rules and regulations have been enacted/drafted or existing ones have been amended, to mimic international laws.

The ICC also has had an appreciable impact on the establishment of institutions and agencies that promote accountability to the law. The ICC, by prosecuting individuals that allegedly bear the greatest responsibility for crimes committed, challenges the culture of impunity in these countries. Although the failure of the ICC to convict top politicians reduces its contributions to the campaign against impunity, the import of indicting, a former president, a sitting president and a sitting vice-president should not be underrated. It strengthens the fight against impunity.

Excluding Côte d'Ivoire, where about 150 persons were prosecuted, the ICC involvement has sparked minimal domestic prosecutions in other countries. In Uganda, the International Crimes Division of the High Court of Uganda has recorded only one prosecution, while in Kenya, though some people have been prosecuted for offences committed during the 2007/2008 post-election violence for smaller offences such as theft and robbery, only fourteen persons have been prosecuted for grievous crimes such as murder, rape and arson (Human Rights Watch 2016).

8.3.2 The Impact of the Intervention of the ICC on Promotion of Reconciliation

The impact of the intervention of the ICC on reconciliation is complex. The ICC became involved in already divided countries with deep animosities, political differences that go back to the early independence years and ethnic politics. The impact of the intervention of the ICC on reconciliation in the short run is not positive. Reconciliation is also situational and a process that is linked to the political and economic history of each country. In Côte d'Ivoire, the long years of conflict and division between the North and the South, and the way the conflict ended, with victory for the North, and the prosecution of only persons from the opposition, influence the reconciliation process. In Kenya, the long-standing political differences among the major ethnic groups and the politics of exclusion and patronage common in the country also have impacted on the interactions between the ICC and the reconciliation. In Uganda, the long-term political animosity and economic inequality between the North and the South, and, the nature of the conflict, which started as one between the North and the South, have impact on reconciliation. In the short term, therefore, prosecutions have not improved the divisions and animosities among contending ethnic, political, religious and economic groups in the three countries. In Côte d'Ivoire, because of the peculiar circumstance of the country, and the ICC's sequential prosecution policy, the ICC intervention seems to be having negative impact on reconciliation.

8.3.3 The ICC and Promotion of Respect for Victims' Rights

In Chapters 4, 5, 6 and 7, the impact of the involvement of the ICC on the promotion of victims' rights was discussed. This can be divided into two categories: the impact of prosecutions by the ICC on promotion of victims' rights and the impact of the TFV projects on victims' rights. Analysis of qualitative evidence shows that the influence of the ICC's prosecutions on the promotion of victims' rights, is to a large extent symbolic, in the sense that the ICC admits very few of the direct and indirect victims of the conflicts to participate in the proceedings at The Hague, and these victims are represented by Counsel at The Hague. For instance, as at January 2019, out of the numerous victims in the three countries, only 4107 (Uganda), 727 (Côte d'Ivoire) and 1463 (Kenya) persons were granted the status of victims authorised to participate in the proceedings. The ICC also contributes to victims' redress by creating awareness of the importance of such redress.

The reparation provisions in the Rome Statute are a novelty in international criminal law because they provide victims of conflicts with actual rights to reparation; thus, it is becoming an expectation in international law that victims of international crimes are entitled to reparation as a right (Clamp 2014). The TFV has worked in Uganda for several years, but (as at March 2018) has not commenced work in Kenya and Côte d'Ivoire. The projects could be grouped into two: community and personal/group projects. On the negative side, the involvement of victims in ICC proceedings, as witnesses, may at times lead to re-victimisation (Fletcher and Weinstein 2002).

Overall, in Chapter 7, it was established through analysis of the data presented in Chapters 4, 5 and 6, and the literature reviews in Chapter 2, that the ICC's interventions have not diminished victims' rights in the three countries, but has little or no impact on the peace processes. The ICC's influence on victims' rights, therefore, does not lead to positive impact on the peace processes in these countries, since its contributions in this area are very minimal at this stage and have not concretised to have any significant impact on peace processes.

8.3.4 Can the ICC Deter Future Atrocities in These Countries?

The results of the interview evidence presented in Chapters 4, 5 and 6 and further discussed in Chapter 7 support the conclusion that the ICC *contributes* to general, but not to specific deterrence. Furthermore, because of the difficulties of measuring deterrence, the claim of deterrence can best be substantiated through specific examples (Mendez and Kelly 2015). A practical result of deterrence is conflict prevention. Evidence shows that violent conflicts in the three countries have been de-escalating. The ICC is contributing to conflict prevention through deterrence, by its various activities. Such actions include but are not limited to, the prosecution of some persons, the ICC's numerous public comments on the situations, its investigations of the violent conflicts, and the issuance of arrest warrants. Also, as a permanent international Court, the ICC is also a constant reminder to all would-be violators of international norms that their conducts can be punished.

The findings are in line with deterrence theory discussed in Chapter 2 that an increase in the likelihood of imposition of sanctions will lead to a decrease in violations. The costs of committing international crimes increased in the three countries, and the benefits have remained relatively constant. In Chapter 5, arguments were proffered to show that the indictment of some high profile persons in Kenya contributed to the relatively peaceful election in 2013, and have had long-lasting deterrent impact. In Côte d'Ivoire, though the prosecutions, which are restricted to the opposition, have been divisive, the ICC has also established that it can punish political leaders and this contributed to the relatively peaceful 2015 election. Viewed against the backdrop of a decade of impunity, the ICC involvement in Côte d'Ivoire is clearly a plus for accountability to the law, which influences deterrence for, at least, the key political leaders. The Ugandan situation presents a similar result: by investigating the situation, issuing warrants of arrest for some rebel leaders and prosecuting one of the leaders, the ICC has established that it can impose sanctions, and that it cannot be easily manipulated like national courts.

8.4 Recommendations

This book has traced how the ICC has struggled to make meaningful impact in the three countries. First, this study notes that the ICC has failed, so far, to expeditiously prosecute those it indicted. The failure of the ICC to speedily deliver justice to victims of violent conflicts has negative impact on its ability to promote peace processes and to facilitate conflict transformation. Secondly, the study highlighted the confrontations between the ICC and some national governments, the African Union, powerful interests/individuals and entrenched cultures of impunity. Also, the study outlined the tension between international accountability and impunity/amnesty and the challenges of deploying an international Court to deal with those who committed atrocities. This study, however, notes that the ICC is still in its embryonic stages, and that time is still needed for the Court to make an impact on the international legal system (Jurdi 2011). In view of the points discussed above, the study makes the following recommendations that will assist the ICC to contribute to international accountability and maybe create new dynamics for change.

8.4.1 The ICC Should Properly and Assertively Promote Its Activities

In all the three countries, the majority of respondents think the ICC needs to improve on its visibility on the ground. This is pertinent because the Head Office of the ICC is located in The Hague, considerably removed from the communities where the conflicts took place. The central question is: How will the ICC provide justice to victims of the conflicts when it is located in a distant country? How will it deter or express international global norms when it so removed from the people it is supposed to have impact on? Thus, how the ICC communicates to communities that are recovering from violent conflict and how it creates awareness about its programmes becomes almost as crucial as its main function of providing justice to victims of atrocities. The ICC's outreach programmes have not been spectacular (Human Rights Watch 2015) as they have not brought home to the victims and to the communities where atrocities took place, clear messages on the mandates, procedures and limitations of the ICC. The result is that there are disconnects among the victims, the communities where mass atrocities took place and the ICC. There are also gaps between victims' expectations and what the ICC has the powers to do, and what it has achieved in each case. There are high expectations in all the countries that the ICC will apprehend people, who are thought to have committed atrocities, deal with them expeditiously and compensate all victims of the crimes committed. The ICC needs to improve on its outreach, to properly manage these expectations by explaining to victims and communities, its mandates and the limits of its powers. Thus, because of the high expectations people have of the ICC to do things national courts have failed to do, and (even to do more) such as taking care of the "victims because it is an international court"[2] there is a sense of disappointment in these countries that the ICC has not delivered. Disappointments have led to a loss of interest in the work of the ICC, and the squandering of goodwill, in both Kenya and Uganda.

Apart from its outreach programmes through field offices, and from its Headquarters, the ICC, to a large extent, still relies on the local media to disseminate information about its activities. This approach is good and even practical, (considering the financial limitations of the ICC and the difficulty of directly reaching out to the victims of mass atrocities, such as language barriers and the sheer number of victims

[2]Interview with a member of Acholi Religious Leaders' Peace Initiative, 2015.

in vast areas). Nevertheless, relying substantially on the local media for the dissemination of information about its activities in each situation may be counter-productive because, in most cases, the local media are divided between pro-ICC media and anti-ICC media, which determine what they disseminate, how they disseminate it, and how much attention they give to each news item (Human Rights Watch 2015).

The ICC should develop more reliable ways to reach victims in communities where it is working. Opening properly equipped and well-staffed outreach stations remains a viable option. The ICC should therefore ensure that its outreach offices are well equipped, well managed and properly staffed with personnel who understand the vast scope of the problems, and how to reach as many people and communities as possible.

8.4.2 The ICC Should Conduct More Rigorous Investigations and Prosecutions

The Office of the Prosecutor is mandated to conduct investigations in situations where any of the crimes that are within the jurisdiction of the ICC are believed to have been committed. The Office first conducts preliminary investigations pursuant to article 54 of the Rome Statute, and if satisfied that there are reasons to conduct further investigations, then the Office of the Prosecutor applies to a Pre-Trial Chamber of the Court for authority to conduct full investigations. Most of the experts interviewed in Kenya in particular were of the opinion that the Office of the Prosecutor did a hasty and poor job in investigating the cases from Kenya, which resulted in the gradual collapse of the cases. They argued that the failure of the Pre-Trial Chamber to confirm the charges against all six persons initially charged in Kenya, and the withdrawal of charges against Francis Muthaura, Uhuru Kenyatta, William Ruto and Sang were also partially because the Office of the Prosecutor did not properly investigate the cases.

Goldston (2016) argues that "formidable as the government obstruction was, the prosecution shares some responsibility for the disappointing outcome, and for the previous failure of its attempted prosecution of Kenyatta". In the same vein, the Trial Chamber in the Kenyatta case observed that the Chamber has "serious concerns regarding the timeliness and thoroughness of prosecution investigations in this case including—in accordance with its responsibilities under Article 54 (l) (a) of the Statute—verifying the credibility and reliability of the evidence upon which it intended to rely at trial. Consequently, the Chamber considers it appropriate to caution the Prosecution in that regard".[3]

The Trial Chamber's "Decision on Defence Applications for Judgment of Acquittal"[4]—a "no case to answer" application, in favour of the Defence, in the Ruto and Sang case—is based on the conclusion that the prosecution does not have enough evidence to prosecute the case, and, according Judge Fremr, "it would be against the interests of justice for a Trial Chamber to abstain from making a credibility assessment at the 'no case to answer' stage where the evidence before it, at the close of the Prosecution case, is of an isolated nature…that would make it unlikely that a conviction in the case could ultimately follow".[5]

In Côte d'Ivoire, the Pre-Trial Chamber had to postpone the confirmation of charges proceeding in the case against Laurent Gbagbo and ordered the chief prosecutor to provide more evidence in relation to some of the crimes, before the Chamber would confirm charges against him. On 15 January 2019, Trial Chamber I acquitted Mr. Gbagbo and Mr. Blé Goudé from all charges against them, and also ordered their immediate release.

Taking due cognisance of the importance of evidence-gathering in prosecuting those who allegedly committed mass atrocities, and noting the difficulties of gathering such evidence in situations of mass atrocities without the assistance of its security officers/police, it is nonetheless important that the Office of the Prosecutor needs to

[3]Decision on Prosecution's applications for a finding of non-compliance pursuant to article 87 (7) and for an adjournment of the provisional trial date, ICC-01/09-02/11-908, 31 March 2014.

[4]Public redacted version of Decision on Defence Applications for Judgments of Acquittal, ICC-01/09-01/11-2027-Red-Corr, 05 April 2016.

[5]Public redacted version of Decision on Defence Applications for Judgments of Acquittal, ICC-01/09-01/11-2027-Red-Corr, 05 April 2016.

deploy more personnel in the field and be more thorough during this process to ensure that it has sufficient evidence to prosecute its cases. For the Office of the Prosecutor to improve in these areas, an important requirement is an increase in its resources. Good and painstaking investigations and prosecutions cannot be undertaken without proper funding (Rigney 2014). The Office of the Prosecutor in the 2012–2015 Strategic Plan complained that "the Office is unable to produce high-quality preliminary examinations, investigations and prosecutions without a substantial increase in resources".[6]

Nevertheless, the abysmal track record of the ICC clearly points to the fact that the Office of the Prosecutor should do more to bring those who committed atrocities to justice. The capability of the Court to deter, to promote victims' rights and accountability to the law, is also largely dependent on its capability to punish. The ICC will be in a stronger position to make more contributions to peace processes if it can successfully sanction some of those whom the Office of the Prosecutor alleged were responsible for international crimes.

8.4.3 Improving the Slow Pace of Justice

The Office of the Prosecutor has, so far, not been able to successfully prosecute any of the accused in the three countries. The ICC intervened in Côte d'Ivoire in 2011 after the post-election violence. Four years afterwards, in January 2016, it commenced the trial of two persons accused of bearing the greatest responsibility for the crimes committed during the post-election violence in the country. In January 2019, Trial Chamber I acquitted Mr. Gbagbo and Mr. Blé Goudé from all charges against them. In Kenya, six years after the intervention of the ICC, the Court failed to successfully prosecute any of the four persons whose indictments were confirmed in 2012. In Uganda, after ten years of work, the ICC commenced the first case in 2016, because the five indicted persons refused to surrender to the jurisdiction of the Court.

[6] Office of the Prosecutor Strategic Plan June 2012–2015, https://www.icc-cpi.int/iccdocs/otp/OTP-Strategic-Plan-2013.pdf. Accessed 24 January 2019.

Two of the accused are now confirmed dead, and the charges against them have been withdrawn. In the three countries, but particularly in Uganda and Kenya, people are generally losing interest in the ICC and its work.

A comparison of the ICC's prosecution record with those of similar international justice mechanisms sheds light on this problem. The ICTY, after twenty-two years of work (1993–2015), has sentenced eighty persons to various terms of imprisonments, acquitted eighteen and referred thirteen to national jurisdictions, while ten cases are currently on appeal. Also, the ICTR, after twenty-one years of work (1994–2015), has sentenced sixty-one people to various terms of imprisonment, acquitted fourteen and referred ten cases to national jurisdictions for trial. Comparatively, the ICC has performed dismally: so far the judges have issued verdicts in 6 cases with 8 convictions and 2 acquittals.[7] As at January 2019 according to information on the website of the ICC, "there have thus far been 28 cases before the Court, with some cases having more than one suspect. ICC judges have issued 34 arrest warrants, and 16 people have been detained in the ICC detention centre and have appeared before the Court, while 15 people remain at large. Charges have been dropped against 3 people due to their deaths. ICC judges have also issued 9 summonses to appear. The judges have issued 8 convictions and 3 acquittals". The slow pace of justice at the ICC has grave implications for peace processes. It narrows the contributions of the ICC, as the Court is unable to make contributions to peace processes as early as possible during the transitional process. The power of the Court to contribute to alleviating some of the problems of the victims will be profound if the ICC is able to convict and is able to order reparations for the victims and/or communities affected by the conflicts. Further, the ability of the ICC to challenge impunity will be reinforced if the Court has actually convicted persons accused of international crimes. Without convictions, the potency of the ICC is reduced, so also is it [illegible] e to peace processes.

[7]This record is at 24 Janu [illegible] nt/about. Accessed 24 January 2019.

8.4.4 Engaging Robustly with the African Union

The ICC has been engaged in a war of attrition with the African Union for some years. The central issues of misunderstanding are: How the ICC should do its work in Africa, and how and when the ICC should intervene in conflict situations on the continent. The misunderstandings have dire consequences for conflict transformation in Africa, including in the three countries. Firstly, they distract the ICC from focusing on its duty of prosecuting those who commit atrocities in Africa. Secondly, they rob the ICC of the cooperation of a powerful ally in the fight against impunity. Thirdly, they force the ICC to waste energy on diplomatic issues and building relationships which ordinarily should be assumed as given, as the ICC and the AU are interested in the same core issues, such as promoting accountability, stability, human rights, peace and good governance. Ongoing consultations between the ICC and the African Union should be strongly supported by both parties. The consultations, which started in 2012, and had their third session in Addis Ababa in October 2015, provide a platform for discussing the contentious issues. The ICC should also encourage consultations with key international figures and players and stop contending that the ICC is only a judicial and not a political institution (Schabas 2012). The foundation of the argument that the ICC should consult more is that international justice mechanisms (unlike national courts) may require consultations with key states, organisations and individuals to succeed. The logic of this argument is rooted in the fact that the ICC does not have its own police and is dependent on the cooperation and support of member states, and the international community to enforce its mandate. Thus, the success of the ICC depends on the willingness of state parties, and the international community to cooperate, and the effectiveness of such cooperation is vital to the fulfilment of its mandate (Williams 2012).

8.4.5 Avoiding Partial o [illegible] e

In Côte d'Ivoire, and to som[illegible]he ICC is dogged by accusations of conducting [illegible]sation is weighty and should not be ignored [illegible] justification for